One-Stop Internet Resources

D0860483

ewow.glencoe.com

Online Study Tools

- eFlashcards
- Drag and Drop
- Concentration
- Answers to Section Reviews
- Portfolio Help

Online Activities

- Math Practice
- Practice Tests
- Internet Activities
- Smart Tips for Feature Activities

glencoe.com/sec/careers

Link to Career City for:

- Career Tools
- Career Research
- Links to Career Web Sites

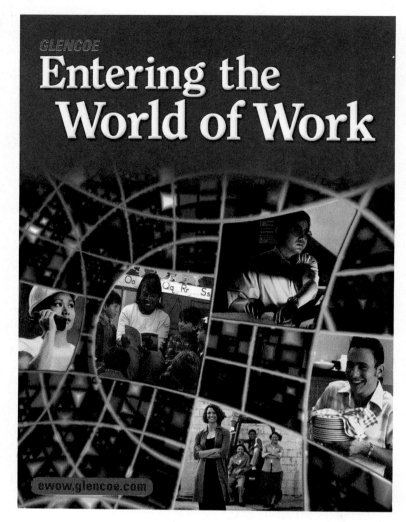

GLENCOE
Entering the World of Work

Fourth Edition

Grady Kimbrell

Educational Consultant
Santa Barbara, California

Ben S. Vineyard

Professor and Chairman Emeritus
Vocational and Technical Education
Pittsburg State University
Pittsburg, Kansas

McGraw Hill **Glencoe**

New York, New York   Columbus, Ohio   Chicago, Illinois   Peoria, Illinois   Woodland Hills, California

Send all inquiries to:
Glencoe/McGraw-Hill
21600 Oxnard Street, Suite 500
Woodland Hills, CA 91367

ISBN 0-07-861458-9 (Student Text)
ISBN 0-07-866497-7 (Teacher Annotated Edition)

Printed in the United States of America

1 2 3 4 5 6 7 8 9 027 08 07 06 05 04

Table of Contents

Welcome to *Entering the World of Work!*

What do you enjoy? What do you do well? What do you want to do with your life? This book will help you answer these questions.

Getting to Know You

You will learn more about yourself. You will learn to make smart decisions and choose the right career for you.

Finding the Right Job

You will learn how to find and get the job you want. You will learn how to be a valuable employee. You will improve skills that will move you ahead in your career.

Developing Skills for Everyday Living

You will learn everyday skills related to working. You will learn what you need to live on your own.

Getting Ready for the Future

The world of work offers you many opportunities. Use your abilities to their fullest. Your entry into the world of work will be easier and more successful.

Understanding the Text Structure

Your textbook has been organized to help you learn about the skills you will need to enter the world of work. Before you start reading, follow this road map to help you understand what you will encounter in the pages of this textbook.

Units help you focus on big ideas.

Unit Preview presents the main ideas.

Reading Preview lists the chapter titles along with questions to guide your learning.

Chapters help you focus on particular areas of learning.

You Already Know helps you recall knowledge you have about the chapter topics.

You Will Learn lists the knowledge you will master after you study the chapter.

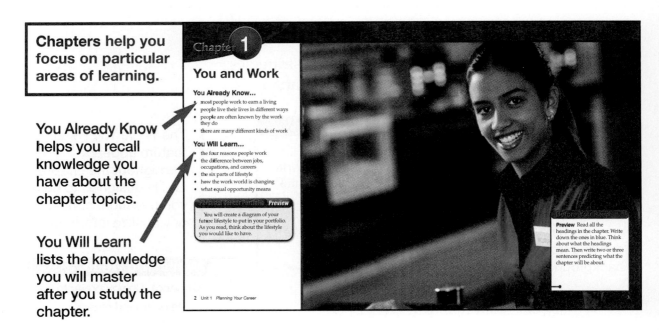

Previewing Your Textbook

The Section Opener

Each chapter is divided into two sections. The section opener helps you understand concepts.

Sections introduce specific skills and knowledge.

Key Terms is a list of important vocabulary terms. The Key Terms are also in boldface type as they are introduced with the text and are accompanied by clear definitions.

Main Idea briefly states the section's meaning and purpose.

Thought Organizer is a tool to help you organize what you learn.

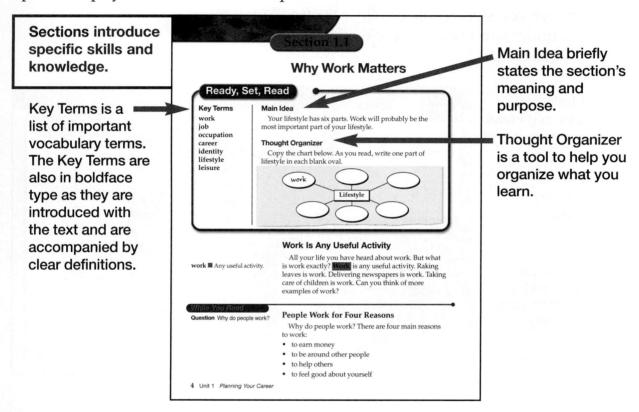

Section 1.1

Why Work Matters

Ready, Set, Read

Key Terms
work
job
occupation
career
identity
lifestyle
leisure

Main Idea
Your lifestyle has six parts. Work will probably be the most important part of your lifestyle.

Thought Organizer
Copy the chart below. As you read, write one part of lifestyle in each blank oval.

work

Lifestyle

Work Is Any Useful Activity

work ■ Any useful activity.

All your life you have heard about work. But what is work exactly? **Work** is any useful activity. Raking leaves is work. Delivering newspapers is work. Taking care of children is work. Can you think of more examples of work?

While You Read
Question Why do people work?

People Work for Four Reasons
Why do people work? There are four main reasons to work:
• to earn money
• to be around other people
• to help others
• to feel good about yourself

4   Unit 1   *Planning Your Career*

Using Reading Strategies

Entering the World of Work contains reading strategies that help you learn the information in each chapter.

The Before You Read feature helps prepare you to learn by previewing information, setting a purpose for your learning, or by drawing from your own background knowledge.

Before You Read

Preview Read all the headings in the chapter. Write down the ones in blue. Think about what the headings mean. Then write two or three sentences predicting what the chapter will be about.

The While You Read feature appears throughout the chapter and is designed to help you question, connect, or visualize information.

While You Read

Connect Do you prefer to be alone or around others?

Focus on the Features

The features in each chapter provide special insights into career topics and challenge your creativity and imagination.

Point of View

Learning Customer Service

Stacy Mignon just started her first full-time job. "I'm a customer service trainee at Kiddy Toys in Memphis. I'm learning to handle calls from customers."

Stacy likes to work with people. She thought doing customer service would be easy. "But there's nothing easy about customer service!" she says. "Dealing with customers' complaints is very hard work."

Stacy has learned a lot about customer service at her job. "I've learned that you have to be flexible too and have great people skills to give good customer service," she says. "Once a customer was missing a part for a model train. We were out of that part, but I found a similar part in the supply room. We sent it to him. That solved the problem and made everybody happy."

It's Your Turn Getting along with others is an important skill. Think of a situation in the past where you showed skill at getting along with others. What was the situation? How did you show your skill?

For help completing this activity, visit **ewow.glencoe.com/tip** the Chapter 1 *Point of*

The Point of View feature presents the experiences of young people beginning their careers along with their tips for success.

Real-World Connection

Handling Criticism

Everyone receives some criticism at work. *Criticism* is a comment about something you could do better. Criticism might hurt your feelings. But it is helpful. If your boss gives you criticism, listen well. You may get criticism from coworkers and customers. It is important to listen to this criticism, too. If you do not understand what they are saying, ask. Ask for suggestions on how you could do your job better.

People sometimes give criticism in an angry way. Do not take this personally. It does not mean you are a bad worker.

Take the Next Step Helpful criticism is called *constructive criticism*. Less helpful criticism is called *destructive criticism*. Research the two types of criticism on the Internet. Explain the differences between them. Describe how to give the criticism.

doing this activity, go to **:oe.com/tips** and find the *Smart Tip* pter 1 *Real-World Connection* feature.

Making Good Choices

Using E-Mail at Work

You work in the billing department of a large insurance company. Every day you read and write many business e-mails. You also write a few messages to friends and family. Your company allows workers to spend a little time using e-mail for personal reasons. Your coworker Farad, however, spends two hours a day e-mailing friends. Farad sometimes falls behind at work and asks you for help. If you do not help, your boss will find out that he is not working hard. You do not want to keep helping Farad, but you do not want him to be fired.

You Make the Call What options do you have in this situation? Which one would you choose?

For help in answering this question, visit **ewow.glencoe.com/tips** and select the *Smart Tip* for the Chapter 1 *Making Good Choices*.

The Making Good Choices feature lets you look at the ethical challenges and choices workers face.

The Real-World Connection feature helps build the communication skills needed on the job.

Focus on the Features

The Career Talk feature provides interviews with people who have jobs in each of the career clusters. The feature offers information about job skills, education or training, and career outlook.

The Study Tip feature provides tips and ideas to help you build your study skills.

Study Tip

Are you close to friends or family? Try "teaching" a friend or family member about what you are learning in school. When you explain something to another person, it helps you remember it.

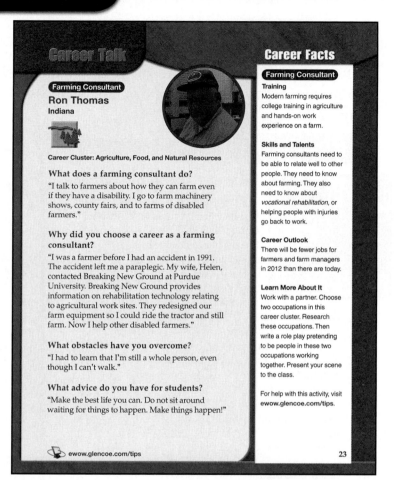

Career Talk

Farming Consultant
Ron Thomas
Indiana

Career Cluster: Agriculture, Food, and Natural Resources

What does a farming consultant do?
"I talk to farmers about how they can farm even if they have a disability. I go to farm machinery shows, county fairs, and to farms of disabled farmers."

Why did you choose a career as a farming consultant?
"I was a farmer before I had an accident in 1991. The accident left me a paraplegic. My wife, Helen, contacted Breaking New Ground at Purdue University. Breaking New Ground provides information on rehabilitation technology relating to agricultural work sites. They redesigned our farm equipment so I could ride the tractor and still farm. Now I help other disabled farmers."

What obstacles have you overcome?
"I had to learn that I'm still a whole person, even though I can't walk."

What advice do you have for students?
"Make the best life you can. Do not sit around waiting for things to happen. Make things happen!"

ewow.glencoe.com/tips

Career Facts

Farming Consultant

Training
Modern farming requires college training in agriculture and hands-on work experience on a farm.

Skills and Talents
Farming consultants need to be able to relate well to other people. They need to know about farming. They also need to know about *vocational rehabilitation*, or helping people with injuries go back to work.

Career Outlook
There will be fewer jobs for farmers and farm managers in 2012 than there are today.

Learn More About It
Work with a partner. Choose two occupations in this career cluster. Research these occupations. Then write a role play pretending to be people in these two occupations working together. Present your scene to the class.

For help with this activity, visit **ewow.glencoe.com/tips**.

23

Resources to Help You Learn

The back of *Entering the World of Work* contains resources that help you find and learn more information.

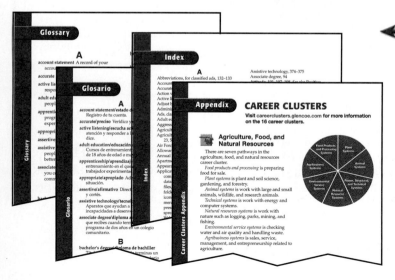

The Glossary allows you to find definitions quickly and easily.

The Glosario/Spanish Glossary provides definitions of all the Key Terms written in Spanish.

The Index lists important terms and ideas.

The Career Clusters Appendix offers detailed information about each career cluster's pathways.

Reviewing What You've Learned

Entering the World of Work guides you to review and reinforce your learning at each step.

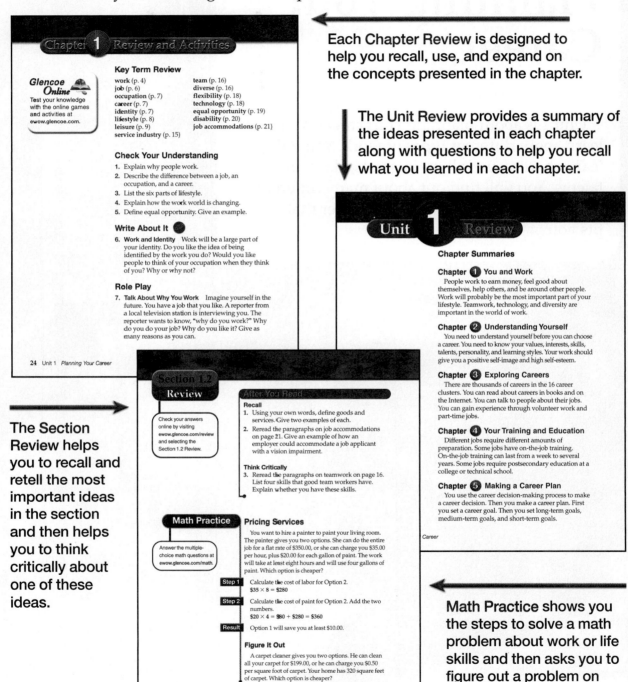

Each Chapter Review is designed to help you recall, use, and expand on the concepts presented in the chapter.

The Unit Review provides a summary of the ideas presented in each chapter along with questions to help you recall what you learned in each chapter.

The Section Review helps you to recall and retell the most important ideas in the section and then helps you to think critically about one of these ideas.

Math Practice shows you the steps to solve a math problem about work or life skills and then asks you to figure out a problem on your own.

Unit 1

Planning Your Career

Unit Preview

Unit 1 is about planning your career. You will learn about different types of work. You will learn about your values, interests, skills, and talents. You will find out about many different careers. Then you will choose a career that fits you.

Reading Preview

These are the topics in this unit. What do you know about them now?

Chapter 1
You and Work
- Why Work Matters
- Today's Workplace

Chapter 2
Understanding Yourself
- Getting to Know Yourself
- Being an Individual

Chapter 3
Exploring Careers
- Narrowing Your Career Choices
- Learning About Careers

Chapter 4
Your Training and Education
- Your Training Options
- Education After High School

Chapter 5
Making a Career Plan
- Making a Career Decision
- Planning Your Career

Chapter 1

You and Work

You Already Know...

- most people work to earn a living
- people live their lives in different ways
- people are often known by the work they do
- there are many different kinds of work

You Will Learn...

- the four reasons people work
- the difference between jobs, occupations, and careers
- the six parts of lifestyle
- how the work world is changing
- what equal opportunity means

Personal Career Portfolio *Preview*

You will create a diagram of your future lifestyle to put in your portfolio. As you read, think about the lifestyle you would like to have.

Preview Read all the headings in the chapter. Write down the ones in blue. Think about what the headings mean. Then write two or three sentences predicting what the chapter will be about.

Why Work Matters

Ready, Set, Read

Key Terms

work
job
occupation
career
identity
lifestyle
leisure

Main Idea

Your lifestyle has six parts. Work will probably be the most important part of your lifestyle.

Thought Organizer

Copy the chart below. As you read, write one part of lifestyle in each blank oval.

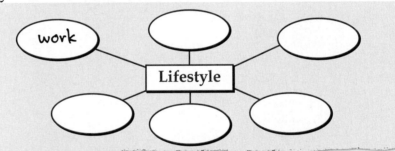

Work Is Any Useful Activity

work ■ Any useful activity.

All your life you have heard about work. But what is work exactly? **Work** is any useful activity. Raking leaves is work. Delivering newspapers is work. Taking care of children is work. Can you think of more examples of work?

While You Read

Question Why do people work?

People Work for Four Reasons

Why do people work? There are four main reasons to work:

- to earn money
- to be around other people
- to help others
- to feel good about yourself

People Work to Earn Money   One reason to work is to earn money. You must earn money to pay for the things you need and want. You need food and housing. You need transportation, medical care, and education. Most people want other things, too. You may want a car, a DVD player, and other things you could live without. These extra things are called *luxuries*. Luxuries help make life fun, but they cost money.

People Work to Be Around Others   The second reason to work is to be around other people. You can meet people who share your interests. You can make new friends. You can learn about other people's ideas and feelings. You can have experiences that you would not have by yourself.

While You Read

Connect Do you prefer to be alone or around others?

People Work to Help Others   The third reason to work is to help other people. You can help people in many ways. You might help a customer buy an item. You might help a coworker do a project. You might help a child learn something new.

There are over 150 million jobs in the United States. Each job is important. Each job helps other people in some way.

People Work to Feel Good About Themselves   The fourth reason to work is to feel good about yourself. You feel good about yourself when you do a job well. You feel proud of yourself when you learn something new. You feel important and valued when other people count on you.

Work helps you take pride in what you do and who you are. It gives you confidence. *Confidence* is the belief that you can do well. When you are confident, you feel satisfied with your life. You feel happy. This is worth more than money.

Work Includes Jobs, Occupations, and Careers

Work includes jobs, occupations, and careers. These are three parts of the same idea.

Study Tip

The more you learn, the more you will earn. Most of the high-paying careers of the future require some education after high school. So the more you know, the higher your pay will be.

job ■ Work you do for pay.

Jobs Are Paid Work   A **job** is work you do for pay. Take the example of Zahra. Zahra gardens at a city park. She gets paid for doing it. Gardening is her job.

People do many different tasks at their jobs. *Tasks* are activities you are assigned. Zahra has many daily and weekly tasks. Her daily tasks include watering and trimming shrubs. Her weekly tasks include mowing grass and planting seeds. Zahra is responsible for completing all these tasks on time.

Jobs Are Paid Work   Gardening is Zahra's job. She feels proud of herself because she does her job well. Describe a time when you felt proud of yourself. Explain why you felt this way.

Occupations Are Activities   An occupation is a little different from a job. An occupation is the type of work you do to earn a living.

People can change jobs and still have the same occupation. For example, imagine that Zahra decides to leave her job at the city park. She starts her own gardening service. She gardens at people's homes instead of at the park. She has a different job, but she is still a gardener. Her occupation is the same. Her occupation is gardener.

occupation ■ The type of work you do to earn a living.

Careers Are Related Jobs   A career is all the related jobs you do during your life. Zahra, the gardener, will have several jobs during her life. All her gardening jobs are part of one career.

You will probably work at many different jobs during your life. You may change jobs to make more money. You may find a job you like better than the one you have. You may want a change of pace. You may want to learn new skills. When you become good at one type of work, you will probably stay with it. Then it will become your career.

career ■ All the related jobs you do during your life.

Work Will Be a Large Part of Your Identity

School is probably a big part of your life right now. Being a student is a part of your identity. If you play a sport, then being an athlete is part of your identity, too. Your identity is the way other people know you.

Later, work will be a large part of your identity. You will often be identified by the work you do. For example, you will be known as a mechanic if you repair cars. You will be known as a writer or journalist if you write for the newspaper. Your job, your occupation, and your career will help identify you to others.

While You Read

Connect Is school a large part of your identity?

identity ■ The way other people know you.

Work Gives You Dignity   Work also gives you dignity. Having *dignity* means being proud of yourself and what you do. It means respecting your own worth. When you respect yourself, others will respect you, too.

Real-World Connection

Handling Criticism

Everyone receives some criticism at work. *Criticism* is a comment about something you could do better. Criticism might hurt your feelings. But it is helpful. If your boss gives you criticism, listen well. You may get criticism from coworkers and customers. It is important to listen to this criticism, too. If you do not understand what they are saying, ask. Ask for suggestions on how you could do your job better.

People sometimes give criticism in an angry way. Do not take this personally. It does not mean you are a bad worker.

Take the Next Step Helpful criticism is called *constructive criticism*. Less helpful criticism is called *destructive criticism*. Research the two types of criticism on the Internet. Explain the differences between them. Describe how to give constructive criticism.

For help doing this activity, go to **ewow.glencoe.com/tips** and find the *Smart Tip* for the Chapter 1 *Real-World Connection* feature.

Your Lifestyle Is How You Spend Your Time, Energy, and Money

Everyone wants to be happy. Each person looks for happiness in a different way. Each person chooses his or her lifestyle. Your **lifestyle** is the way you spend your time, energy, and money. Your lifestyle reflects what is important to you.

As you think about your future, picture the way you would like to live. This will help you decide what kind of lifestyle you want.

lifestyle ■ The way you spend your time, energy, and money.

Your Lifestyle Has Six Parts

All the parts of a person's life combine to form a lifestyle. For most people, lifestyle includes six parts:

- family
- friends
- leisure
- health
- spirituality
- work

Family Is Part of Lifestyle   Families can be all types and sizes. Families can be large or small. We can be born into a family, and we can also create a family. Family members may live together in one household, or they may live many miles apart.

Is family an important part of your life? What size and type of family would you like? Do you want to live with your family, or would you rather live alone? Would you like to build a family around a committed relationship, such as marriage? Would you like to raise a child? These are important lifestyle questions.

Friends Are Part of Lifestyle   Friends are important, too. *Friends* are people to talk with and do things with. Good friends help you and care about your thoughts and feelings. They encourage you during good times and bad times. Do you see friends every day? How important are friends to you?

While You Read

Connect What does the word *friend* mean to you?

Leisure Is Part of Lifestyle   Free time is known as leisure. Everyone needs leisure time to rest. Many people like to spend leisure time doing recreational activities, such as playing sports or pursuing hobbies. A *hobby* is an activity that you do for your own pleasure.

Some people like to have a lot of leisure time. Others are content with only a little. Are hobbies important to you? Do you like to travel? Do you like to read books? Do you want time to help in your community? Think about these questions as you plan your career.

leisure ■ Free time.

Everyone Has a Different Lifestyle Pattern

Everyone values different things. So everyone's lifestyle pattern is different. A *lifestyle pattern* shows the importance of each part of your lifestyle.

Look at **Figure 1.1.** It shows two different lifestyle patterns. Each circle represents a different part of a person's lifestyle. The lifestyle pattern on the left belongs to Kaina. All six parts of lifestyle are equally important to her. So all six circles are the same size.

The lifestyle pattern on the right belongs to Antonio. Work, health, and family are the most important parts of Antonio's lifestyle. They are the largest. Spirituality is a little less important. Leisure and friends are the least important.

Figure 1.1

Lifestyle Patterns

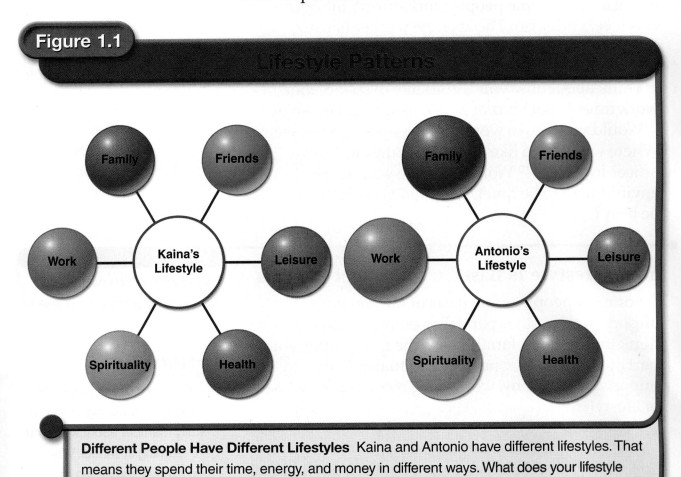

Different People Have Different Lifestyles Kaina and Antonio have different lifestyles. That means they spend their time, energy, and money in different ways. What does your lifestyle pattern look like? What do you want it to look like in the future?

Your Work Affects Your Lifestyle

For most of us, work has a bigger effect on lifestyle than any other part. Let's look at how work affects your time and your money.

Work Affects Your Time Most people plan their daily lives around their work. For example, they may need to get up early to be at work on time. They may eat dinner early or late, depending on when they get home from work. They may spend a lot of time *commuting*, or going to work and coming home. How you spend your free time may also depend on where and when you work. You may find new things to do near work. New friends from work may get you involved in new activities. Some workplaces even have social clubs or fitness centers.

Work Affects Your Money Your work will determine how much money you earn. You need to earn enough to pay your bills and to save money for the future. Housing, food, and transportation cost thousands of dollars each year. If you earn enough money, you can buy luxuries. Luxuries are things that you do not need but would like to have. For example, you might be able to buy an expensive car or a bigger house. You might be able to take a vacation.

While You Read

Connect How does work affect your money?

Plan Your Work to Fit Your Lifestyle

Work can control your lifestyle. For example, a night job can keep you from being able to spend time with your family or friends. A job on weekends can keep you from attending some religious services. If you work long hours, you may not have time for a movie. You many not have much time for leisure.

Think about how different careers would affect your lifestyle. Pick a career that will let you have the lifestyle you want. Do you sometimes daydream about the future? If so, you are trying out ideas for an adult lifestyle. This is good. It is the first step in planning your future. It gives you a starting point.

Check your answers online by visiting ewow.glencoe.com/review and selecting the Section 1.1 Review.

After You Read

Retell

1. Reread the section titled, "Careers are Related Jobs." Using your own words, define the term *career*. Give an example of a career.

2. Explain how work affects a person's time. Use your own words.

Think Critically

3. List the four reasons for working. Explain which of the four reasons is the most important to you.

Math Practice

Answer the multiple-choice math questions at ewow.glencoe.com/math.

Figuring Hours Worked

Today you arrived at work at 9:00 a.m. You took lunch from 12:30 p.m. to 1:15 p.m. Then you worked from 1:15 p.m. to 5:45 p.m. How many hours and minutes did you work today?

Step 1 Calculate how long you worked before lunch.
12:30 − 9:00 = 3:30

Step 2 Calculate the time you worked after lunch.
5:45 − 1:15 = 4:30

Step 3 Add the two times together.
3:30 + 4:30 = 8:00

Result You worked 8 hours today.

Figure It Out

Tomorrow you arrive at work at 8:30 a.m. You take lunch from 12:30 p.m. to 1:00 p.m. Then you work from 1:00 p.m. to 5:30 p.m. How many hours and minutes have you worked?

Today's Workplace

Ready, Set, Read

Key Terms

service industry
team
diverse
flexibility
technology
equal opportunity
disability
job accommodations

Main Idea

Today's workers need skills in teamwork, technology, and getting along with others. Today's employers must give workers and job applicants equal opportunity.

Thought Organizer

Make a list like the one below. As you read, write down at three different skills you will need to succeed.

Skill	Why I Need This Skill
teamwork	to work well in teams
flexibility	
technology	

The World of Work Is Changing

The world is always changing. Changes affect the kinds of jobs you can choose. Changes also affect the way you will do your job.

The Service Industry Is Growing

Businesses sell goods and services. *Goods* are objects such as groceries, cars, and clothing. Goods workers have jobs such as miner, manufacturing worker, and carpenter. These jobs are becoming harder to find.

Services are activities. Services include transportation, education, and health care. The **service industry** is all the businesses that provide activities for a fee. Jobs in the service industry include waiter, police officer, and health care technician. These jobs are becoming easier to find.

service industry ■ All the businesses that provide activities for a fee.

Teamwork Is Becoming More Important

team ■ A group of people who have a common goal.

Today, many workers work in teams. A **team** is a group of people who have a common goal. Team members share skills and ideas with one another. This helps everyone do a better job.

Employers want workers who know how to work in teams. Good team members do their fair share of the work. They communicate well and share ideas. They have a positive attitude. They treat other people as they would like to be treated.

While You Read

Question What is the workforce?

diverse ■ Varied and different.

The Workforce Is Becoming More Diverse

The *workforce* is all the people who have jobs or are looking for jobs. The workforce is growing. It is also becoming more diverse. **Diverse** means varied and different.

The workforce is becoming more ethnically diverse. This means that there are more workers of different *ethnicities*, or races and cultures.

At work you will meet people who come from cultures different from yours. You will meet people who speak languages different from yours. You will meet people who act differently from you. You will need to respect all these differences.

Common Goals
Each member of a team brings important skills. This helps the team reach its goal. What is the goal of this team?

Workers Need New Skills to Succeed

Employers want workers with excellent skills. *Skills* are abilities to do specific tasks. Employers want workers who can do many tasks well.

In the past, many employers hired unskilled workers and trained them. Today, most employers look for workers who already have solid skills.

Point of View

Learning Customer Service

Stacy Mignon just started her first full-time job. "I'm a customer service trainee at Kiddy Toys in Memphis. I'm learning to handle calls from customers."

Stacy likes to work with people. She thought doing customer service would be easy. "But there's nothing easy about customer service!" she says. "Dealing with customers' complaints is very hard work."

Stacy has learned a lot about customer service at her job. "I've learned that you have to be flexible too and have great people skills to give good customer service," she says. "Once a customer was missing a part for a model train. We were out of that part, but I found a similar part in the supply room. We sent it to him. That solved the problem and made everybody happy."

It's Your Turn Getting along with others is an important skill. Think of a situation in the past where you showed skill at getting along with others. What was the situation? How did you show your skill?

For help completing this activity, visit **ewow.glencoe.com/tips** and go to the *Smart Tip* for the Chapter 1 *Point of View.*

Workers Need to Be Flexible

flexibility ■ The ability to change when the world around you changes.

Workers need to have flexibility. **Flexibility** is the ability to change when the world around you changes.

Let's say there is a big change at your workplace. Perhaps you get a new boss. Perhaps your company offers a new service. What do you do? You cannot do things the same way. You need to be flexible.

While You Read

Question Why do employers want workers with technology skills?

technology ■ Knowledge and tools that make it possible to do new things.

Workers Need Technology Skills

Today, technology is part of every job. **Technology** is knowledge and tools that make it possible to do new things.

Computers are the most common form of technology. Millions of workers use computers. Even *entry-level* (beginning) workers need skill with computers.

Making Good Choices

Using E-Mail at Work

You work in the billing department of a large insurance company. Every day you read and write many business e-mails. You also write a few messages to friends and family. Your company allows workers to spend a little time using e-mail for personal reasons. Your coworker Farad, however, spends two hours a day e-mailing friends. Farad sometimes falls behind at work and asks you for help. If you do not help, your boss will find out that he is not working hard. You do not want to keep helping Farad, but you do not want him to be fired.

You Make the Call What options do you have in this situation? Which one would you choose?

For help in answering this question, visit **ewow.glencoe.com/tips** and select the *Smart Tip* for the Chapter 1 *Making Good Choices*.

Equal Opportunity Means Fair Treatment for Everyone

Equal opportunity is an important part of today's workplace. **Equal opportunity** is fair treatment for everyone. Workers are chosen for jobs for their skills and not for how they look or who they are.

Equal opportunity is the opposite of discrimination. *Discrimination* is unfair treatment. For example, people may be treated unfairly because they have a certain skin color, or because they were born in a certain place. This is discrimination. It is against the law.

equal opportunity ■ Fair treatment for everyone.

Equal Opportunity Is the Law

Employers must give all workers equal opportunity. This is the law. It does not matter what a worker's sex, religion, or ethnicity is. It only matters whether a worker can do the job. Employers cannot turn down a job applicant just because she is a woman. They cannot turn down a job applicant just because he or she has a disability. Because of these laws, people can choose any career they wish.

Women and Men Have Equal Opportunities

In the past, women had fewer career choices than men. In the past some jobs were called "men's work." Other jobs were called "women's work."

Today women and men can choose any career they wish. Women work as truck drivers, engineers, and construction workers. They work as firefighters and police officers. These are jobs that were once only for men. Men work as child care workers, dental assistants, and flight attendants. They work as nurses and secretaries. These are all jobs that were once thought proper only for women.

Today more women also work outside the home. In 1950, one third of all American women had a job outside the home. Today, more than half of all women have a job outside the home. **Figure 1.2** on the next page shows how the percentage of women in the workplace has grown.

While You Read

Question Why do you think most police officers always were men in the past?

People With Disabilities Have Equal Opportunities

disability ■ A long-lasting impairment that limits a major life activity.

People with disabilities have more career choices than ever before. A **disability** is a long-lasting impairment that limits a major life activity. Major life activities include caring for yourself, walking, reading, learning, and working.

While You Read

Question How common are disabilities?

Disabilities Can Affect the Body and the Mind   Some disabilities affect parts of the body. For example, some disabilities limit vision or hearing. Some disabilities limit movement.

Some disabilities affect parts of the mind. For example, some disabilities cause behavior difficulties. Some disabilities affect the ability to learn.

How common are disabilities? About 20 percent of Americans have a disability. That means that one out of every five people has a disability.

Figure 1.2

Men and Women at Work

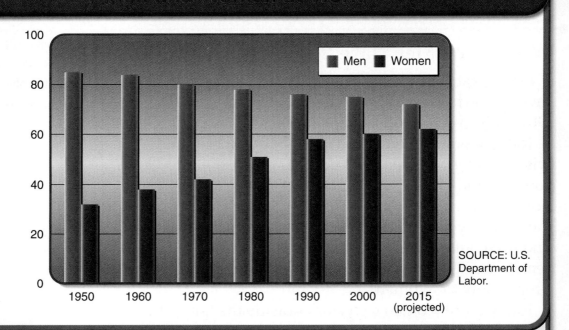

SOURCE: U.S. Department of Labor.

More Women Are Working In 1950, about a third of American women had jobs outside the home. In 2000, more than half of American women had jobs outside the home. Why do you think there are more women working at jobs today than in the past?

Careers Are Open to All This woman has a physical disability. She chose a career as an accountant. What other careers could she have chosen?

Employers Must Provide Accommodations to Workers

Job accommodations are things that help workers with disabilities to do their jobs.

Employers must give you job accommodations if you need help doing your job. However, you must have the skills to do most of the job tasks.

Most job accommodations are simple. For example, a person who uses a wheelchair might need a desk that adjusts in height. A person with a breathing difficulty might need an office where perfumes are not allowed. Most people with disabilities do not need any job accommodations.

job accommodations ■
Things that help workers with disabilities to do their jobs.

Employees Must Provide Accommodations to Job Applicants

Employers must also provide accommodations to job applicants with disabilities. A *job applicant* is a person who is applying for a job.

Imagine that you have a disability and want to apply for a certain job. You can do most of the tasks for that job. The employer must help you work around the disability. For example, the employer could give you forms in large type if you have a limited vision.

While You Read

Question What job accommodations might help you?

Check your answers online by visiting **ewow.glencoe.com/review** and selecting the Section 1.2 Review.

After You Read

Recall

1. Using your own words, define goods and services. Give two examples of each.

2. Reread the paragraphs on job accommodations on page 21. Give an example of how an employer could accommodate a job applicant with a vision impairment.

Think Critically

3. Reread the paragraphs on teamwork on page 16. List four skills that good team workers have. Explain whether you have these skills.

Math Practice

Answer the multiple-choice math questions at **ewow.glencoe.com/math**.

Pricing Services

You want to hire a painter to paint your living room. The painter gives you two options. She can do the entire job for a flat rate of $350.00, or she can charge you $35.00 per hour, plus $20.00 for each gallon of paint. The work will take at least eight hours and will use four gallons of paint. Which option is cheaper?

Step 1 Calculate the cost of labor for Option 2.
$35 × 8 = $280

Step 2 Calculate the cost of paint for Option 2. Add the two numbers.
$20 × 4 = $80 + $280 = $360

Result Option 1 will save you at least $10.00.

Figure It Out

A carpet cleaner gives you two options. He can clean all your carpet for $199.00, or he can charge you $0.50 per square foot of carpet. Your home has 320 square feet of carpet. Which option is cheaper?

Farming Consultant

Ron Thomas
Indiana

Career Cluster: Agriculture, Food, and Natural Resources

What does a farming consultant do?

"I talk to farmers about how they can farm even if they have a disability. I go to farm machinery shows, county fairs, and to farms of disabled farmers."

Why did you choose a career as a farming consultant?

"I was a farmer before I had an accident in 1991. The accident left me a paraplegic. My wife, Helen, contacted Breaking New Ground at Purdue University. Breaking New Ground provides information on rehabilitation technology relating to agricultural work sites. They redesigned our farm equipment so I could ride the tractor and still farm. Now I help other disabled farmers."

What obstacles have you overcome?

"I had to learn that I'm still a whole person, even though I can't walk."

What advice do you have for students?

"Make the best life you can. Do not sit around waiting for things to happen. Make things happen!"

Farming Consultant

Training
Modern farming requires college training in agriculture and hands-on work experience on a farm.

Skills and Talents
Farming consultants need to be able to relate well to other people. They need to know about farming. They also need to know about *vocational rehabilitation*, or helping people with injuries go back to work.

Career Outlook
There will be fewer jobs for farmers and farm managers in 2012 than there are today.

Learn More About It
Work with a partner. Choose two occupations in this career cluster. Research these occupations. Then write a role play pretending to be people in these two occupations working together. Present your scene to the class.

For help with this activity, visit **ewow.glencoe.com/tips**.

Key Term Review

work (p. 4)
job (p. 6)
occupation (p. 7)
career (p. 7)
identity (p. 7)
lifestyle (p. 8)
leisure (p. 9)
service industry (p. 15)

team (p. 16)
diverse (p. 16)
flexibility (p. 18)
technology (p. 18)
equal opportunity (p. 19)
disability (p. 20)
job accommodations (p. 21)

Check Your Understanding

1. Explain why people work.
2. Describe the difference between a job, an occupation, and a career.
3. List the six parts of lifestyle.
4. Explain how the work world is changing.
5. Define equal opportunity. Give an example.

Write About It

6. **Work and Identity**   Work will be a large part of your identity. Do you like the idea of being identified by the work you do? Would you like people to think of your occupation when they think of you? Why or why not?

Role Play

7. **Talk About Why You Work**   Imagine yourself in the future. You have a job that you like. A reporter from a local television station is interviewing you. The reporter wants to know, "why do you work?" Why do you do your job? Why do you like it? Give as many reasons as you can.

Teamwork Challenge

8. **Do a Lifestyle Interview**   Team up with a partner. Choose five workers you would like to interview. Ask each worker, "How does work affect your time?" Ask each worker to explain how many hours he or she spends on work each day. Include time spent working and getting ready for work. Also include time spent commuting and caring for work tools or clothing. Create a chart showing how many hours the workers spend on work each day.

Computer Lab

Do a Diversity Survey   Diverse means varied and different. How diverse are people? In how many ways are they different from one another? Using a computer, make a list of all the ways people differ from one another. Think of how people look, how they think, and how they act. Make your list as long as you can. Format your list using bullets or numbers.

Personal Career Portfolio

Draw Your Lifestyle Pattern   Sketch the lifestyle pattern you would like to have in the future. Think about how large to make each of the six circles. Below the pattern, add a paragraph explaining why you would like to have this lifestyle pattern. Write the title "My Future Lifestyle" at the top of the page. If possible, use a computer to do this portfolio project.

Go to **ewow.glencoe.com/portfolio** for help.

Chapter 2

Understanding Yourself

You Already Know...

- there are many career possibilities
- everyone is interested in different things
- your skills and talents make you special
- everyone has a unique personality

You Will Learn...

- why you need self-awareness to set career goals
- why it is important to know your values
- how you can identify your interests and talents
- why you should consider your personality and learning styles when choosing a career
- why it is important to have a positive self-image

Personal Career Portfolio *Preview*

For your portfolio you will make a list of your values, interests, skills, and talents. As you read, think about what you will include in your list.

Draw From Your Own Background Draw a figure that represents you. Write words that describe you around the figure. Write as many different words as you can. Think about the kind of person you are. Think about what is important to you. Think about what you like to do.

Getting to Know Yourself

Key Terms

self-awareness
values
interests
experiences
volunteer work
skills
knowledge
talents

Main Idea

You need to know yourself to choose the right career. You need to know your values, interests, skills, and talents.

Thought Organizer

Draw the chart below. As you read, write the definition of each key term. Then give an example.

Key Term	Definition	Example
values	things that are important to you	helping others
interests		
skills		
talents		

Self-Awareness Means Knowing Yourself

self-awareness ■ Knowing your thoughts, feelings, and actions.

There are so many careers. Which one is right for you? To answer this question, you need self-awareness. **Self-awareness** means knowing your thoughts, feelings, and actions. Self-awareness is about knowing yourself. When you know yourself, you can make good choices.

It is up to you to choose your career and your path in life. Other people can make suggestions, but they should not make decisions for you.

To be self-aware, you need to know a lot about yourself. You need to know what things are important to you. You need to know what you like to do. You need to know what you do well. When you know these things, you can pick a career that is right for you.

Your Values Are What Is Important to You

You can become more self-aware by thinking about your values. **Values** are things that are important to you. Like lifestyles, values differ from person to person. Values help you make choices that are right for you.

You learn your values as you grow up. You learn them from your family, your teachers, and your friends. When you were a child, you probably learned the values of the adults you knew.

As young adults, we begin to choose our own values. We keep some of the values we learned in childhood. We also add some new values of our own.

You need to think about your values before you choose a career. Certain careers match up well with certain values. Certain careers conflict with certain values. You want to make a good match between your values and your career.

values ■ Things that are important to you.

Different Values Match Different Careers

Look at the values listed below. Which ones are most important to you?

• helping other people

• being part of a family

• earning a lot of money

• having good health

• being a spiritual or religious person

Try to decide which of these values are yours. Then think about which careers match your values.

Helping Other People Is a Value   Helping others is very important to some people. You can help people in many careers. You might help people stay healthy by working as a nurse or a physical therapist. You might help people feed themselves by working at a supermarket or a restaurant. You might help people learn by working as a teacher or teacher aide.

While You Read

Visualize Think of two people who are important to you. Describe these people.

Being Part of a Family Is a Value   Do you like to spend time with your family? Would you like to have a life partner? Would you like to raise children? If family is important to you, think about your family when you set your career goals. Choose a career that will allow you to spend time with your family.

While You Read

Connect Would you choose an occupation if it did not pay well?

Earning a Lot of Money Is a Value   Will you need a lot of money to live the way you want? If so, you place a high value on earning money. You will want to learn about careers that pay well. If you want a simpler life, money may not be so important.

Having Good Health Is a Value   When you are healthy, you enjoy life more. How important is your health to you? Do you take great care to stay healthy? Do you eat the right foods? Do you exercise?

If your health is important to you, you may not want to do some types of work. Some jobs are more dangerous to your health than others. Workers on some jobs breathe dangerous dust. Some workers must lift and carry heavy things. These types of jobs can cause health problems.

Having a Lot of Friends Is a Value   Do you like to be around people? Do you want to have a lot of friends? Some people do. Others do not. Most people like to have at least one or two good friends. Friends may be members of your family. Romantic partners often consider each other best friends. School is a great place to make friends. There are many people your same age. You will also meet people at your job. Some of them may become close friends. You can meet people by pursuing your hobbies, too. For example, you might make friends when you join a club or team. You might make friends when you volunteer.

If having a lot of friends is important to you, you could look for a career where you can meet lots of people. You might also look for a career that will allow you to spend time with your friends.

Helping Others
Helping other people is important to Karine. She chose a career as a physician assistant so she could help hospital patients. What other careers give you the opportunity to help people?

Being a Spiritual or Religious Person Is a Value   If spirituality or religion is important to you, you might want to work in a religious organization. Helping people is important in many religions. If helping others is important in your religion, you may want to choose a career that lets you help others.

Some people do not like to work where people do things that go against their religious beliefs. For example, some people do not like to work where alcohol is sold or used. You may not want to work on the days you attend religious services.

Study Tip

Before turning in an assignment, look it over a final time to catch any errors. When you look at something a second time, you can often find small mistakes that you did not see before.

You Should Be Proud of Your Life

When you live by your values, you can be proud of your life. Most happy people are proud of their lives. They take pride in their work. They enjoy what they do in their free time. They do not give up the values that are important to them.

Being proud of how you do your job is very satisfying. It carries over into other parts of your life. It makes you a happier person at home, too.

Your Interests Are the Things You Like to Do

interests ■ Things you like to do.

Understanding your interests is another part of understanding yourself. Your **interests** are things you like to do. Knowing your interests will help you choose a career. It will help you plan other parts of your life, too.

Look at **Figure 2.1** below. Do you share any of these interests? What interests do you have that are not pictured here?

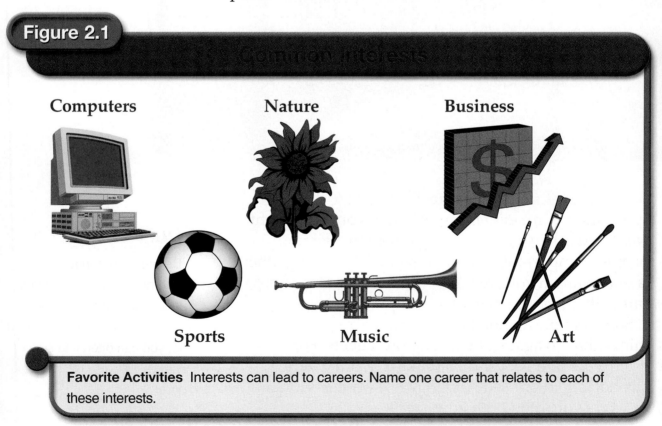

Figure 2.1

Common Interests

Computers

Nature

Business

Sports

Music

Art

Favorite Activities Interests can lead to careers. Name one career that relates to each of these interests.

Your Experiences Tell You About Your Interests

You can also figure out your interests by thinking about your experiences. **Experiences** are activities you have tried. You have tried many activities at school, at home and in your community, and maybe at a job.

experiences ■ Activities you have tried.

School Experiences   You have had many experiences at school. What subjects have you taken in school? Which ones did you enjoy? Do you really like math? Or marketing? Or machine shop? There are many jobs in each of these fields.

Other school activities tell about your interests. Imagine that you join the photography club at school. You will learn how to take pictures and develop film. You may find you have an interest in photography. You might even like a photography career.

Home and Community Experiences   You have also had many experiences at home and in your community. What activities do you enjoy with family members? What neighborhood activities do you like to do? Are there cultural activities that you enjoy? You see people doing many different kinds of work in your community. Do any of them have jobs that interest you?

While You Read

Connect Think of two activities you have tried with your family.

Work Experiences   You can also learn about your interests from the work that you do. Household chores are one type of work. Do you enjoy cooking, gardening, sewing, decorating, caring for pets, or repairing broken items? Many people earn a living doing such work.

Jobs are another type of work. They help you learn about a certain career and see if it interests you. You may find that you enjoy one part of a job but not another part.

Imagine that you work in a restaurant. You may find that you like helping customers. But you may not like preparing food.

Some young people try three or four types of work. This gives them a chance to see what interests them most.

volunteer work ■ Work you do without receiving pay.

Volunteer Work Is Work Experience   Volunteer work is also helpful work experience. **Volunteer work** is work that you do without receiving pay. Imagine that you volunteer at your local library. You will find out if you would enjoy working there full time. If you volunteer in a nursing home, you will see if you enjoy working with older people.

Point of View

Helping Animals and People

Tamara Johnson, a high school senior, volunteers at an animal shelter in Orlando, Florida. "I love cats and dogs," she says, "but we can't have pets at home because my brother has allergies. So I do my community service at the shelter."

Because of her experiences at the shelter, Tamara began to think about a career working with animals. "I got interested in watching the veterinary technicians treat the animals. I talked to them about their job and decided it might be a good match for me. Right now I'm applying to the veterinary technology program at Brevard Community College. In two years I would qualify to be a veterinary technician. It's a satisfying career because you get to help both animals and people."

It's Your Turn   Tamara's volunteer work led to a great career idea. What volunteer activities could you do in your community to explore your interests?

For help completing this activity, visit **ewow.glencoe.com/tips** and click on the *Smart Tip* for the Chapter 2 *Point of View*.

Look at What You Do for Fun

How you spend your leisure time is another clue to your interests. *Leisure time* is free time that you use to do what you like. What do you like to talk about? What do you like to read about? What kinds of TV shows and movies do you watch? What do you want to learn more about? Your answers to these questions are your interests.

Hobbies Are Fun Activities   Interest in a hobby can give you ideas for your career. A *hobby* is an activity that you do for fun. If you like woodworking, for example, you might consider a career as a carpenter. Do you work on your own car? Maybe a career as a mechanic is right for you. If you are good at a sport, you could train other people how to play that sport.

Trying things is the best way to see if you like them. The more things you try, the better you will know what you like to do. Then you will have a better chance of finding a career that will make you happy.

While You Read

Connect Name a hobby you would like to try.

Interest Surveys Help You Learn About Your Interests

There is another good way to learn about your interests. You can take an interest survey. An *interest survey* is a list of questions about your likes and dislikes. An interest survey is not a test. There are no right or wrong answers.

The purpose of an interest survey is to learn which jobs would be right for you. Let's say you like animals. You might enjoy a career in farming or animal medicine. If you like cars, you might enjoy a career in manufacturing or auto repair. Take an interest survey and then look at the results. You might learn something new about yourself. You might discover interests you did not know about. You might get a good idea for a career. Your teacher or counselor can help you find out more about interest surveys.

Your Skills Are Your Specific Abilities

You have looked at your interests. Now think about your skills. **Skills** are abilities to do specific tasks. A skill is something special you know how to do. Taking care of children is a skill. Operating a car or a wheelchair is a skill.

There Are Two Types of Skills

There are two types of skills. Job-specific skills are one type of skill. Job-specific skills are abilities you need to do a specific job. Using a table saw is a job-specific skill. Programming a computer is a job-specific skill.

While You Read

Connect List five of your strongest transferable skills.

Transferable skills are the second type of skill. *Transferable skills* are general abilities. Many transferable skills involve communicating and thinking. How many of these transferable skills do you have?

- reading
- writing
- adding, subtracting, multiplying, dividing
- listening
- speaking
- thinking logically
- thinking creatively
- making decisions
- solving problems
- picturing things in your mind

Transferable skills can also be *personal qualities*, or ways of acting. How many of these personal qualities do you show?

- responsibility
- self-esteem
- friendliness
- self-management (setting goals and reaching them)
- honesty

Build Your Skills Through Knowledge and Practice

Skills come from knowledge and practice. **Knowledge** is understanding facts. *Practice* means repeating something again and again. You have knowledge about all kinds of subjects, not just things you have learned in school. You might know about languages, basketball, or music.

knowledge ■
Understanding facts.

You also have practice doing many activities. You might have practice with Spanish or basketball.

When you put knowledge and practice together, you get a skill. So to improve a skill, you need to learn more and practice more.

You can build your skills in many places. You can build them at school. You can build them on the job. You can build them at home.

Making Good Choices

Handling Job Competition

Sarah and Joo-Ri are good friends who have a lot in common. They both play the trumpet in band class. They both have a lot of experience baby-sitting their younger brothers and sisters. Last summer, Joo-Ri worked at her father's day-care center, while Sarah helped the neighbors with yard work. This summer, they are hoping to get jobs to pay for new instruments.

One day, Sarah sees a great job posting on the Internet. It is an ad for a summer counselor at a musical day camp. Sarah would love to have this job. However, Sarah thinks that her friend Joo-Ri might be better at this job because of her day-care experience.

You Make the Call Should Sarah tell her friend about the job? Why or why not?

For help in answering this question, visit **ewow.glencoe.com/tips** and select the *Smart Tip* for the Chapter 2 *Making Good Choices*.

Your Talents Are Your Natural Gifts

talents ■ Natural gifts.

Your **talents** are your natural gifts. A talent is the ability to do something easily or to learn something easily. The greater your talent for something, the easier it is for you to do.

To set career goals, you should be aware of your talents. You will be happier if you choose a career that lets you use your special talents.

There Are Three Types of Talents

There are three different types of talents. There are mental, physical, and social talents.

Mental Talents Involve the Mind   Mental talents are talents that involve thinking and creativity. If you are good at writing, art, music, math, science, or any other subject, you have mental talents. Do you work hard in school? If so, your grades probably show your mental talents. If not, you may have more talent than your grades show. All jobs require mental talents, so it is important to work hard to develop them.

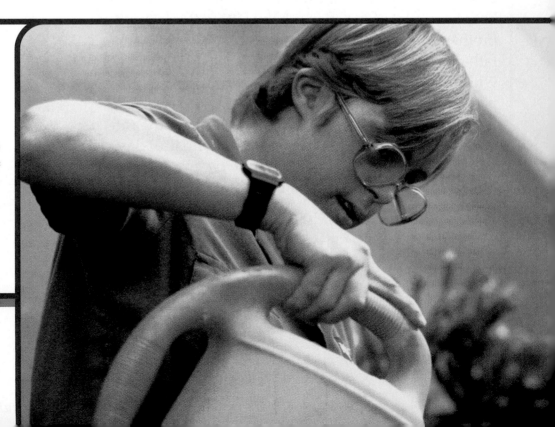

Your Natural Gifts
Everyone has different talents. Some people are good with plants and animals. Others have an excellent sense of touch or an eye for color. How can you find out what your physical talents are?

Physical Talents Involve the Body Physical talents are talents that involve using your body. If you are good at sports, dance, shop, gardening, or cooking, you have physical talents. Do you have steady hands? Are you strong? Can you run fast? Can you throw a ball straight? Can you move your hands and fingers quickly? These skills show physical talents. Many jobs require physical talents. You need physical talents to work as an athlete, sculptor, or gardener.

Social Talents Involve Getting Along Social talents involve getting along with other people. Most people can learn to get along well, but it is easier for some than for others. People with social talents understand others. They have a gift for saying things that make people feel good. Salespersons, social workers, and teachers are examples of people who need social talents.

While You Read

Connect List the social talents of three people you know.

Use Your Talents on the Job Most jobs require a mix of talents. For example, cashiers need mental talents to make change. They need physical talents to handle goods and use store machines. They need social talents to help customers and get along with their coworkers.

Understand Your Talents by Trying Many Things

You can learn what your talents are by trying many different things. Is a certain subject at school easy for you? Do you find certain tasks easier than others? Are you good at sports, music, art, repairs, or math? Are you good at talking to people or solving problems? By paying attention to what you can do quickly and easily, you will learn what your talents are.

Sometimes other people can help you see talents that you never thought about. Notice when people say you did a good job with a certain task. Listen to what people praise you for. Have you ever won an award? If so, you are sure to have a talent in that area.

Study Tip

Routines can help you stay organized. Organize your schoolwork in the same way each evening. That way you won't forget anything you need.

Check your answers online by visiting **ewow.glencoe.com/review** and selecting the Section 2.1 Review.

Retell

1. Using your own words, explain why you need to understand yourself to choose a career.

2. Reread the first two paragraphs of the section titled Types of Skills. Retell the information in your own words.

Think Critically

3. You read that people with social talents have a gift for saying things that make people feel good. Give an example.

Math Practice

Answer the multiple-choice math questions at **ewow.glencoe.com/math**.

How Much Will Housing Cost?

Most Americans spend about 32% of their yearly income on housing. If you earn $27,000 per year, how much will you need to spend on housing? Here's how to figure it out.

Step 1 Convert the percentage to a decimal.
$$32\% = 32 \times 1\% = 32 \times .01 = .32$$

Step 2 Multiply the decimal by your yearly salary.
$$\$27,000 \times .32 = \$8,640.00$$

Result You will spend $8,640.00 per year on housing.

Figure It Out

Most Americans spend about 17% of their yearly income on food. If you earn $43,000 per year, how much will you need to spend on food?

Being an Individual

Key Terms

personality
learning styles
self-image
self-esteem

Main Idea

Everyone is different. Your personality and your self-image make you an individual.

Thought Organizer

Draw the chart below. As you read, fill each empty oval with one key term.

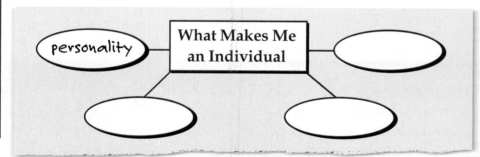

personality — What Makes Me an Individual

Your Personality Is How You Think, Feel, and Act

Everyone is different. Everyone has different ways of thinking, feeling, and acting. The way you think, feel, and act is your **personality**. Your personality is an important part of who you are. Understanding your personality will help you pick a career you will like.

personality ■ The way you think, feel, and act.

You Have a Unique Personality

Everyone is an individual. For example, some people like to talk. These people have outgoing personalities. Other people talk less. They often listen better than people with outgoing personalities. These people have quieter personalities.

Your Personality and Your Career   When you know your personality, you can choose a career that will suit you. Do you like to talk to other people? If so, you might like a career as a salesperson, a tour guide, or a teacher. Do you prefer to spend time alone? If so, you might not enjoy these jobs. Instead, you might want to work with computers or cars or plants.

Think of other parts of your personality. How do they make you suited for some jobs and not others? For example, let's say that you like routine. You find it satisfying to do the same tasks again and again, getting the task right each time. In this case, you might like to work on an assembly line or checking groceries. Let's say that you do not like routine. You like a variety of tasks. In this case, you might like to work in a busy office or retail store.

While You Read

Visualize Picture two people you know who have very different personalities.

The Real You It is important to choose a career that fits your personality. Jo is outgoing and energetic, which is a perfect match for her career as a third grade teacher. What careers might be good for a person who is quieter and prefers to work alone?

Learning Styles Are Part of Personality

How you think and learn is also part of your personality. The different ways people naturally think and learn are called **learning styles**. When you know your learning style, you can figure out the best way to learn something new. You can also figure out which jobs are right for you.

Read the descriptions of the eight different learning styles. Which one sounds most like you?

Verbal-Linguistic Learners Verbal-linguistic learners are good with words. They like to read, write, and tell stories. They are good at remembering names and dates. A verbal learner learns best by saying, hearing, and seeing words. Does this sound like you? If so, you might enjoy a career as a writer, a radio announcer, or a lawyer.

Logical-Mathematical Learners Logical-mathematical learners are good with numbers. They like to learn, do experiments, and solve problems. Does this sound like you? If so, you might enjoy a career as a scientist, a repairperson, or an accountant.

Visual-Spatial Learners Visual-spatial learners are good at imagining things. They like to draw, build, design, and create things. This makes them good at doing puzzles and mazes. They also have a talent for reading maps and charts. A visual learner learns well by working with colors and pictures. If you are a visual-spatial learner, you might enjoy a career as an architect, a designer, or an airplane pilot.

Musical-Rhythmic Learners Musical-rhythmic learners have musical talent. They like to sing, hum, play an instrument, and listen to music. They are good at remembering melodies and noticing rhythms. Musical-rhythmic learners enjoy careers related to music, such as guitarist, disc jockey, or music therapist.

learning styles ■ The different ways people naturally think and learn.

While You Read

Question What jobs involve reading maps or charts?

Bodily-Kinesthetic Learners Bodily-kinesthetic learners like to touch things and move around. They are good at using their hands to do things such as craft projects and repairs. A bodily-kinesthetic learner learns best by touching objects and moving. Does this sound like you? If so, you might enjoy a career as a dancer, a carpenter, or a physical therapist. You will probably enjoy a career where you can move around or work with your hands.

Interpersonal Learners Interpersonal learners are good with people. They have social talents. They usually like having lots of friends, talking to people, and joining groups. They are good at understanding people, leading, and communicating. They are also good at helping people solve their problems. An interpersonal learner learns best by working with others. If you are an interpersonal learner, you might enjoy a career as a teacher, a psychologist, or a manager.

While You Read

Connect Do you prefer to study alone or in a group?

Intrapersonal Learners Intrapersonal learners are usually very self-aware. This means they know themselves well. They are confident about their thoughts and feelings. Intrapersonal learners often like to work alone and go at their own pace. They would rather learn alone than join a study group. Does this sound like you? If so, you might enjoy a career as a small business owner, a therapist, or a politician. You will want a career where you can express yourself. You may also like to work alone sometimes.

Naturalistic Learners Naturalistic learners enjoy nature. They like spending time outdoors and working with plants, animals, and the environment. They are good at hearing and seeing things in nature. Naturalistic learners often have collections of things. They are good at sorting things into different categories. A naturalistic learner would enjoy a career as an astronomer, a gardener, or a chef.

Use Your Learning Styles to Succeed

Strong learners are successful at school and at work. You can become a strong learner by understanding the way you learn best. You may be very strong in one learning style. You may be equally strong in two or three learning styles. Either way, you can use this knowledge about yourself to succeed.

Let's say that you are talented at learning new faces but have trouble learning names. You probably have a visual learning style. You can improve your learning by using your visual talents. When you meet a new person, you could write that person's name down in colored ink. You could make a sketch of the person's face or clothing. You could also create a mental movie of the person saying his or her name. You could play this movie in your mind when you need to recall the person's name.

Focus on what you do well. Use your learning style to succeed.

It's Your Decision
Make the choices that are right for you. This will help you feel happy with yourself and your life. What are some things you can do to feel good about yourself?

Your Self-Image Is How You See Yourself

Another part of you is your self-image. Your **self-image** is how you see yourself. It is how you picture yourself in your mind.

The way other people see you affects the way you see yourself. However, it is important to feel good about yourself even if other people are not friendly toward you. It is good to be aware of your flaws so that you can improve yourself. But do not let other people's words and actions damage your self-image. Remember that you have the right to be an individual.

When you are proud of yourself as an individual, it shows in your personality. You act yourself. You do not pretend to be something you are not. You like who you are, even if some people do not like you.

While You Read

Connect Do you have a positive or a negative self-image?

Your Self-Image and Work Affect Your Career

Your self-image affects the way you feel about yourself. It affects the way you act around other people. It also affects what you think you can do at school and at work. If you do not think much of yourself, you will have trouble setting career goals. You will have trouble succeeding in a career.

You want to have a good self-image. But it must be a true self-image. Know what you can do. Know your limits, too. Everyone has strengths and weaknesses. Be proud of your strengths. Be realistic about your limits. Do not pick a career based on a false image of yourself.

If you see yourself as a great athlete, you may decide on a professional career with a sports team. If you have the talent, this is a good goal. If you do not have the talent, your false self-image may cause you some trouble. Your career choice can cause you a lot of unhappiness.

Compare your self-image with how others see you. If you do not know how they see you, ask. This will give you a clearer picture of yourself. You can make good career choices if you know who you really are.

Self-Esteem Is Feeling Good About Yourself

It is important to have a positive self-image. When you have a positive self-image, you feel good about yourself. You can picture yourself doing what you want to do in life.

When you see yourself in your mind, do you like what you see? If so, you probably have high self-esteem. **Self-esteem** is a positive feeling about yourself. It is respect for yourself as a person.

self-esteem ■ A positive feeling about yourself

Self-esteem gives you many advantages. It helps you feel confident. It helps you try new things. It helps you learn. It helps you get along with other people. It helps you succeed at school and on the job.

Real-World Connection

Understanding Empathy

Each person has a unique way of communicating. This can sometimes make it hard for people to understand each other. To communicate well, it is important to use empathy. *Empathy* is caring about the feelings, thoughts, and experiences of others. Use empathy when you talk and when you listen. If someone makes you upset, stay calm and ask what the person meant to say. Communicating with empathy is very important on the job. It helps you get along with customers, coworkers, and supervisors.

Take the Next Step Interview an adult about good communication on the job. What should a worker do to communicate well with customers, coworkers, and supervisors?

For help doing this activity, go to **ewow.glencoe.com/tips** and find the *Smart Tip* for the Chapter 2 *Real-World Connection*.

Check your answers online by visiting ewow.glencoe.com/review and selecting the Section 2.2 Review.

After You Read

Retell

1. Reread the first paragraph of the section titled You Have a Unique Personality. What example does this paragraph give of people having different personalities?

2. Explain how learning styles can help you succeed. Use your own words.

Think Critically

3. Which learning style do you think is your strongest? Why?

Math Practice

Answer the multiple-choice math questions at ewow.glencoe.com/math.

Is It a Bargain?

You need a pair of work shoes that cost $89.99. A store near you is selling the shoes at 20% off. How much will the shoes cost after the discount?

Step 1 Convert the percentage to a decimal.
$20\% = 20 \times 1\% = 20 \times .01 = .20$

Step 2 Multiply the decimal by the price of the shoes.
$\$89.99 \times .20 = \$18.00$

Step 3 Subtract the discount from the original price.
$\$89.99 - 18.00 = \$71.99$

Result The shoes will cost $71.99.

Figure It Out

The regular price of a set of pots and pans is $119.99. A department store is offering the set for 35% off. How much will the pots and pans cost after the discount?

Construction and Maintenance Worker

Melissa Wood

Georgia

Career Cluster: Architecture and Construction

What does a construction and maintenance worker do?

"I'm the groundskeeper and maintenance worker for an apartment complex. I do all the maintenance work, even the electrical and plumbing."

Why did you choose a career in construction?

"I'm a non-traditional person. I don't like sitting behind a desk. I'm a bodybuilder, so I'm strong. When I was a little girl, my grandfather taught me about tools. I like construction work."

What obstacles have you overcome?

"I had emotional problems and I couldn't do numbers. I went to the New Choices for Women at the Goodwill Industries of Northern Georgia. They train women for nontraditional jobs. They taught me fractions so I could work in construction."

What advice do you have for students?

"Don't give up. Stay strong. Men in construction used to harass women. It's better now."

Construction and Maintenance Worker

Training
Construction and maintenance workers learn their work through on-the-job training and apprenticeship programs. A high school diploma is helpful.

Skills and Talents
Construction and maintenance workers need to be physically fit. They need good math skills, mechanical skills, and problem-solving skills.

Career Outlook
Employment for construction and maintenance workers should be good through 2012. Jobs vary by season and by area.

Learn More About It
Draw vertical lines on a piece of paper to make three columns. Label each column with the name of one career pathway in the architecture and construction career cluster. Work with a classmate to make a list of five jobs in each pathway.

For help with this activity, visit **ewow.glencoe.com/tips**.

Glencoe Online

Go to ewow.glencoe.com to find online games and activities for Chapter 2.

Key Term Review

self-awareness (p. 28)
values (p. 29)
interests (p. 32)
experiences (p. 33)
volunteer work (p. 34)
skills (p. 36)

knowledge (p. 37)
talents (p. 38)
personality (p. 41)
learning styles (p. 43)
self-image (p. 46)
self-esteem (p. 47)

Check Your Understanding

1. Explain why you need self-awareness to set career goals.
2. Tell why it is important to know your values.
3. List three ways to identify your interests and talents.
4. Explain why you should consider your personality and learning styles when choosing a career.
5. Describe why it is important to have a positive self-image.

Write About It

6. **Get to Know Yourself** You have read about understanding yourself. Now that you have finished reading this chapter, make a list of things that you still would like to learn about yourself. List four things you would like to understand better about yourself. Then write a short paragraph about an activity you could do to learn each of these things about yourself.

Role Play

7. **Describe Yourself**   Pretend that you are on a job interview. The interviewer wants to know more about you. Describe yourself to the interviewer. Tell him or her about your skills, interests, and talents. Explain how these could help you on the job.

Teamwork Challenge

8. **Personality and Careers**   Ask your partner about his or her personality. Which words does your partner use to describe his or her personality? Write these words down. Think of a job that might fit your partner's personality. Tell your partner about the job and the reasons it would be a good fit. Ask your partner to do the same for your personality.

Computer Lab

Make a Chart   Use a word-processing program to make a chart with your top three learning styles. In the first column, list the learning style. In the second column, list the things you like to do using this learning style. In the last column, write down one job that would be good for this learning style.

Personal Career Portfolio

Personal Inventory   Make a list of your values, interests, skills, and talents. Include values, interests, skills, and talents you have in school, at home, or at work. File this list in your Personal Career Portfolio.

Go to **ewow.glencoe.com/portfolio** for help.

Chapter 3

Exploring Careers

You Already Know...

- work will be an important part of your life
- there are thousands of occupations
- knowing yourself helps you choose the right career
- you can learn about careers in many ways

You Will Learn...

- what career clusters are and how they can help you make a career choice
- what to find out when you do career research
- how to find career information in books and on the Internet
- what informational interviews and job shadowing are
- how to try the work that interests you

Personal Career Portfolio *Preview*

For your portfolio, you will profile three occupations that interest you. As you read, think about which occupations appeal to you.

Preview Find the photos in this chapter. Read the caption below each photo. Based on the photos and captions, write three sentences predicting what this chapter will be about.

Narrowing Your Career Choices

Key Terms

career cluster
business
management
training
finance
health science
hospitality
   and tourism
information
   technology
manufacturing
marketing
engineering

Main Idea

You need to narrow your career choices before you can make a career decision. You can narrow your career choices by learning about the 16 career clusters.

Thought Organizer

Make a chart with two columns. As you read, write each career cluster name in the first column. Write two occupations from each cluster in the second column.

Career Cluster	Sample Occupations
Agriculture, Food, and Natural Resources	farmer, food-processing worker
Architecture and Construction	
Arts, Audio/Video Technology, and Communications	

Narrowing Your Career Choices Means Picking Options

There are thousands of occupations. With so many options, how do you choose? By narrowing your choices. Narrowing your choices means picking some options and putting aside the rest. Narrowing your career choices will help you make decisions about your future occupation.

Learning About Careers Helps You Narrow Your Choices

How do you narrow your career choices? By learning about careers.

You cannot choose a career without knowing what careers there are. Can you imagine trying to order food in a new restaurant without a menu? You would not know where to begin. The same is true for choosing a career. You need to know what types of careers there are.

In this section you will learn about many different occupations. As you read, think about which occupations appeal to you. Which seem fun and interesting? Which do you want to know more about?

Career Clusters Are Groups of Occupations

It would be pretty hard to learn about every single occupation. Luckily, you do not have to learn about them all. You can learn about many kinds of work by learning about career clusters. A **career cluster** is a group of related occupations.

Read about the 16 career clusters. Then choose two or three clusters that seem interesting. Right away you will have narrowed your choices.

career cluster ■ A group of related occupations.

Agriculture, Food, and Natural Resources

Agriculture is growing plants and raising animals for people to use. People who work in agriculture are called farmers or agriculturists.

Agriculture is the first step in making food. The second step is food processing. *Food processing* means turning farm products into foods you can eat. As a baker, you would make grain into bread. As a butcher, you would cut and prepare pieces of meat.

Natural resources are useful things found in nature. Coal, metal, soil, trees, and water are natural resources. You could harvest natural resources as a logger or fisher. You could protect natural resources as a conservationist or ecologist.

While You Read

Question What do agriculture and natural resources have in common?

Architecture and Construction

Workers in architecture and construction design and build structures such as houses and bridges.

As an architect or civil engineer, you would design structures. You would make sure they are safe, useful, and attractive.

As a construction worker, you would build structures. There are many specialties in construction. A *specialty* is a focus on one type of work. For example, as a carpenter, you would build and install things made of wood.

Arts, Audio/Video Technology, and Communications

The arts are about sharing thoughts and feelings. As an artist, you could make objects with your hands. You could express yourself with your body, face, or voice.

As a journalist, you would write news stories. As a printing equipment operator, you would operate machines that make books, magazines, or newspapers.

Audio/video technology means knowledge and tools to make sounds and pictures. As a camera operator, you would take pictures with a television or movie camera. As a cable installer, you would hook up cable television systems.

Communications Technology This worker is holding telephone wires. She works in the arts, audio/video technology, and communications career cluster. List several ways people use technology to communicate.

Business, Management, and Administration

Business is selling goods or services. The goal of business is to make a profit. You make a profit when you receive more money than you spend.

Management is a big part of business. Management means making decisions and planning. As a manager, you would tell workers what tasks to do. You would check that workers are doing a good job. You could work at a company, a government, a school, or a charity.

Administration means making sure that an organization runs smoothly. Administrative workers take care of the day-to-day work. As a receptionist, you would greet people and answer the phone. As a bookkeeper, you would keep records of money.

business ■ Selling goods or services.

management ■ Making decisions and planning.

Education and Training

Over ten million people work in education and training. *Education* means teaching and learning. Training is education in a specific skill, such as computer programming.

The biggest career in education and training is teaching. There are nearly four million teachers for kindergarten through 12th grade.

Schools also need workers besides teachers. For example, they need counselors and librarians. As a counselor, you would answer students' career and personal questions. As a librarian, you would run a library and help people find information.

While You Read

Connect Think of five jobs that people do at your school.

training ■ Education in a specific skill.

Finance

We all use money to pay for goods and services such as food, housing, and transportation. Because money is so important, finance is a very important field. Finance means managing money.

Finance workers help people and businesses use their money wisely. As a bank teller, you would help customers at a bank. As a financial planner, you would help people handle their money. As a tax preparer, you could help people fill out their tax forms.

finance ■ Managing money.

Government and Public Administration

The government keeps order and provides services. What do government workers do? As a legislator, you would vote on laws. As a soldier, you would protect the country.

In public administration, you would do tasks that keep the government running. As a mail carrier, you would deliver mail. As a census clerk, you would collect information about the population.

Public administration also includes nonprofit organizations. Unlike businesses, *nonprofit organizations* do not try to make a profit. The Red Cross and the Salvation Army are large nonprofit organizations.

Making Good Choices

Reporting Illegal Behavior

José has a summer job as a receptionist at a small financial company. He answers the phone and greets visitors. The company helps people handle their money wisely. As part of their job, the workers at the company give money advice.

José overhears two workers talking about the president of the company. They say that she has a lot of money invested in a certain stock. She wants this stock to rise in value so she can earn money from it. The president pressures the workers to tell their clients to buy that stock. The workers know it is illegal to do this, but they do it anyway. They want to protect their jobs.

You Make the Call What should José do with the information he heard? What would you do?

For help in answering this question, visit **ewow.glencoe.com/tips** and select the *Smart Tip* for the Chapter 3 *Making Good Choices*.

 ewow.glencoe.com/tips

Health Science

Health science is about helping people stay healthy and recover from sickness. There are many specialties in health science.

Some health science workers work in hospitals. As a surgeon, for example, you would perform operations in a hospital operating room. Some health science workers work in labs. As a laboratory technician, you would use lab equipment to test blood and other samples. Some health science workers work in offices. As a medical records technician, you would work in an office organizing medical files.

health science ■ Helping people stay healthy and recover from sickness.

Hospitality and Tourism

Hospitality and tourism includes services for people who are traveling. What do people do when they travel? They stay at hotels and eat at restaurants. They rent cars. They relax and go to special events. There are jobs in all these areas.

As a travel agent, you would help people plan their vacations. As a front desk clerk, you could check guests into and out of hotels. As a chef or waiter, you would cook or serve food in a restaurant. As a guide, you would show visitors through a museum, a city, or even a whole country.

While You Read

Visualize Recall a time when you went to a hotel or restaurant. What jobs did you see workers doing?

hospitality and tourism ■ Services for people who are traveling.

Hospitality and Tourism Is Growing Hospitality and tourism is a growing career field. List three activities people like to do when they are on vacation. Then list two jobs that relate to each activity.

information technology ■ Designing and using computer systems.

Human Services

Human services are services that improve people's lives. Human service workers help people in all kinds of ways. As a social worker, you would help people live better at home, school, and work. As a consumer credit counselor, you would help people who have money problems. As a child care worker, you would look after children. As a hairstylist, you would help people look their best. You could even work as an event planner, a soup kitchen manager, or a spa attendant.

Information Technology

Information technology means designing and using computer systems. Why are computer systems called information technology, or IT? Because computers are information machines. They store, sort, and use information.

Some IT workers work with computer *hardware*, or parts. As a network manager, for example, you would set up and run office computers.

Other IT workers work with *software*, or programs. As a programmer, for example, you would write computer programs. As a web designer, you would create Web sites.

Law, Public Safety, and Security

Workers in law, public safety, and security protect people and property. They prevent crimes and help during emergencies.

Important occupations in this career cluster include lawyer, police officer, firefighter, and security guard. As a lawyer, you would answer people's questions about the law. You would help them write legal papers. You would stand up for them in court. As a police officer, you would see that people obey the law. You would catch and arrest people who break the law. As a firefighter, you would put out fires and help during medical emergencies. As a security guard, you would protect people and property.

Manufacturing

Manufacturing means making products by hand or machine. Many manufacturing jobs are in factories. Factories make things. Each factory makes just a few kinds of things, but it makes many of them.

Most manufacturing workers use tools and machines. As a welder, you would use a torch to bond metal pieces together. As a material mover, you would use a forklift to move heavy objects.

Today, many manufacturing workers work with computers. For example, some workers use computers to control robots.

manufacturing ■ Making products by hand or machine.

Point of View

Designing Cities on Mars

One year ago, Patrick Wong had no interest in science. Then he learned about the International Space Settlement Design Competition.

Building a city in outer space isn't easy. "It is 100 degrees below zero on Mars, so we had to keep 10,000 people from freezing," says Patrick. "We had to pump in oxygen and grow enough plants to feed everybody. It all had to be based on science."

Patrick's team didn't make it to the finals in the competition. However, Patrick gained a lot. Today Patrick is planning to study engineering after high school. "In engineering you can do practically anything. It's a good job, and you learn a lot."

It's Your Turn Patrick built his science and math skills by joining a school team. What activities could you join at your school? What skills could they help you build?

For help completing this activity, visit **ewow.glencoe.com/tips** and go to the *Smart Tip* for the Chapter 3 *Point of View*.

Marketing, Sales, and Service

marketing ■ Deciding which goods and services people will want to buy.

Marketing is about deciding which goods and services people will want to buy. As a marketer, you would decide what your company should sell. You would decide how and where you should sell it and what the price should be.

Sales, or selling, is helping people decide to buy. As a salesperson, you would tell customers what is good about what you sell. As a store manager or assistant manager, you would make sure your store is a success.

Science, Technology, Engineering, and Mathematics

Science is the study of our world. As a scientist or science technician, you could study animals, plants, atoms, oceans, or even the stars.

engineering ■ Using science and mathematics to make things that help people.

Engineering is using science and mathematics to make things that help people. *Mathematics* is the study of numbers, shapes, and patterns. As an engineer or engineering technician, you would look for better, faster, and cheaper ways to do things.

While You Read

Connect What kinds of vehicles have you seen on land, in the air, and on the water?

Transportation, Distribution, and Logistics

Transportation involves moving people and things. As a pilot, you would fly planes.

Distribution involves getting goods to customers. As a warehouse worker, you would organize goods and send them to customers.

Logistics is planning the movement of people, objects, information, and money. As a logistics manager, you would make sure that the right things get to the right places at the right time.

Choose Two or Three Career Clusters

You now have a general idea of the 16 career clusters. Which ones are most interesting to you? Make a list.

Read more about the career clusters that interest you. The more you know, the better your career choice will be.

Check your answers online by visiting **ewow.glencoe.com/review** and selecting the Section 3.1 Review.

After You Read

Retell

1. Explain why learning about careers helps you make a career choice.

2. Using your own words, explain what workers in information technology (IT) do.

Think Critically

3. List three career clusters that interest you. Explain what interests you about them.

Math Practice

Answer the multiple-choice math questions at **ewow.glencoe.com/math**.

Paying for Advertising

You want to print an advertisement in your local newspaper. Your budget is $100.00. Advertisements cost $23.00 per inch on weekdays and $32.50 per inch on weekends. The newspaper sells space in whole inches only. What size advertisement could you afford on a weekday? What size could you afford on a weekend?

Step 1 Divide your budget by the price per inch on weekdays.
$$23 \div 100 = 4.3 = 4$$

Step 2 Divide your budget by the price per inch on weekends.
$$32 \div 100 = 3.1 = 3$$

Result You can afford a 4-inch advertisement on weekdays. You can afford a 3-inch advertisement on weekends.

Figure It Out

In a neighborhood newsletter, advertisements cost $13.00 per inch during the school year and $18.00 per inch during the summer. What size advertisement could you afford during the school year? What size could you afford during the summer?

Learning About Careers

Ready, Set, Read

Key Terms

research
Internet
informational
  interview
job shadowing
part-time job
cooperative
  education
service
  learning

Main Idea

You can learn about careers by reading, by talking to people, and by working.

Thought Organizer

Draw the chart below. As you read, give an example of each method of research.

Way to Research Careers	Examples
reading	researching careers online
talking to people	
working	

Your Next Step Is to Research Careers

Do you have a list of occupations that you think you might like? Good! Now it is time to find out more about these occupations. It is time to do research. **Research** means collecting information. Collect as much information as you can about each occupation on your list.

There are many things to look for in a career. There are many ways to find out career information. Before you begin your research, write down what you want to find out. What is important to you in your work? What is not so important?

research ▉ Collecting information.

There Are Many Important Questions to Ask

There is a lot to learn about every job. There are many different questions you can ask. Here are some basic questions to ask about the occupations that interest you.

You may have other questions, too. For example, you may want to know what kinds of job accommodations you will need to do a certain job. You may want to know what kinds of technology you will need to do a certain job. As you do your research, you may think of more questions. Write them down as you think of them.

While You Read

Connect Which of these eight things is most important to you in a job?

Duties   What do people in this occupation do? What are the tasks? What will be expected of you?

Working Conditions   Where will you work? Will you work by yourself or with others? Is the workplace noisy or quiet? Is it dangerous? How will you need to dress and act in this workplace?

Work Hours   When will you work? Are the hours long or short? Will you work during the day or during the night? Will you work the same hours every week?

Skills and Talents   What skills and talents do you need for this job?

Education and Training   What education do you need to do this job? Can you learn to do this job after you are hired? Will you need special training? College?

Pay   What pay can you expect to earn? Will you be able to have the lifestyle you want?

Career Path   If you have this job, can you expect to work up to a better job in the future?

Job Outlook   Will this type of job be available in the future? Is this a growing field?

There Are Three Ways to Research Careers

There is a lot of information about careers. How do you find it? Three ways to research careers are to:

- read
- talk with people
- try jobs yourself

While You Read

Connect Is there a library close to your home? Where is it?

You Can Read About Careers in Books

Books are good sources of career information. Visit your school library or public library. Look up the occupation or career cluster that interests you. A librarian can show you how to look up books in the library's catalog.

Larger libraries usually have a career section. Career sections include books related to work, occupations, careers, and jobs. Your library may also have career information on CDs, DVDs, or CD-ROMs. Ask your librarian to show you.

Finding Information Books, magazines, newspapers, and the Internet are all good sources of career information. Why is up-to-date career information more helpful to you than career information from the past?

Reference Books Make Information Easy to Find

Look at the reference books on careers. *Reference books* are books that you use to look up information in the library. They are usually kept in a section near the librarian's desk. Ask for these books:

- *Occupational Outlook Handbook.* This handbook describes hundreds of occupations. It is printed by the U.S. government and has very accurate information. A new version of this book comes out every two years.

- *Encyclopedia of Careers and Vocational Information.* This encyclopedia tells you about over 650 different occupations. It also gives you information on industries and career areas.

You Can Read About Careers on the Internet

The **Internet** is a worldwide network of computers. A *network* is two or more computers linked together. It lets people all over the world share information.

You need the Internet to get to the World Wide Web. The *World Wide Web* (the Web) is a collection of words, images, and sounds. The Web has billions of pages. A *Web page* is a document on the World Wide Web. A *Web site* is a group of Web pages.

The World Wide Web is easy to use. It is fast. You can find the answer to almost any question.

Ask whether you can use the Internet on a computer at your school. Your public library may have computers that allow you to use the Internet.

Type in a Web Address to Find a Web Site There are several ways to find information on the Internet. One way is to type in the address of the Web site you want. Web site addresses usually begin with the letters *www.* You can find Web site addresses in books and magazines. You can also ask a counselor or librarian. Type in the address of the Web site. The computer finds the Web site for you.

There are many good career Web sites. Monster.com is a useful career Web site.

While You Read

Question What is the World Wide Web?

Internet ■ A worldwide network of computers.

Study Tip

Do you know how to read a reference book? Do not start reading from the beginning. Instead, skim the table of contents. Skim the index. Then go directly to the pages that have the information you want.

Use a Search Engine to Search by Keywords Another way to find information on the Internet is to do a search. You do searches with a search engine. A *search engine* is a tool that finds Web sites for you. Type in keywords, and the search engine finds Web pages that have these words on them.

Let's say you are interested in careers in advertising. You type in *advertising careers*. Now the search engine finds Web sites about advertising and careers. Look at the list of sites. Click on ones that look helpful.

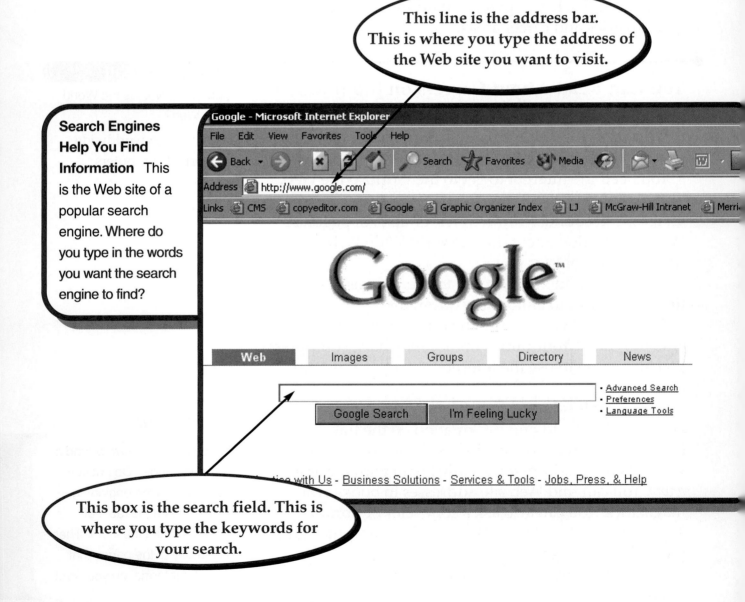

This line is the address bar. This is where you type the address of the Web site you want to visit.

Search Engines Help You Find Information This is the Web site of a popular search engine. Where do you type in the words you want the search engine to find?

This box is the search field. This is where you type the keywords for your search.

You Can Research Careers by Talking to People

Talking to people is another excellent way to learn about careers. Do you know someone who works at a job you like? Ask if he or she will talk about the work.

Talk to friends or family members. Talk to neighbors. Talk to anyone you can. Ask them what tasks they do in their jobs. Find out what they like about their jobs. Find out what they do not like.

Informational Interviewing Is Talking to a Worker on the Job The best way to learn about a specific occupation is to do an informational interview. An **informational interview** is a discussion with a person who has a job that interests you.

Informational interviews are very useful. You learn what it is like to have a certain occupation. This helps you see whether the occupation would be a good fit for you.

Job Shadowing Is Spending Time on the Job Job shadowing is another good way to learn about careers. **Job shadowing** is spending time with a worker on the job. It can last a few hours, a day, or a few days. Job shadowing is more in-depth than informational interviewing. You learn what a job is really like.

informational interview ■
A discussion with a person who has a job that interests you.

job shadowing ■ Spending time with a worker on the job.

You Can Set Up a Meeting by Phone or Letter How do you find people to interview? Ask your family members, friends, neighbors, teachers, and advisers. Ask people you see in your daily life, such as your doctor or your mail carrier. You can even look in the phone book. Look for a worker who has several years of experience.

If you know the person, telephone him or her. If you do not know the person, send a letter. Introduce yourself. Say why you would like to meet. Explain that you want to learn more about a career. Ask to set up an informational interview or a job shadow. Use the letter in **Figure 3.1** on the next page as a guide.

While You Read

Question How can you find a worker to job shadow?

Figure 3.1   Informational Interview Letter

John Singh
1236 Orlando Terrace, Apt. 8
Austin, TX 78757-3596
johnsingh@school41.org

October 13, 20--

Zeenat Walker
Loan Officer
People's Bank
100 Landmark Plaza
Austin, TX 78750

Dear Ms. Walker:

I am a senior at LaClare Technical High School and am completing a career preparation program. I interested in learning about careers in banking. Your client Michelle Kim visited our school last week and mentioned that you were very knowledgeable about banking.

Would you be willing to meet with me for an informational interview of about 20 minutes? I would like to find out about your job and what it is like to work at a bank. I would also like to learn about the skills necessary to succeed as a loan officer.

I will telephone you next Wednesday, October 19, to schedule a time that is convenient for you.

Sincerely yours,

John Singh

John Singh

Show Your Writing Skills Introduce yourself in writing to a worker you would like to interview. Make sure your letter is polite and well written. Why does a well-written letter make a better impression than a sloppily written letter?

Be Prepared for Your Interview   Do research before an informational interview or before you spend time job shadowing. Read about the job. Read about the industry. Learn the basics. This will give you ideas for good questions. Here are some useful questions to ask in an informational interview or during job shadowing:

- What is a typical day like for you?
- What do you like most about your job?
- What do you like least about your job?
- What kind of person would enjoy this job?
- How did you get started in this field?
- What kind of training did you have for this job?
- What advice would you give to a person starting a career?

While you ask questions, pay attention to what your host says. Show that you are interested in what he or she is saying. If you do not understand something, ask questions. Take notes so you will remember what you learn.

You Can Research Careers by Trying the Work Yourself

The best way to find out if a job is right for you is to try it. Of course, you do not have time to try every job. Start your research by reading and talking to people. Make a list of the jobs that interest you the most. Then try the work yourself.

Why try a job yourself? You can find out if you like a certain type of work. You can see if your personality is a good match. You can find out whether you want to continue.

You may not have enough training for the jobs that interest you. In that case, look for work that is in the same career cluster. Look for work where you can meet people who have the occupation that interests you. If you are interested in being a doctor, for example, look for a job at a hospital.

While You Read

Question What could you learn at a job that you could not learn by reading or by talking to people?

part-time job ■ A job where you work up to 30 hours per week.

cooperative education ■ A program that combines school with a part-time job.

service learning ■ A program that combines school with volunteer work.

Part-Time Jobs Give You Work Experience   One way to get work experience is to look for a part-time job. A part-time job is a job where you work up to 30 hours per week. Part-time jobs are usually entry-level jobs. An *entry-level job* is a job that requires little training. Many retail stores hire part-time workers. Many restaurants also hire part-time workers.

Cooperative Education Gives You Work Experience
A cooperative education program can also give you work experience. A cooperative education program is a program that combines school with a part-time job. Cooperative education programs are sometimes called co-op programs or work study programs. In these programs, you can work at a job while you are going to school. You learn skills at school and then apply them on the job.

Volunteering and Service Learning Give You Work Experience   Volunteer (unpaid) work is another kind of work experience. Many organizations use volunteer workers. You could volunteer at a library, a hospital, or a nursing home. You could volunteer at a nonprofit organization, such as Big Brothers Big Sisters™.

Look for service learning programs at your school. Service learning is a program that combines school with volunteer work. Service learning helps the community. It also helps you build your skills.

While You Read

Question What does "keeping an open mind" mean?

Keep an Open Mind as You Do Career Research

Keep an open mind as you do your research. Look at all the facts. You may find that a certain occupation is not right for you. Let's say that you are interested in being a veterinarian. You learn about the work and see that you need many years of science courses. This does not appeal to you. That is okay. Use this information to find a job that you like better. Maybe you would rather work as an animal trainer. Research can show you different options.

...ating With Adults

Com...
at ... ...bably used to talking to people
...e. When you start to look for a job,
... have to communicate with adults a
...e. You will have to communicate
... when you are at work, on an
... or just talking to someone about their
... nportant to show respect for anyone
... ht be your boss, your customer, or your
...er. This will show them that you are

...ways you can communicate with respect
...ulture include:
... the person to whom you are speaking.
...n carefully to what the other person is
...
... interrupt.
... adults as "Ms." or "Mr.," plus their
... unless they ask you to use their

... work is a great place to learn
... different kinds of people.
... come confident in your
... h adults.

... et up a short informational
... t you know. During the
... to how you are speaking
... to how the adult is
... el you are being
... or why not?
... go to
... d the *Smart Tip*
... nnection.

...rview
... (p. 69)
... (p. 72)

...ucation

...ing (p. 72)

... learning about
... e a career decisi
... tions that you
... r research.
... nformation in ...oks

... e information... interview

... in work experience.

...wing Letter Choose a job that
...k in your local yellow pages for a
...res workers in that job. Write a
... set up a half day of job shadowing.
... letter to the human resources
... of the company. Use the letter in
...s a guide.

...w
...ether,
...son. Make
...and your
...h ask some
...iew. Write up your
...esentation.

ewow.glencoe.com

For help with this activity, visit
ewow.glencoe.com/tips.

Study Tip

Taking notes helps you pay attention. It also helps you remember information. Make your notes brief. Focus on key words and topics. Circle questions you want to ask and words you need to look up.

Check your answers online by visiting **ewow.glencoe.com/review** and selecting the Section 3.2 Review.

After You Read

Retell

1. Reread the section titled, "A Sea___ You Find Information on t___ what a search engine___

2. Write five spe___ during a___

Answe___
choice m___
ewow.glenc___

Glencoe Online

Test your knowledge with the online games and activities at **ewow.glencoe.com**.

Chapter 3 Review and Activities

Key Term Review

career cluster (p. 55)
business (p. 57)
management (p. 57)
training (p. 57)
finance (p. 57)
health science (p. 59)
hospitality and tourism (p. 59)
information technology (p. 60)
manufacturing (p. 61)

marketing (p. 62)
engineering (p. 62)
research (p. 64)
Internet (p. 67)
informational inte___
(p. 69)
job shadowing (___
part-time job (___
cooperative e___
(p. 73)
service lear___

Check Your Understanding

1. Define *career cluster*. Explain why___ career clusters can help you mak___

2. List the eight categories of que___ should ask when you do care___

3. Describe how to find career___ and on the Internet.

4. In your own words, defin___ and *job shadowing*.

5. Name three ways to ga___

Write About It

6. **Write a Job-Shad___**
   interests you. Lo___
   company that hi___
   letter asking to___
   Address your___
   department___
   Figure 3.1 a___

Role Play

7. **Practice an Informational Interview** Practice doing an informational interview with a partner. Pick an occupation you would like to research. Make a list of ten questions to ask a worker in that occupation. Then interview a partner, who should play the role of the worker. Switch roles.

Teamwork Challenge

8. **Visit a Workplace** Find a local company or nonprofit organization in a career cluster that interests you. Arrange a visit with the help of a teacher. Find out what the company or organization does. Create a presentation for the class.

Computer Lab

Use a Search Engine Visit the Web site of a search engine such as Google. In the search field, type in the word *careers* plus a word that describes one of your interests. For example, you could type in *careers sports* or *careers marketing*. Click on several search results. Make a list of ten careers related to your interest.

Personal Career Portfolio

Do a Career Critique Write profiles for two occupations that interest you. Make a chart for each occupation. List the eight categories of questions that you should ask when you do career research. Under the name of each category, write one or two sentences that summarize the information in that category. For example, under *Work Hours* one answer might be, "Work hours are usually eight hours a day, 9:00 a.m. to 5:00 p.m."

Go to **ewow.glencoe.com/portfolio** for help.

Chapter 4

Your Training and Education

You Already Know...

- education and training build skills
- you need to prepare for your career
- many occupations require education after high school

You Will Learn...

- the benefits of on-the-job training
- the difference between short-term, medium-term, and long-term on-the-job training
- which occupations you can learn through an apprenticeship, an internship, or military training
- the benefits of postsecondary education
- five types of secondary schools

Personal Career Portfolio *Preview*

For your portfolio, you will describe the preparation you need for three careers that interest you. As you read, think about what kind of training and education you would need for each.

Set a Purpose Complete this sentence: "I need to know about training or education because…." List as many reasons as you can. Add to your list after you have read the chapter.

Your Training Options

Key Terms

on-the-job
   training
apprenticeship
internship
adult education
distance
   education

Main Idea

Different jobs require different amounts of education and training. On-the-job training can last from a few weeks to a few years. Adult education and distance learning let you study while you work.

Thought Organizer

Copy this list of occupations. As you read, look for these occupations in the text. In the right-hand column, write the type of training you need for each occupation.

Occupation	Type of Training
cashier	short-term on-the-job
veterinary assistant	
ambulance driver	
tax preparer	
police officer	
carpenter	
tank driver	

You Have Many Education and Training Options

In Chapter 3 you researched careers. One of the things you researched was education and training. Now you can learn more about your education and training options. Learning your options will show you what you need to do to prepare for your career. It will also help you make a good career decision.

Every Occupation Requires Preparation

Every occupation requires preparation. *Preparation* means getting ready. However, different occupations require different amounts of preparation. Higher-paying jobs usually require more preparation.

Different Occupations Require Different Amounts of Preparation   Every job requires some preparation. Preparation means getting ready. It means learning the skills you need to do the job.

For some occupations, you can get a job after high school and then learn while you work. For example, you could get a job as a dental assistant. You could learn the job as you work.

For other occupations, you need a year or two of preparation after high school. To be a dental hygienist, for example, you need to take courses for two years at a college.

You need years to prepare for some occupations. If you want to work as a dentist, for example, you need to go to school for several years.

While You Read

Question Why would a dentist need more training than a dental assistant?

Different Preparation for Different Occupations Some jobs require almost no preparation after high school. Other jobs require several years of preparation. What might the worker in this auto plant have to learn before he can do his job well?

On-the-Job Training Is Learning While You Work

There are many ways to get training for the job you want. One way is to learn while you work. Training at work is called **on-the-job training**.

On-the-job training is an excellent option. First, it is free. Second, you are usually paid while you are training. Third, it teaches you exactly what tasks you need to do. It shows you exactly what your employer expects from you.

There Are Six Types of On-the-Job Training

There are six types of on-the-job training, as shown in **Figure 4.1** below. These are:

- short-term on-the-job training
- medium-term on-the-job training
- long-term on-the-job training
- apprenticeships
- internships
- military training

Figure 4.1

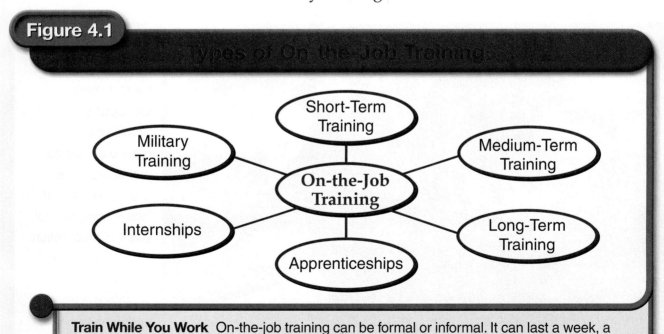

Types of On-the-Job Training

Short-Term Training
Military Training
Medium-Term Training
On-the-Job Training
Internships
Long-Term Training
Apprenticeships

Train While You Work On-the-job training can be formal or informal. It can last a week, a month, or years. Jobs that require long-term training often pay more than jobs that require short-term training. Why do you think this is true?

Short-Term On-the-Job Training Takes a Few Weeks

Some on-the-job training is short-term, or brief. It lasts only a few weeks. Your boss or coworkers show you what to do. You practice, and they help. Soon you are able to do the job on your own.

Imagine that you get a job as a cashier. Your supervisor shows you how to use the cash register. You practice until you are comfortable. You then start to work with customers. If you have questions, you ask your boss or coworkers. In a few weeks, you are doing your job with confidence.

Short-Term On-the-Job Training Teaches You to Do Basic Tasks   Short-term on-the-job training prepares you for jobs that involve doing a few basic tasks. Here are some kinds of work you could do with short-term on-the-job training:

- baggage checker, handling people's luggage at an airport
- bellhop, carrying bags at a hotel
- crossing guard, helping children cross the street
- gas station worker, helping people pump gas
- mail clerk, delivering mail to workers in offices
- projectionist, showing movies in a movie theater
- ticket taker, helping people find their seats at a theater
- veterinary assistant, feeding animals and cleaning cages at an animal hospital

Medium-Term On-the-Job Training Takes a Few Months

Some on-the-job training is medium-term. It lasts from a few months to a year. When you do medium-term on-the-job training, you may learn how to use safety equipment. You may learn how to use certain tools. You may learn to fill out forms. You may even take a class.

While You Read

Visualize Imagine that you are training as a projectionist. Would you be nervous? Calm? Excited?

Study Tip

To build your thinking skills, ask the questions, "why?" and "how?" When you are reading, ask yourself, "Why does the author say that?" "How do I know this is true?" When you are in class, ask yourself, "Why are we learning this?" "How can this information help me?"

Medium-Term On-the-Job Training Teaches You to Do More Complex Tasks Medium-term on-the-job training is more in-depth than short-term on-the-job training. It teaches you to do more complex tasks.

Here are some of the jobs you could do with medium-term on-the-job training:

- ambulance driver, driving sick or injured people to the hospital
- animal control worker, handling lost animals
- construction worker, building and repairing fences
- factory worker, using machines to manufacture parts
- tax preparer, helping people complete tax papers

Real-World Connection

Being a Great Trainee

On-the-job training gives you time to learn. It also gives you the chance to show your employer what you can do. Your training period is a trial period. It is a time for your employer to see how well you fit the job. Your employer wants to know: Are you a good learner? Are you responsible? Do you have a good attitude?

Use your first weeks on the job to make a good impression. Pay close attention during training. Listen carefully. Take notes. Ask when you do not understand something. Come to work on time. Return on time from breaks. Show a positive attitude. Be enthusiastic. Enjoy doing your job.

Take the Next Step Interview an adult worker about being a good trainee. Ask: How can you be a good learner? How can you show responsibility? How can you show a good attitude?

For help doing this activity, go to **ewow.glencoe.com/tips** and find the *Smart Tip* for the Chapter 4 *Real-World Connection*.

Military Training Can Help You Get Ahead The military provides high-quality training. You can learn many job skills. Why do you think the military might train people to work in a warehouse?

Long-Term On-the-Job Training Takes a Year or More

Some jobs require long-term on-the-job training. This kind of training lasts a year or more. Long-term on-the-job training requires commitment. You must be willing to study and work hard.

To be a police officer, for example, you need to learn how to use police equipment and weapons. You need to learn about the law. You need to learn self-defense. You need to learn how to handle emergencies.

Long-Term On-the-Job Training Teaches You to Do Very Complex Tasks Long-term on-the-job training is for jobs that involve very complex skills. You need to learn a lot of information to build these skills. You need to practice for many months.

Here are some of the jobs you could do with long-term on-the-job training:

- carpenter, making things out of wood
- engraver, scratching words and designs into metal
- sheriff's deputy, enforcing the law in your county
- telephone line installer, putting in new telephone lines

While You Read

Connect Would you be interested in a career as a sheriff's deputy?

Apprenticeships Are a Form of On-the-Job Training

apprenticeship ■ An on-the-job training program in which you learn from an expert worker.

Working as an apprentice is another way to gain training and work experience. An **apprenticeship** is an on-the-job training program in which you learn from an expert worker. As an *apprentice*, you work alongside a master worker. The skilled worker helps you become better and better at your job. Some apprenticeships can last for two, three, or even more years. When you complete an apprenticeship, you are highly skilled in your field.

Are you interested in plumbing, carpentry, painting, or sheet metal work? You can learn these occupations and many others as an apprentice.

Making Good Choices

Making a Positive Impression

You have worked at a restaurant for four years. A month ago you were promoted from head waiter to assistant manager. The restaurant is now going out of business. You apply for a job as the manager of a café. The café owner wants to hire someone with experience in management. You had only one month of management experience at the restaurant. You are tempted to stretch the truth on your application. You think, "Maybe I should say that I was the assistant manager for the past year. The restaurant is closed now, so the owner will not be able to check. Plus, I know I can do the job."

You Make the Call Should you stretch the truth on your job application? Why or why not? Would it make a difference if the café owner was able to check your story? Why or why not?

For help in answering this question, visit **ewow.glencoe.com/tips** and select the *Smart Tip* for the Chapter 4 *Making Good Choices*.

Internships Are Another Form of On-the-Job Training

Another way to get on-the-job training is to do an internship. An **internship** is a short-term job or work project. Internships usually last a few months. They are usually for college students or recent graduates. They are usually in professional fields such as management, finance, and marketing.

As an *intern*, doing an internship, you might not receive pay. An internship, however, helps you develop job skills. It also helps you learn what it is like to work full-time.

internship ■ A short-term job or work project.

Military Training Offers Excellent On-the-Job Training

The United States armed services offer excellent training. There are five branches of armed services. These branches are the Army, the Navy, the Marines (or the Marine Corps), the Air Force, and the Coast Guard. Each branch has training programs in hundreds of areas. These include health science, vehicle repair, construction, human services, and broadcasting.

The Army, Navy, Marines, Air Force, and Coast Guard train people for hundreds of different jobs. Each member of the armed forces is assigned to a specific job. For example, you could learn to be a court reporter. You could learn to use construction equipment. You could learn how to pilot a helicopter. You could learn to be a firefighter or a metalworker. You could conduct search-and-rescue missions. You could be a tank driver or a cook.

To receive military training, you must *enlist*, or sign up to serve. Your service will last for four or five years. You will receive pay for your service. When your service is over, you may choose to stay in the military. You may choose to find a job outside the military. Military training will help you develop skills for many different careers.

While You Read

Visualize Picture yourself as a member of the armed forces. Would you be proud to serve in uniform?

Study Tip

Note-taking is an important study skill. It helps you pay attention. In class, write down the most important points of the lesson. Write down key terms. Write down words you want to look up. Write down questions you want to ask.

Learn While You Earn With Adult Education and Distance Learning

Not all jobs come with on-the-job training. However, there are many ways to train while you work. You can work full-time while you prepare for a career. Adult education and distance learning offer many classes.

Adult Education Classes Let You Work and Study

Another way to learn while you work is to take adult education classes. **Adult education** is training courses for people age 18 and older. Adult education courses are usually offered through high schools.

Adult education gives you skills that will help you find a job. For example, you could learn accounting or Web design. You can find classes that fit your work schedule. That way, you can earn money and improve your skills at the same time.

adult education ■ Training courses for people age 18 and over.

Distance Education Is Learning Over the Internet

You can also prepare for a career at home. How? Through distance education. **Distance education** is education in which the teacher and the student are not together in a classroom. You learn on your own and send assignments and tests to your teacher. You learn by reading, listening to recordings, or watching videos.

Today, most distance education takes place on the Internet. You visit the class Web site for notes and assignments. You communicate with your teacher by e-mail. You have discussions with other students online. You can even take tests online.

distance education ■ Education in which the teacher and the student are not together in a classroom.

While You Read

Connect Which would you like better, distance learning or classroom learning?

Distance Education Has Many Benefits   With distance education, you can study where you choose. You can usually study when you choose, too. If you work during the day, for example, you can study in the evening. You can study almost anything through distance education.

Check your answers online by visiting ewow.glencoe.com/review and selecting the Section 4.1 Review.

After You Read

Retell

1. What kind of training do police officers receive? List four things you need to learn before you can become a police officer.

2. In your own words, describe the difference between an apprenticeship and an internship.

Think Critically

3. Why do you think some occupations require so much more training and education than others? For example, dental assistants are trained on the job. Dental hygienists need two years of college.

Math Practice

Answer the multiple-choice math questions at ewow.glencoe.com/math.

Calculating Loan Interest

You decide to attend technical school. You take out a student loan to pay tuition and expenses. You borrow $5,000 from the federal government. The loan charges 8.25% interest, compounded every six months. How much will you owe after the first six months?

Step 1 Rewrite the interest rate and the time as decimals.
8.25% = .0825; 6 months = ¹/₂ year = .5

Step 2 Multiply the principal (the loan amount) by the interest rate by the time.
$5,000 × .0825 = $412.50 × .5 = $206.25

Step 3 Add the interest to the principal.
$5,000 + $206.25 = $5,206.25

Result After six months you will owe $5,206.25.

Figure It Out

How much will you owe after six more months? Use the amount you owe after six months as the principal.

Education After High School

Key Terms

postsecondary education

college

career college

tuition

technical school

community college

associate degree

bachelor's degree

Main Idea

There are many options for education after high school. These include career college, technical school, community college, and four-year college.

Thought Organizer

Copy the chart below. As you read, fill in the names of three occupations that you can learn at each type of school.

Type of School	Possible Occupations
career college	*hairstylist*
technical school	
community college	
four-year college	

Postsecondary Education Is Study After High School

On-the-job training is one good way to prepare for a job. Postsecondary education is another good way. **Postsecondary education** is study after high school. When you complete a postsecondary program, you receive a certificate or a degree. This proves that you have completed a specific program of study. It shows employers that you have the skills they need. It also shows them that you can finish what you start.

postsecondary education
■ Study after high school.

Postsecondary Education Has Many Benefits

Continuing your education after high school has many benefits. You will develop better thinking skills. You will be able to do a wider variety of tasks on the job. You will probably get a promotion faster. You will probably receive higher pay. You will probably enjoy your job more.

Postsecondary Schools Offer Many Career Programs

While You Read

Question What are the five major types of postsecondary schools?

There are five major types of postsecondary schools:

- career college
- technical school
- vo-tech center
- community college
- four-year college

A college is a postsecondary school that offers classes in several interest areas.

college ■ A postsecondary school that offers classes in several interest areas.

Career Colleges Offer Certificate Programs

A career college is a private postsecondary school that offers training for service occupations. Most of these programs take less than a year.

Career colleges are businesses that make a profit. They do not receive money from the government. Because of this, the tuition is sometimes high. Tuition is the fee you pay to a school for each unit or course.

career college ■ A private postsecondary school that offers training programs for service occupations.

tuition ■ The fee you pay to a school for each unit or course.

A Career Certificate Can Prepare You for a Career

If you train at a career college, you can enter many growing occupations. Many of these occupations are in the service industry. For example, you could work as a:

- florist, arranging and selling flowers
- hairstylist, cutting and styling hair
- licensed practical nurse, helping sick people
- secretary, doing administrative work in an office
- travel agent, helping people plan vacations

Technical Schools Teach Hands-On Skills

technical school ■ A private postsecondary school that offers training programs for specific occupations.

A **technical school** is a private postsecondary school that offers training programs for specific occupations. Technical schools are sometimes known as trade schools or trade colleges.

Like career colleges, technical schools offer certificates.

While You Read

Question What is the difference between a career college and a technical school?

A Technical Certificate Can Prepare You for a Career

Courses at technical schools prepare you for jobs using tools and machines. Many of these occupations are in the goods industry. If you attend a technical school, you could learn an occupation such as:

- auto mechanic, repairing cars and trucks
- carpenter, making things out of wood
- chef, cooking and preparing food
- electrical installer, putting in electrical systems
- computer technician, repairing computers

Vo-Tech Centers Also Offer Technical Training Vo-tech centers are another option. *Vo-tech centers* are training schools for high school students and adults. They are similar to technical schools, but they are public. Their courses are usually free. Vo-tech centers offer training for working adults and for students.

There are over 1,400 area vocational-technical (vo-tech) centers in the United States. One may have a program that will help you reach your career goal.

Point of View

Mechanic-in-Training

Celia Yee has always been good at building and fixing things. "I always liked art and science, because of the hands-on projects," she remembers. "But I had no idea what I wanted to do for a career. Then I took auto tech at the Ross Vo-Tech Center. The teacher, Mr. Brown, really encouraged me and the two other girls in the class. He gave me the idea for a career as an automotive technician."

Celia is happy with her choice. "Being an auto mechanic is a great career for me. The pay is good. You can open your own business. You can move to a new city and find work right away."

To prepare, Celia spent half a year at the Vo-Tech Center. "I did auto-tech classes during the day. I also worked at a Volkswagen dealership three days a week." Now Celia works as a junior mechanic at the dealership.

It's Your Turn Find a local vo-tech center, technical high school, or technical college. Make a list of ten occupations that you can learn at this school.

For help completing this activity, visit **ewow.glencoe.com/tips** and select the *Smart Tip* for the Chapter 4 *Point of View*.

Community Colleges Offer Associate Degree Programs

community college ■ A public postsecondary school that offers two-year programs in many subjects.

Community colleges are another good option. A **community college** is a public postsecondary school that offers two-year programs in many subjects. Community colleges are sometimes called *junior colleges*.

Community colleges are nonprofit organizations, not businesses. They receive money from the government. Because of this, the tuition is usually very low.

An Associate Degree Program Can Prepare You for a Career   When you complete a two-year program at a community college or junior college, you receive an

associate degree ■ A title you receive when you complete a two-year program at a community college.

associate degree. You can enter many interesting occupations with an associate degree. For example, you could work as an:

- auto mechanic, fixing cars and trucks
- bookkeeper, keeping financial records
- court reporter, writing down what people say in court
- dental hygienist, cleaning people's teeth
- physical therapy assistant, helping people recover from injuries
- X-ray technician, taking X-rays of patients

Community Colleges Offer Educational Programs Many four-year colleges accept course credits earned at community colleges. Why might you start your education at a community college and then transfer to a four-year college?

Four-Year Colleges Offer Bachelor's Degree Programs

Are you interested in learning even more? If so, a four-year college might be for you. When you complete a four-year program at a college or university, you receive a **bachelor's degree**.

bachelor's degree ■ A title you receive when you complete a four-year program at a college or university.

A Bachelor's Degree Program Can Prepare You for a Career What kinds of jobs require a bachelor's degree? Jobs that require specialized knowledge. Jobs that require thinking skills. For example, teachers need a bachelor's degree. Engineers need a bachelor's degree. Other jobs you could do with a bachelor's degree are:

- accountant, keeping track of a company's money
- computer programmer, writing computer programs
- journalist, writing news stories
- marketing manager, deciding what to sell and how to sell it
- social worker, helping people solve problems and live better

Research Your College Options

There are so many education options. How do you choose? You do research. Research the postsecondary schools with programs in your interest area. Find out as much as you can. Answers these questions:

- How much will the program cost?
- How long will the program take?
- How much career counseling is there?
- How many students are in each class?
- How much experience do the instructors have?
- Is distance learning available?

There are many ways to pay for postsecondary education. For example, the government lends students money for college. Many colleges also offer scholarships. Remember that the more education you have, the more money you will probably earn later.

Check your answers online by visiting **ewow.glencoe.com/review** and selecting the Section 4.2 Review.

Retell

1. Why would an employer want to hire a worker who has a degree? Explain in your own words.

2. Explain why teachers and engineers need a bachelor's degree. Describe a situation in which an engineer would need to use thinking skills.

Think Critically

3. Many community colleges offer distance learning courses. If you had a choice between going to a classroom and learning over the Internet, which would you choose? Why?

Math Practice

Answer the multiple-choice math questions at **ewow.glencoe.com/math**.

Calculating Student Loan Payments

You finish technical school and get a job. You need to repay your student loan. With interest, you owe $5,655.63. How many months will it take to repay this loan if you pay $100.00 a month? How many months will it take to repay the loan if you pay $150.00 a month?

Step 1 Figure out how many payments of $100.00 it would take to pay the loan. Round the total up.
$5,655.63 ÷ $100 = 56.5 = 57

Step 2 Figure out how many payments of $150.00 it would take to pay the loan. Round the total up.
$5,655.63 ÷ $150 = 37.7 = 38

Result It will take 57 months (four years and nine months) if you pay $100.00 a month. It will take 38 months (three years and two months) if you pay $150.00 a month.

Figure It Out

How many months will it take to pay off the loan if you pay $250.00 a month? How many months will it take if you pay $300.00 a month?

 ewow.glencoe.com

Community Relations Director

Christi Jones

Florida

Career Cluster: Business, Management, and Administration

What does a community relations director do?

"A community relations director does public relations. I am the spokesperson for Ability 1st, a resource for people with disabilities. I am the link between the business community and the people who come to Ability 1st for help."

Why did you choose a career in public relations?

"I enjoy public speaking and being out in the community. As a person with a disability I wanted to harness my abilities for good, so I went into nonprofit work."

What obstacles have you overcome?

"People's perceptions. I am visually impaired. People think that I won't be able to do the work. I have to work twice as hard to fulfill my goals."

What advice do you have for students?

"To stay focused on your goals. Reaching your goals may be challenging, but you can find a way to accomplish your goals."

Community Relations Director

Training
Most public relations directors have a college degree. Accreditation by the Public Relations Society of America (PRSA) is helpful.

Skills and Talents
Public and community relations directors need strong communication skills and to understand community trends.

Career Outlook
This industry is projected to be one of the fastest growing through the year 2012. Half of all jobs are in managerial, business, financial, and professional occupations.

Learn More About It
Work with a partner. Interview a worker in business management and a worker in business administration. Ask the people you interview what makes a good manager or a good administrative worker. Together, make a chart that compares and contrasts the traits of a good manager and a good administrator.

For help with this activity, visit **ewow.glencoe.com/tips**.

 ewow.glencoe.com/tips

Key Term Review

on-the-job training (p. 82)
apprenticeship (p. 86)
internship (p. 87)
adult education (p. 88)
distance education (p. 88)
postsecondary education (p. 90)

college (p. 91)
career college (p. 91)
tuition (p. 91)
technical school (p. 92)
community college (p. 94)
associate degree (p. 94)
bachelor's degree (p. 95)

Check Your Understanding

1. List three benefits of on-the-job training.

2. Describe the kinds of occupations you can learn during short-term, medium-term, and long-term on-the-job training.

3. List two occupations you can learn through an apprenticeship, two occupations you can learn through an internship, and two occupations you can learn through military training.

4. List four benefits of postsecondary education.

5. List and define the five types of postsecondary schools that offer career preparation.

Write About It

6. **Share Your Opinion**   Sometimes there are two ways to learn an occupation. For example, you might be able to learn an occupation on the job or in school. Which way would you prefer? Would you rather go to school, or would you rather "work your way up"? Why? Write about your thoughts.

Role Play

7. **Research a College** Work with a partner. Pretend that you are visiting a college. You want to know if the school is right for you. Your partner pretends to be a counselor at the college. Describe the career you would like. Practice asking questions about the programs at the college. Switch roles.

Teamwork Challenge

8. **Interview a Manager** Find a large restaurant, a large retail store, or a company near you. Ask to interview the manager. Ask the manager about his or her career preparation. Did he or she have on-the-job training? Did he or she have postsecondary education? What preparation does he or she recommend for a student who would like to be a manager? Is a bachelor's degree necessary to be a manager? Why or why not? Report your findings to the class.

Computer Lab

Find Training Programs Choose an occupation that interests you. Find the Web site of a postsecondary school that trains students for this occupation. Make a list of the answers to the six questions on page 95. If you cannot find the answers on the Web site, call or e-mail the school. Use a computer to type and print your list.

Personal Career Portfolio

Research Career Preparation Choose three occupations that interest you. Find out what preparation you would need for each. Use the Internet, interviews, and library resources. For each occupation, write a short paragraph about the training or education you would need.

Go to **ewow.glencoe.com/portfolio** for help.

Chapter 5

Making a Career Plan

You Already Know...

- learning about careers helps you narrow your options
- there is a lot of information about jobs and careers
- you should research several careers before making a choice
- you can change your job and your career

You Will Learn...

- why it is important to make a career decision
- the four steps to making a career decision
- how to create a personal career profile and a career evaluation
- why you need a career plan
- the difference between short-term, medium-term, and long-term goals

Personal Career Portfolio *Preview*

For your portfolio, you will make a career plan. As you read, think about your career goal and how you will reach it.

Before You Read

Draw From Your Own Background Think about the last time you made an important decision. Describe how you made that decision. Explain whether you are happy with your decision.

101

Making a Career Decision

Ready, Set, Read

Key Terms

decision
tentative
decision-making process
personal career profile
career evaluation

Main Idea

It is important to make a tentative career decision. The career decision-making process has four steps.

Thought Organizer

Draw the chart below. As you read, fill in the four steps in the decision-making process.

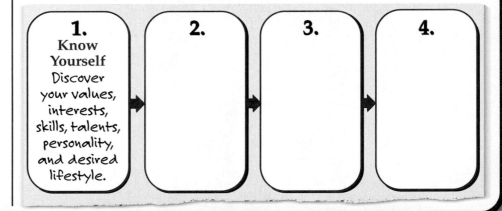

1.
Know Yourself
Discover your values, interests, skills, talents, personality, and desired lifestyle.

2.

3.

4.

Create Opportunities With a Career Decision

Your career will be a big part of your life. It will affect your whole lifestyle.

Do not leave your career to chance. Start planning right now by making a career decision. A **decision** is a choice among several options.

Many people never take the time to make a career decision. Instead, they fall into careers by chance. They work for years at jobs they do not really like. They wait for opportunities that never come. If you plan, you can make your own opportunities!

decision ■ A choice among several options.

Your Career Decision Is Tentative

Choosing a career can be difficult. You may think you are not ready to decide. You may be afraid of making the wrong decision.

Do not worry. The career decision you make now is tentative. **Tentative** means flexible and not final. You can change a tentative decision later. You can make a new decision if you are not happy with your decision.

tentative ■ Flexible and not final.

Experience Is the Best Teacher How do you know whether you have made the right career decision? You know through your experiences. You learn that there are some things you like. You learn that there are some things you do not like. You get to know yourself better through experience.

What if you change your career decision later? Have you wasted your time? No. Every job teaches you valuable things. You learn skills that will help you in another job.

While You Read

Question How will you know if you have made the right career decision?

Every Job Builds Skills You learn something at every job. You build skills that you can use at your next job. What skills would you learn at this job?

People Change Jobs, Occupations, and Careers

Changing careers is more common today than it used to be. In the past, workers often had the same job for many years. Today, most people change jobs and careers. The average person changes jobs eight times between age 18 and age 34.

Many people change occupations also. A teacher might become an administrator. A farmer might become a businessperson.

Imagine that you are a cook in a restaurant. After a few years you want to try something new. You do research on your career options. You make a new decision. Perhaps you become a magazine writer. Perhaps you become a nurse in a hospital.

Real-World Connection

Getting the Job You Want

You found a job that would be a perfect fit for you. Now you have to convince the employer to hire you. It is up to you to show the employer that you have the skills he or she wants in an employee.

Look at all your experiences. Think about how your experiences have prepared you for this new job. Make a list of skills you can use to succeed in the new job. You may have learned these skills at school, at work, or at a volunteer job. Be confident about your skills and personal qualities.

Take the Next Step Think of a job that you would like to do. Write a short script describing the skills that you could use in that job. Have a practice interview with an adult. Have the adult ask you why you are right for this job.

For help doing this activity, go to **ewow.glencoe.com/tips** and find the *Smart Tip* for the Chapter 5 *Real-World Connection*.

The Career Decision-Making Process Has Four Steps

You make a good career decision by following a decision-making process. A **decision-making process** is a series of steps that you take to make a good decision. The decision-making process helps you stay focused. It helps you make a good decision.

The career decision-making process has four steps:

1. Know yourself.
2. Explore.
3. Evaluate.
4. Decide.

Figure 5.1 shows these four steps.

decision-making process ■
A series of steps that you take to make a good decision.

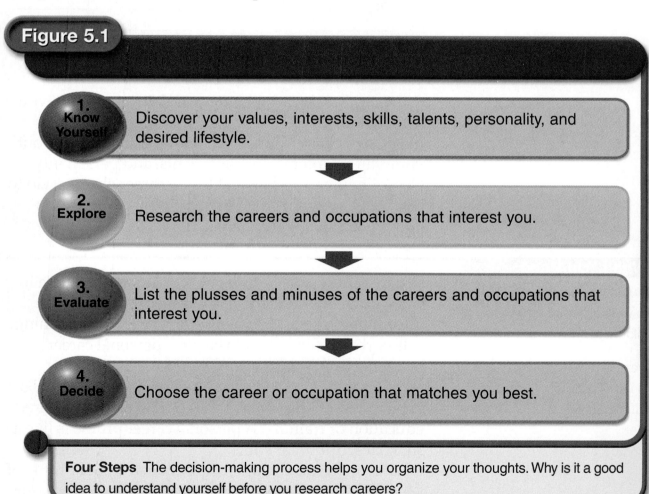

Figure 5.1

1. Know Yourself Discover your values, interests, skills, talents, personality, and desired lifestyle.

2. Explore Research the careers and occupations that interest you.

3. Evaluate List the plusses and minuses of the careers and occupations that interest you.

4. Decide Choose the career or occupation that matches you best.

Four Steps The decision-making process helps you organize your thoughts. Why is it a good idea to understand yourself before you research careers?

Step One Is to Know Yourself

Step one in the career decision-making process is to know yourself. Do you know yourself? See if you can complete the following sentences:

- My *values* are _____

  _____

- My top *interests* are _____

- My strongest *skills* are _____

  _____

- My *talents* are _____

  _____

- I would describe my *personality* as _____

  _____

- The *lifestyle* I want is _____

  _____

- The *training or education* I would like is _____

  _____

Can you answer these questions? If you cannot, you need to know yourself better. Review the parts of lifestyle in Chapter 1. Go to Chapter 2 and think about your values, interests, skills, talents, and personality. Go to Chapter 3 and look at the 16 career clusters. Go to Chapter 4 and think about the training or education you would like.

While You Read

Question Why is it a good idea to write down your personal information?

personal career profile ■
A list of your career information.

Create a Personal Career Profile   It is a good idea to write down your personal information. Writing information down keeps you from forgetting anything.

Use your information to create a personal career profile. A **personal career profile** is a list of your career information. It lists your values, interests, skills, talents, personality traits, desired lifestyle, and desired education or training. A personal career profile is like a short description of you.

Look at **Figure 5.2** to see the personal career profile of Mike Martinez. Create a chart like this one. Fill in your own answers.

Figure 5.2

Personal Career Profile

Name: Mike Martinez

Values

- helping other people
- helping my community
- being part of a family

Interests

- computers
- airplanes
- martial arts
- movies
- jazz music

Skills

- responsibility
- honesty
- solving problems
- mathematics
- computer programming
- playing piano

Talents

- reasoning
- memory
- physical strength
- using my hands

Personality

- quiet
- sensitive
- thoughtful
- dependable

Desired Lifestyle

- time to spend with family
- money to buy a comfortable home
- free time to do volunteer work in my community

Desired Training and Education

- on-the-job training or technical school

Put It on Paper Your personal career profile shows the information you have learned about yourself. You can add to your profile as you discover new things about yourself. Do you think your interests will change as you get older? Why or why not?

Step Two Is to Explore Careers

Step two in the decision-making process is to explore careers. You explore careers by learning about career clusters and doing career research.

Do you have the information you need about the careers that interest you? If not, do more research. Read more. Ask more questions. Talk to more people.

Step Three Is to Evaluate Careers

Now you are ready for step three. Step three is to evaluate careers. To *evaluate* something means to look at its good points and bad points. Evaluate the careers that you have researched. This will show you which careers are the best match for you.

While You Read

Connect Do you think there is a career that is a perfect match for you?

career evaluation ■ A chart showing the plusses and minuses of a career.

Create a Career Evaluation   Use your personal career profile form to create a career evaluation. A career evaluation is a chart showing the plusses and minuses of a career for you.

Make a career evaluation for each career that interests you. Evaluate how well the career matches your values, interests, skills, talents, personality, desired lifestyle, and desired training and education. Ask yourself:

- How well does this career support my *values*?
- How well does this career match my *interests*?
- How well do my *skills* match the skills I need for this career? If they do not match, can I build the skills I need?
- How well does this career match my *talents*?
- How well does this career match my *personality*?
- How well does this career match the *lifestyle* I want?
- How well does this career match the *training and education* I want?

Figure 5.3 on the next page shows a career evaluation by Mike Martinez. He wrote this career evaluation for the job of air traffic controller. Green plus signs show where the job is a good match for him. Red minus signs show where the job is not a good match.

Figure 5.3

Name: Mike Martinez   **Job: Air Traffic Controller**

My Values • helping other people • helping my community • being part of a family	**Values of the Job** + helping other people: air traffic controllers help keep people safe
My Interests • computers • movies • airplanes • jazz music • martial arts	**Job Tasks** + airplanes: air traffic controllers direct the movement of airplanes + computers: air traffic controllers use computers to do their work − movies, jazz music: air traffic control is not an artistic job
My Skills • responsibility • honesty • solving problems • computer programming • playing piano	**Skills Needed** + responsibility: air traffic controllers have to take their jobs seriously + solving problems: air traffic controllers have to be able to solve problems in a crisis + computer programming: air traffic controllers use computers
My Talents • reasoning • physical strength • memory • using my hands	**Talents Needed** + reasoning: air traffic controllers have to do complex thinking + memory: air traffic controllers must remember a lot of details
My Personality • quiet • thoughtful • sensitive • dependable	**Personality Needed** − sensitive: air traffic controllers work under a lot of stress and pressure + dependable: air traffic controllers must come to work on time
Desired Lifestyle • time to spend with family • money to buy a comfortable home • free time to do volunteer work in my community	**Hours, Pay, Working Conditions** − time to spend with family: I might have to work overtime and in the evening + money to buy a comfortable home: pay is relatively high
Desired Training or Education • on-the-job training or technical school	**Training or Education** + on-the-job training combined with classroom training
Result:	11 plusses (+) 3 minuses (−)

Plusses and Minuses A career evaluation lets you add up the plusses and minuses of an occupation. If you were Mike Martinez, would you choose this career? Why or why not?

Step Four Is to Make a Decision

The last step is to decide. Look at your career evaluations. Which career is the best for you?

It can be hard to choose. After all, no career is a perfect match. Every occupation has something you may not like. Look for the career that matches you best. Make a decision! Remember that your decision is tentative. You can change it later.

Point of View

Getting a Good Start

Carole Russo is a professional actor. She acts on stage. She also plays roles in movies and on television shows.

Carole says she struggled in high school. "I have dyslexia. Because of the learning disorder, I felt like I was a poor student. I needed something to help my self-esteem." Carole was interested in acting, so she took a class to build her confidence. She enjoyed it and learned that she was good at acting.

Acting class also helped Carole with her reading. "In school I was the girl who had trouble reading," Carole says, "so I had to memorize a lot. Acting class helped me learn how to memorize my lines."

In high school, Carole made a career plan to be an actor. She knew that acting was competitive. She also knew that having a plan would help her succeed.

It's Your Turn Carole's learning disorder caused her to seek ways to make her feel better about herself. She found her own special talents. What classes could you take that might help you build confidence? How might the classes lead to a career?

For help completing this activity, visit **ewow.glencoe.com/tips** and go to the *Smart Tip* for the Chapter 5 *Point of View* feature.

Check your answers online by visiting **ewow.glencoe.com/review** and selecting the Section 5.1 Review.

After You Read

Retell

1. Reread the section on page 103 titled "Experience is the Best Teacher." Summarize this section in your own words.

2. How are a personal career profile and a career evaluation similar? How are they different?

Think Critically

3. Why would a person want to change occupations? Describe a situation in which you would want to change occupations.

Math Practice

Answer the multiple-choice math questions at **ewow.glencoe.com/math**.

The Cost of Training

You earn $6.25 an hour as a park ranger. You would like to change jobs to Forest Ranger I. That job pays $10.75 an hour. To qualify, you need more training, which will cost $500. How many 8-hour days will you have to work as a Forest Ranger I to pay for the training class?

Step 1 Figure out how much you will earn per day as a Forest Ranger I.
$10.75 × 8 = $86.00

Step 2 Divide the cost of the training by your daily pay. Round up.
$500.00 ÷ $86.00 = 5.81 = 6

Result You will have to work for six days as a Forest Ranger I to pay for the training class.

Figure It Out

You can become a Forest Ranger II and earn $11.50 an hour if you take a second training class. This class costs $650. How many 8-hour days will you have to work as a Forest Ranger II to pay for the second training class?

Section 5.2

Planning Your Career

Ready, Set, Read

Key Terms

goal
career goal
career plan
long-term goal
short-term goal
medium-term goal

Main Idea

Goals give you direction in life. A career plan is a plan for how you will reach your career goals.

Thought Organizer

Draw the chart below. As you read, write the definition of each key term. Then write an example of each term.

Key Term	Definition	Example
long-term goal	a goal that will take a year or more to reach	become a restaurant manager
medium-term goal		
long-term goal		

Making a Decision Helps You Set Goals

goal ■ Something you want to achieve.

You have made a decision. Now you can set goals.

A **goal** is something you want to achieve. Goals give you direction. They motivate you. You feel proud of yourself when you achieve a goal.

Goals can be big or small. You can set goals in any area of your life. Your goal might be to learn to swim. Another goal might be to visit another country. Perhaps you want to go to cooking school. Perhaps you want to earn a certain amount of money. Perhaps you want to have a family. These are all goals.

Career Goals Give You Direction

It is important to set career goals. A **career goal** is a goal for the work you want to do. Career goals give you direction. They help you plan what you will do after high school.

Career Goals Can Be General or Specific

Career goals can be general or specific. General career goals are goals for the type of work you want to do. Here are some general career goals:

- "I want to work with children."
- "I want to work outdoors with tools."
- "I want to work in public safety."

Specific career goals are goals for the specific occupation you want. Here are some specific career goals:

- "I want to be a preschool teacher."
- "I want to be a construction worker."
- "I want to be a police dispatcher."

Read your career goal. Is it very general? If your goal is general, you will not know where to start. Make your goal more specific.

A Career Plan Helps You Reach Your Career Goal

You have a career goal. You know where you want to go. How do you get there? By following a career plan. A **career plan** is a chart showing all the steps you will take to reach your career goal.

Suppose that your career goal is to become a kindergarten teacher. Are you ready to teach the day you finish high school? Of course not. You need to take several steps first. For example, you need to go to college. You need to work as a student teacher. You need to get a license from your state. A *license* is permission from the government to do a certain job. All of these steps will go on your career plan.

career plan ■ A chart showing all the steps you will take to reach your career goal.

Making Good Choices

Changing Career Paths

Morgan works in a family-owned sporting goods store. She began working there part-time in high school. For the last five years, Morgan has worked full-time as a sales associate at the store. She is well liked and was promoted to assistant manager and then to manager. The company's owner promised Morgan that she would have a job for as long as she wants.

Morgan likes the people she works for. She likes the job security. But she does not like the job any more. She would like to return to school to study to be a travel agent. Being a travel agent sounds more exciting to her than her current job.

You Make the Call Should Morgan change careers? Why or why not?

For help in answering this question, visit **ewow.glencoe.com/tips** and select the *Smart Tip* for the Chapter 5 *Making Good Choices*.

List Your Long-Term Goals

Start your career plan by listing the biggest steps you need to take. These steps are your long-term goals. A **long-term goal** is a goal that will take a year or more to reach.

Write down your long-term goals. Write how long each one will take. Then arrange them in the order you plan to reach them.

Kanisha Porter's career goal is to become a real estate agent. Kanisha has three long-term goals. She puts her goals in time order and gives each one a time period:

- finish high school and get job as salesperson (1 year)
- complete training in real estate (2 years)
- pass real estate licensing exam (2 years)

She now sees what she will need to do over the next two years.

List Your Short-Term and Medium-Term Goals

You have a career goal and some long-term goals. Now add short-term goals and medium-term goals to your career plan.

A **short-term goal** is a goal that will take three months or less to reach. It is a goal you can get started on right now. A **medium-term goal** is a goal that will take between three months and a year to reach.

List all the steps you need to take in order to reach your long-term goals. Then sort these steps into medium-term goals and short-term goals.

For example, one of Kanisha's long-term goals is to work as a salesperson. She also set two short-term goals for this long-term goal: research sales jobs (2 months) and write résumé (1 month). These are steps she can start right now and finish soon.

Kanisha also sets two medium-term goals: take marketing class (4 months) and apply for sales jobs (3 months). These are goals she will start working on a little later.

While You Read

Visualize Picture yourself in two years. Where are you? What are you doing?

short-term goal ■ A goal that will take three months or less to reach.

medium-term goal ■ A goal that will take between three months and a year to reach.

Create a Career Plan

You now have the information you need to create your career plan. You have decided on a career goal. You have made a list of all your goals. You have figured out how long it will take for you to reach or complete each goal. You know which goals are short-term, medium-term, and long-term goals. You can organize this information into your career plan.

Write down all your goals in a chart. Write your career goal at the top of the chart. Make three rows. Write your short-term goals in the first row. Write your medium-term goals in the second row. Write your long-term goals in the third row. Put a check box next to each goal. Check off each goal as you reach it.

Figure 5.4 shows Kanisha's career plan. Remember that her longest long-term goal is two years. She has added a timeline with a time period of two years.

While You Read

Connect What can you do this week to reach one of your short-term goals?

Get Started!

You have a career plan. Your goals are fresh in your mind. Now is the time to get started!

Take action on your short-term goals. For example, sign up for courses that will help you. Look for a part-time job. Volunteer your time. Talk with people about their jobs.

Do not wait until tomorrow or next week. Get started on your goals today.

Review Your Career Plan Often

Review your career plan often. Check off the goals you have reached. Each time you reach a goal, you will feel proud of yourself. Look at what you need to do next. Reviewing your career plan will help motivate you and keep you moving toward your goal.

Reviewing your career plan is important for another reason. It helps you see whether you are on the right track. You may decide that your career goal is not right for you. That is all right. Set new goals for yourself. Then make a new plan.

Figure 5.4

Name: Kanisha Porter **Career Goal: Real Estate Agent**

	Now	1 Year	2 Years
Short-Term Goals	☑ Research sales jobs. ❑ Write my résumé.	❑ Research real estate training programs.	
Medium-Term Goals	❑ Take marketing class. ❑ Apply for sales jobs.	❑ Save money for tuition. ❑ Enroll in training program.	❑ Form study group to prepare for exam. ❑ Talk to several real estate agents who have passed the exam.
Long-Term Goals		❑ Finish training in real estate.	❑ Pass real estate licensing exam.

Organize Your Goals Organize your short-term, medium-term, and long-term goals into a career plan. Now you can easily see what you need to do to reach each goal. When should Kanisha start working on her short-term goals?

Check your answers online by visiting **ewow.glencoe.com/review** and selecting the Section 5.2 Review.

After You Read

Retell

1. Explain why specific career goals are more useful than general career goals.

2. Give two reasons why it is important to review your career plan often.

Think Critically

3. Some people like to plan. Other people like to live one day at a time. How do you live? Which way do you think is better?

Math Practice

Answer the multiple-choice math questions at **ewow.glencoe.com/math**.

Calculating Extra Pay

You have a part-time job at a movie theater collecting tickets. You earn $7 per hour. Your boss asks you to work next Sunday. You will be paid overtime (1.5 times your regular rate). How much will you earn if you agree to work eight hours on Sunday?

Step 1 Multiply your hourly pay by the rate of overtime pay.
$7.00 × 1.5 = $10.50

Step 2 Multiply your hourly overtime pay by the number of hours you plan to work.
$10.50 × 8 = $84.

Result You will earn $84 on Sunday.

Figure It Out

Your boss at the movie theater asks you to work Saturday night. You will be paid overtime (1.5 times your regular rate). How much will you earn if you agree to work six hours on Saturday night?

Director of Disabled Student Services

John Harris
Tennessee

Career Cluster: Education and Training

What do you do in your job?

"I help students at Middle State Tennessee University who have disabilities. I also help the university meet the needs of students with disabilities."

Why did you choose a career in education?

"In high school I wanted to work where I could help people. Education was a career where I could assist others. I get to help students determine their future."

What obstacles have you overcome?

"I come from a large family. My mother raised eight children alone. I grew up poor in a rural area. I've been visually impaired since birth. The state vocational program helped me with my education. Being visually impaired has given me the opportunity to do my job."

What advice do you have for students?

"Learn to be okay with who you are. Society may not be laid out for you. Learn to live with the situation you have and navigate through it. Success goes to the people who learn to live with the situation they have. Be flexible."

Director of Disabled Student Services

Training
People in education careers often need at least a bachelor's degree. A master's degree is helpful.

Skills and Talents
People in education careers need to be creative and have good communication skills.

Career Outlook
Educational services is the second-largest industry in the United States. Employment is expected to grow through 2012.

Learn More About It
Work with a classmate to brainstorm a list of jobs in education. Choose three of these jobs. Write about what values, interests, skills, talents, personality, and education are needed for each of the jobs.

For help with this activity, visit **ewow.glencoe.com/tips**.

Key Term Review

decision (p. 102)	**goal** (p. 112)
tentative (p. 103)	**career goal** (p. 113)
decision-making process (p. 105)	**career plan** (p. 114)
personal career profile (p. 106)	**long-term goal** (p. 115)
career evaluation (p. 108)	**short-term goal** (p. 115)
	medium-term goal (p. 115)

Check Your Understanding

1. Explain why it is important to make a career decision.

2. List the four steps in the career decision-making process.

3. Describe how to create a personal career profile and a career evaluation.

4. Define a *career plan* and explain why it is useful.

5. Explain the difference between short-term, medium-term, and long-term goals.

Write About It

6. **Write About Setting Goals**   It feels good to reach a goal. It shows that you can achieve what you want to achieve. Explain whether you set goals, and why. Do you think that goals are important? Why or why not? Write a paragraph with your ideas.

Role Play

7. **Describe Yourself**   Pretend that you are interviewing for a job. Describe your values, interests, skills, talents, personality traits, desired lifestyle, and desired education or training. Fill in your answers on personal career profile forms.

Teamwork Challenge

8. **Make a Goal List**   Pick a long-term goal related to your career goal. Work with a group of fellow students to make a list of short-term and medium-term goals that relate to this long-term goal. Think of all the goals you can. Write them down on a piece of paper. Circle one goal that you can start on right away. List three things you can do this week to start on this goal.

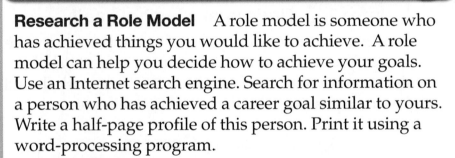

Computer Lab

Research a Role Model   A role model is someone who has achieved things you would like to achieve. A role model can help you decide how to achieve your goals. Use an Internet search engine. Search for information on a person who has achieved a career goal similar to yours. Write a half-page profile of this person. Print it using a word-processing program.

Personal Career Portfolio

Make a Career Plan   Create a career plan. Make a chart like the one on page 116. The chart should include your career goal. The chart should also include your short-term, medium-term, and long-term goals. You can also add a timeline to your chart.

Go to **ewow.glencoe.com/portfolio** for help.

Unit 1 Review

Chapter Summaries

Chapter 1 You and Work

People work to earn money, feel good about themselves, help others, and be around other people. Work will probably be the most important part of your lifestyle. Teamwork, technology, and diversity are important in the world of work.

Chapter 2 Understanding Yourself

You need to understand yourself before you can choose a career. You need to know your values, interests, skills, talents, personality, and learning styles. Your work should give you a positive self-image and high self-esteem.

Chapter 3 Exploring Careers

There are thousands of careers in the 16 career clusters. You can read about careers in books and on the Internet. You can talk to people about their jobs. You can gain experience through volunteer work and part-time jobs.

Chapter 4 Your Training and Education

Different jobs require different amounts of preparation. Some jobs have on-the-job training. On-the-job training can last from a week to several years. Some jobs require postsecondary education at a college or technical school.

Chapter 5 Making a Career Plan

You use the career decision-making process to make a career decision. Then you make a career plan. First you set a career goal. Then you set long-term goals, medium-term goals, and short-term goals.

These are the topics you read about in this unit. What did you learn?

Chapter 1
You and Work
- Why Work Matters
- Today's Workplace

Chapter 2
Understanding Yourself
- Getting to Know Yourself
- Being an Individual

Chapter 3
Exploring Careers
- Narrowing Your Career Choices
- Learning About Careers

Chapter 4
Your Training and Education
- Your Training Options
- Education After High School

Chapter 5
Making a Career Plan
- Making a Career Decision
- Planning Your Career

Unit 2

Getting the Job You Want

Unit Preview

Unit 2 is about finding and getting a job. You will learn how to find available jobs. You will learn how to apply for a job using a job application form or a résumé and cover letter. You will also find out how to make a good impression during a job interview.

Chapter 6

Finding Job Openings

You Already Know...

- working is a good way to gain experience
- you need a career goal before you can find a job
- it takes time and effort to find a job
- you can find information about jobs on the Internet

You Will Learn...

- three good sources of job listings
- how to find job listings on the Internet
- about contacts, networking, and referrals
- why networking is your best job-search tool
- the four steps in networking

Personal Career Portfolio *Preview*

For your portfolio, you will make a contact list. As you read, think about all the people you know who might be able to help you find a job.

Draw From Your Own Background If you already have a job, describe how you found your job. If you do not have a job, describe how someone you know found his or her job. Tell whether you think it is easy or difficult to find a good job.

Gathering Job Leads

Ready, Set, Read

Key Terms

job opening
job lead
job listing
employment
    agency
temp job
temp-to-hire job
classified ad
job board

Main Idea

A job lead is information about a job opening. Employment agencies, classified ads, and Internet job boards are good sources of job leads.

Thought Organizer

Copy the chart below. As you read, fill in the names of three sources of job leads.

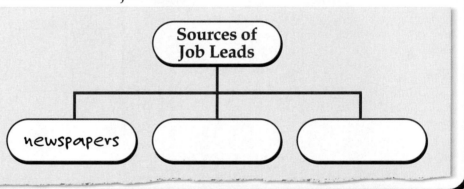

Sources of Job Leads

newspapers

Job Openings Are Available Jobs

Finding a job is a big task. Being prepared and organized will help.

Before you can apply for a job, you need to know where the jobs are. You need to know which jobs are available. You need to look for job openings. A **job opening** is a job that is vacant.

How do you know what jobs are available? You gather job leads. A **job lead** is information about a job opening. The more job leads you have, the more likely you are to get a good job.

job opening ■ A job that is vacant.

job lead ■ Information about a job opening.

Job Listings Are Good Sources of Job Leads

There are many ways to find job leads. One of the easiest ways to find job leads is to look at job listings. A **job listing** is a written notice of a job opening.

There are three good places to find job listings:

- employment agencies
- newspapers
- the Internet

job listing ■ A written notice of a job opening.

Employment Agencies Are a Good Source of Job Leads

An **employment agency** is an organization that matches workers with jobs. Employers pay employment agencies to find good workers. Employment agencies collect job listings.

People who want work may go to an employment agency. So the agency also has lists of people who want jobs. Then the agency matches workers with jobs.

There are two types of employment agencies. One type is private. The other type is public. Most cities have both private and public employment agencies.

employment agency ■ An organization that matches workers with jobs.

Private Employment Agencies Are Businesses

Private employment agencies are businesses. They charge a fee if they help you get a job. They earn their money by matching people to jobs.

Private agencies ask you to sign an agreement. It says that you will pay a fee if they send you for a job where you are hired. The fee may be part of your first wages. Sometimes the employer pays the fee.

Some private employment agencies specialize in a certain career field. For example, some agencies specialize in computer jobs. Some agencies specialize in child care jobs.

You can find private employment agencies in the yellow pages. Look under "employment."

While You Read

Question Why do private employment agencies charge a fee?

temp job ■ A job that is not
permanent.

temp-to-hire job ■ A job
that changes from a temp job
to a permanent job.

Temporary Employment Agencies Find Workers

Short-Term Jobs Many private employment agencies
specialize in temp jobs (temporary jobs). A **temp job** is
a job that is not permanent. Some temp jobs last only a
day or two. Other temp jobs last a month or longer.

Many people do temp work while they look for a
permanent job. Temp workers are usually paid by the
hour. The employer pays the temp agency. The temp
agency keeps some of the money for itself. The agency
then gives the rest to the worker.

Some temp jobs are also temp-to-hire jobs. A
temp-to-hire job is a job that changes from a temp job
to a permanent job. You begin a temp-to-hire job as a
temp worker. Your employer evaluates you during this
time. If your employer likes your work, he or she hires
you. You stop working for the employment agency and
start working for the employer.

Public Employment Agencies Are Government Services   Public employment agencies are run by the government. Taxes pay for their services.

Go to the public employment agency near you. Fill out an application form. Someone there will talk to you. The person will find out what you can do best. He or she will try to find you a job. The agency will contact you when the right job comes along.

Find Your Public Employment Agency in the Phone Book or on the Internet   You can find your public employment agency in the phone book. Look in the blue pages at the front of the book. Look under the name of the state.

You can also find your state public employment agency on the Internet. Visit the Web site of your state government to find a link.

While You Read

Question Where can you find the phone number of your public employment agency?

Making Good Choices

Temping for a Living

Lee works as a security guard at Via Mall. Lee's employer is Ace Temps, even though he works at Via Mall. Lee's temp job was to last three months. Instead, it has lasted seven. Lee does not receive any benefits through Ace Temps. Guards who work directly for Via Mall receive health insurance and paid vacation. They also receive more pay than Lee does.

Lee would like to keep working at Via Mall. However, he wants a job with benefits and more pay.

You Make the Call   Do you think it is fair for temp agencies to use temporary employees for long periods? What would you advise Lee to do?

For help in answering this question, visit **ewow.glencoe.com/tips** and find the *Smart Tip* for the Chapter 6 *Making Good Choices*.

Newspapers Are a Good Source of Job Leads

Newspapers are another good place to find job listings. Job listings are part of the classified ads. A `classified ad` is a short notice that appears in a section of the newspaper. These ads are paid advertisements organized in classes, or groups. Most newspapers print hundreds of classified ads on Sundays. Some newspapers may print classified ads every day.

Classified ads appear in alphabetical order. First find the employment section. Then look under the name of the job you want. Also look under the name of your career field. Let's say that you want to work as a hotel desk clerk. Look under "clerk" or "clerical." Also look under "hotel" and "hospitality."

classified ad ■ A short notice that appears in a section of the newspaper.

While You Read

Question What six facts usually appear in job ads?

Classified Ads Teach You About Jobs   Read the classified ads for job listings in your newspaper. You will learn a lot about jobs. You will learn how much different jobs pay. You will find out what skills you need for different jobs.

What is in a classified ad? Classified ads are usually short. Most ads for jobs give these basic facts about a job:

- job title
- job tasks
- pay
- location
- skills, education, and experience required
- how to apply

Classified Ads Use Abbreviations   Ads often use abbreviations to save space. Abbreviations are shortened forms of words. Read the abbreviations at the top of **Figure 6.1.** They will help you understand ads for jobs. Then read the job ads at the bottom of the figure. They were taken from several newspapers. Do you understand what they say? If you have questions about the ads, talk about them with your teacher or counselor.

Figure 6.1

Common Abbreviations

appl. = applicant or application	immed. = immediate	PT, P/T = part time
appt. = appointment	k = $1,000	qual. = qualified or
asst. = assistant	incl. = included	qualifications
ATTN = attention	lic. = license or licensed	ref. = reference
ben., bnfts. = benefits	M-F = Monday through Friday	rep. = representative
c/o = in care of	mfg. = manufacturing	req. = required
dept. = department	mgr. = manager	sal. = salary
DOE = depending on experience	min. = minimum	svc. = service
	nec. = necessary	w/ = with
EOE = equal opportunity employer	ofc. = office	wk. = week
	PC = personal computer	wpm = words per minute
exc. = excellent	pd. = paid	
exp. = experience	ph. = phone	xlnt. = excellent
FT, F/T = full time	pos. = position	
hr. = hour	pref. = preferred	

BOOKKEEPER/SECRETARY

P/T, Wed–Fri, 8am–5pm. Asst. to controller. Self-starter w/ xlnt computer and communication skills. Type 50–60 wpm, use spreadsheets. West Alhambra. Min. 2 yrs. exp. req. Fax résumé, refs to (347) 555-0124

PRINTING

Copy operators, shift mgrs. w/digital exp. PT & FT $10–$12 DOE. Customer svc. exp. preferred. East Worthington location. Fax (347) 555-0155

NURSING

Busy ofc. looking for RN. FT. Night shift. Competitive pay and bnfts. Exp. in pain treatment pref. Downtown, 4th and Hill. Call (347) 555-0191

RESTAURANT

Italian restaurant needs servers FT & PT. Min. 2 yrs. exp., nonsmoker. Fast and friendly. Flexible shifts. English/Spanish speaker pref. Call Miguel (347) 555-0180 after 2pm

Reading Abbreviations Classified ads tell you the basics about a job. You will need to learn more about a job before you decide whether it is right for you. Why do you think some employers ask applicants to send their information by fax instead of calling?

The Internet Is a Good Source of Job Leads

The Internet is a very good place to find job leads. Look at an Internet job board. A **job board** is a collection of job listings on the Internet. Job listings on the Internet are often called *job postings.*

Some job boards list all kinds of jobs. Other job boards list jobs in one career cluster. For example, some job boards list only jobs in health science. There are job boards for every career cluster.

Some Web sites offer a job board plus career advice. For example, the Web site Monster.com gives advice on writing a résumé. Web sites that have job boards and career advice are called *career Web sites.*

Use an Internet search engine to find job boards and career Web sites. Type "jobs" or "careers" into the search field. Then click on some of the search results.

Search for Jobs by Location, Industry, or Keyword
Job boards allow you to search for job listings that interest you. You can search in several ways.

You can search by location. For example, you could look for jobs in your city or county. You can look for jobs in a different city, state, or even a different country.

You can search by industry. For example, you could look for jobs in manufacturing or engineering. You could search for jobs in information technology.

You can also search by keyword. A keyword is a word that appears in the job description. For example, you could search for keywords such as "sales" or "retail." Remember to search by specific keywords that have to do with the job area that interests you. Do not search by general keywords like "job" or "career."

Learn to Read Job Postings   Job postings on the Internet have the same basic information as job ads in the newspaper. Online ads are longer than newspaper ads, however. They are more detailed. For example, they may give you extra information about the employer. Read a sample job posting in **Figure 6.2.**

Figure 6.2 Internet Job Posting

Job Title: Medical Records Clerk
Position Type: Permanent, full-time
(40 hours per week)

Date Posted: June 14, 2008
Salary: Starting at $29,000 DOE

Job Description:
The medical records clerk organizes the Medical Center's patient records. The clerk organizes files in numerical order, retrieves files and provides staff with medical records, answers telephone calls, and processes incoming correspondence.

Requirements:
- High school diploma.
- Bilingual English/Spanish.
- Good communication skills and word-processing skills.
- Ability to file by number and color code.
- Ability to maintain patient confidentiality.
- Availability to work some Saturdays.
- Medical office experience preferred.

About Us:
Playa Nueva Medical Center is a full-service hospital in downtown Santa Rosa. We have over 3,000 employees and serve a varied community. Visit our Web site at **www.playanuevamedctr.org.**

To Apply:
E-mail résumé, cover letter, and salary requirements to **employment@playanuevamed.org.** Put "Medical Records Clerk" in subject line of the e-mail.

EOE

Lots of Information Job postings on the Internet have more details than job ads in the newspaper. Some job postings are two pages or more. Why would it be a good idea to visit a company's Web site before you apply for a job there?

Government Web Sites List Government Jobs Are you interested in a job with the government? All cities have city government agencies that hire workers. Most cities have county, state, and federal offices, too. These agencies hire workers to do hundreds of different jobs.

You may be surprised by all the workers an agency needs. You know that schools need teachers. They also hire many other workers. These include cooks, office workers, bus drivers, crossing guards, and mechanics.

Most government agencies have job boards on the Internet. For example, the federal government has a job board called USAJOBS. Visit the Web site of your city or county. Look at the home page of the Web site. The *home page* is the first Web page you see when you visit a site. Look for words such as "employment," "personnel," and "human resources." These will take you to the job postings.

Government Jobs

There are government jobs in every career cluster. There are government jobs in public safety, finance, and science. Public school workers are government employees. Name three jobs that you see workers doing at your school.

...ers

Check you

online ...com/review

ewow the

and Review.

Retell

1. Explain the difference between a temp job and a temp-to-hire job. Use your own words.

2. List three ways to search for job listings on a job board. Give an example of each search.

Think Critically

3. Employment agencies, classified ads, and Internet job boards are all sources of job leads. Which of these sources would you use first? Why? Which do you think would be most successful?

Math Practice

Answer the multiple-choice math questions at ewow.glencoe.com/math.

Working for a Temp Agency

You work for a temp agency. Your job pays $6.00 an hour. You work 20 hours each week. The agency receives 12% of your total weekly wages. How much does the temp agency receive each week?

Step 1 Calculate your weekly pay. Multiply your hourly wage by the number of hours you work.
$6 × 20 = $120

Step 2 Convert the agency's fee to a decimal.
12% = 12 × 1% = 12 × 0.01 = .12

Step 3 Multiply the decimal by your wages.
.12 × 120 = $14.40

Result The temporary agency is paid $14.40 weekly.

Figure It Out

You are paid $5.50 an hour at your at your job through a temp agency. You work 25 hours a week. The agency receives 13% of your earnings. How much will the temp agency receive weekly?

Networking

Ready, Set, Read

Key Terms

contact
networking
referral
contact list
contact
   information
cold-calling

Main Idea

Contacts are your best source of job leads. Networking helps you find jobs that are not advertised.

Thought Organizer

Copy the diagram below. As you read, think of the types of people who could be contacts. Fill in the blank ovals with words for these people.

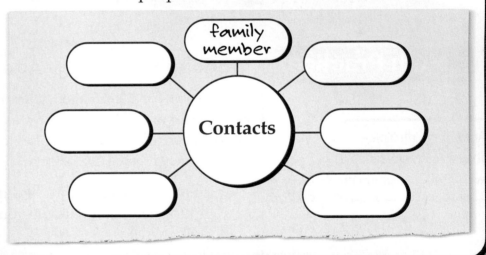

family member

Contacts

Contacts Are Good Sources of Job Leads

You can find job leads at employment agencies, in the newspaper, and on the Internet. Those are all good starts. There is another important source of job leads. This source is your contacts. A **contact** is a person you know who can give you information about jobs.

A contact can be almost anyone. A contact could be a friend or a family member. A contact could be a neighbor or a relative. A contact could even be a person you have met only once.

contact ■ A person you know who can give you information about jobs.

Contacts Help You Find Jobs on the Hidden Job Market

Contacts can be your best source of job leads. They can help you find jobs on the hidden job market. The *hidden job market* is all the jobs that are not advertised.

Your contacts can tell you about a job opening before it is advertised. Your contacts can also tell you about job openings that are not advertised at all.

Most Jobs Are Not Advertised   Most jobs are not advertised. Why? It costs money to advertise a job. It also takes time. The employer needs to write the job listing. The employer then needs to read many applications. He or she needs to interview people. It is easier for employers to hire people they already know.

Employers would rather hire someone they know than someone they do not know. Employers might hire a friend. They might hire a family member. They might hire a neighbor.

Network to Find a Job

What do you do with contacts? You network. **Networking** means asking your contacts for help and information about jobs. Networking helps you find a job. It is not the same as asking for a job.

You can learn a lot from networking. You can learn new information about careers. You can get suggestions about how to find a job. You can get job leads. You can also get referrals. A **referral** is a new contact that you get from an old contact.

When you network, you are not just asking for help. You are also giving help. People in a network share information and advice. You are probably in someone else's network. You could give him or her a referral. You could give him or her the name of a Web site that has a good job board.

Some young people do not want to get a job through networking. They think it is unfair. There is nothing wrong with getting a job through networking. In fact, it is the way most people find jobs.

While You Read

Question What can you learn through networking?

networking ■ Asking your contacts for help and information about jobs.

referral ■ A new contact that you get from an old contact.

There Are Four Steps in Networking

Networking is not difficult. However, you need to prepare. There are four basic steps in networking: **Step 1** is to make a contact list. **Step 2** is to prepare an introduction. **Step 3** is to talk to your contacts. **Step 4** is to follow through.

While You Read

Question What is a contact list?

contact list ■ A list of all your contacts.

contact information ■ How to reach a contact: a phone number, an address, or an e-mail address.

Step One Is to Make a Contact List

Start by making a contact list. A **contact list** is a list of all your contacts. Write down the name of every person who could give you information about jobs.

List the names of all your contacts. Write their contact information so you can reach them. A person's **contact information** is a phone number, an address, or an e-mail address.

Set up your contact list like the one in **Figure 6.3.** Make a column for names. Make a column for contact information. Make a column for notes. Label this column "Contact Date/Outcome." You will use this column later.

Figure 6.3

Name/Relationship	Contact Information	Contact Date/Outcome
Gerardo Lopez, Paul's neighbor, salesperson	**Phone:** (123) 555-0167 **E-mail:** l@ccsales.com	
Barbara Jenkins, sister's friend, computer programmer	**Phone:** (678) 555-0112 (H) (698) 555-0193 (O)	
Adriano Raditz, computer teacher	**Office:** 56-A, Main Building	

Get Organized Write down the names and contact information of everyone you know. You never know who will be able to help you. Would you prefer to keep your contact list on paper or on a computer? Why?

Your Community Is a Source of Contacts Where do you find contacts? One of the best sources of contacts is your community. Friends and family members may know of job openings. A friend or family member might even be able to hire you.

Think of other people you have met in your neighborhood. For example, a neighbor might know of a job. The father or mother of a friend might know of a job. Your mail carrier might even know of a job.

Your School Is a Source of Contacts Your school is another good place to find job leads.

Visit your school's work placement office. Talk to the leader of the work experience program. Talk with your counselor and your teachers. Talk to former teachers.

While You Read

Connect Name two people at your school who might be able to help you find a job.

School and Community Contacts Employers like to hire people they can trust. That is why networking is a good way to find a job. If you were an employer, what would you do to fill a job opening?

Step Two Is to Prepare an Introduction

Step two is to write and memorize a brief description of yourself. Include your year in school, the job you want, your work experience, and your skills.

Josie Rodriguez is looking for a summer job at Computer Corporation. Here is her introduction: "My name is Josie Rodriguez. I will be a senior at Fairfield High School this fall. I have skills in computer programming and repair. I am interested in a summer job or internship at Computer Corporation."

Memorize your introduction. Practice it with your friends and family members.

Real-World Connection

Showing Yourself at Your Best

As you network, you will contact people you have never met. They will know you by your communication skills. You must present yourself well. Speak with confidence and in a clear voice. Use proper grammar. Listen when the other person speaks. Make eye contact.

Briefly describe you skills. State the type of job you seek. Explain why you will make a good employee. Ask if the person knows of a job opening that fits your skills. Ask for referrals. Thank the person for his or her time and help.

Take the Next Step Write an introduction that you will use with your contacts. Include your name and your skills. Also include the job you want. Ask two different adults to listen to your introduction. Ask the adults for advice on how to give your introduction. Summarize their suggestions in a paragraph.

For help doing this activity, go to **ewow.glencoe.com/tips** and find the *Smart Tip* for the Chapter 6 *Real-World Connection*.

Step Three Is to Talk to Your Contacts

Contact your contacts. Talk to them in person if you can. You can also call or write a letter on the computer.

Talk with as many referrals as you can. The more you talk to, the better your chance of getting a job.

While You Read

Visualize How would you feel about asking a person for help?

Ask Your Contacts for Help and Referrals   Begin with your introduction. Then ask for what you need. Be direct. Be specific. Do you need job leads? Information about a specific company? Ask for what you want. Most people are happy to help.

Josie wants a job at Computer Corporation. She asked her contacts, "Do you know of any jobs there?" She also asked, "Do you know anyone else who can help me?" She then asked for permission to use the person's name. She said, "May I tell Mr./Ms. _____ that you referred me?" She thanked each contact at the end of the conversation and sent a thank-you note.

Keep a Record of Your Conversations   Write down all the information you receive. Write down each referral's name and contact information. Ask how to spell and pronounce the contact's name.

Write down job leads you receive. Write the name of the business and its address and phone number. Write the name of the person to see. If you know the person's job title, write that down too.

Write your notes in the third column on your contact list. Turn the page to see how Josie did this in **Figure 6.4.**

Step Four Is to Follow Through

Step four is to follow through on what you have learned.

Follow through on job leads immediately. Contact the employer. Introduce yourself. Explain how you got the job lead. Ask if the job is still available. If so, ask to apply. If not, ask if there are any other job openings. Thank the employer. Send a thank-you note.

Follow Through on Your Referrals   Add your referrals to your contact list. Contact them. Ask them for help and information. Send them a thank-you note, too.

While You Read

Connect How comfortable do you feel when talking with people you do not know?

cold-calling ■ Calling without a lead or referral.

Find Job Openings by Cold-Calling Employers

There is another way to find jobs on the hidden job market. You can find them by cold-calling companies that interest you. **Cold-calling** means calling without a job lead or referral.

Read through the sections of the yellow pages that interest you. Write down the names and phone numbers of businesses where you might like to work. Find out more about these employers. Then call or visit these businesses.

Figure 6.4

Name/Relationship	Contact Information	Contact Date/Outcome
Gerardo Lopez, Paul's neighbor, salesperson	**Phone:** (123) 555-0167 **E-mail:** l@ccsales.com	12/7: Called and left message for GL. 12/9: GL referred me to Mira Latrice at Computing Warehouse, (555) 567-8910.
Barbara Jenkins, sister's friend, computer programmer	**Phone:** (678) 555-0112 (H) (698) 555-0193 (O)	12/8: Talked to BJ at holiday party. She invited me to visit her office after the new year.
Adriano Raditz, computer teacher	**Office:** 56-A, Main Building	12/19: Talked to AR at his office. He said he would call his friend at Computer Corp.

Keep Records of Your Job Search Take notes each time you speak to a contact. This will help you follow through on job leads and referrals. Why do you think it is best to talk to a contact in person?

Ask Employers About Job Openings

Introduce yourself. Ask if there are any job openings for someone with your skills. For example, Josie Rodriguez introduced herself and said, "Does your company have a part-time opening for someone with my skills?"

Write down what the person says. Make notes about the company. You may find a job opening. You may get a referral. Either way, you are one step closer to finding a job.

Point of View

Getting Your Foot in the Door

Damali Elinger always wanted to work for the government in her hometown of Knoxville, Tennessee. Her uncle works for the state government.

Damali began her job search in her last year of high school. "I wrote an introduction and practiced it with my mom and my older brother," she says. Then Damali made a list of contacts. "In school I learned that many jobs are not advertised. I decided to find the job I wanted by networking." Damali's uncle was her first contact. He took her résumé to his department head. He also gave her three referrals.

Damali called each of the referrals. One gave her two more referrals. "I met so many nice people who wanted to help me," Damali says. "I also found the perfect job. I'm now a clerk in the mayor's office."

It's Your Turn Make a list of two contacts who you could talk to about a job. Ask each of these people to give you two referrals. Make a contact list with the names and contact information of all six people.

For help completing this activity, visit **ewow.glencoe.com/tips** and select the *Smart Tip* for the Chapter 6 *Point of View*.

Check your answers online by visiting **ewow.glencoe.com/review** and selecting the Section 6.2 Review.

After You Read

Retell

1. Describe the elements a contact list should have. Sketch a blank contact list.

2. Explain how to find job openings by contacting employers directly. Use your own words.

Think Critically

3. Imagine that you are an employer. You have a job opening. Do you advertise for the job opening? Do you try to find someone you know for the job? Explain.

Math Practice

Answer the multiple-choice math questions at **ewow.glencoe.com/math.**

Which Is a Better Deal?

To find a job, you can subscribe to your local newspaper. You can also register with an employment agency. Both require a three-month commitment. The paper is $10.50 per month. The agency is $5 per week. Is the paper or the agency a better deal?

Step 1 Calculate the cost of the paper for 3 months.
$10.50 × 3 months = $31.50

Step 2 Calculate the monthly cost of the employment agency. Multiply this total by the number of months (3).
$5 × 4 = $20 × 3 = $60

Result The newspaper costs less and is a better deal.

Figure It Out

You are an employer with a job opening. You want to post the job opening on an Internet job board and with an employment service. The job board costs $22.95 a month. The employment service's fee is 75 cents per day. How much will it cost to list the job in both places for one month (30 days)?

Mortgage Banker

Lydia Graber

Michigan

Career Cluster: Finance

Mortgage Banker

Training

Bankers need at least a high school diploma. A bachelor's degree is recommended for management positions.

What does a mortgage banker do?

"We provide mortgages, which are loans for people to buy homes."

Skills and Talents

Bankers need to be good with people and have good communication skills. They also need to be knowledgeable about accounting and banking.

Why did you choose a career in banking?

"I began as a file clerk and worked my way up to being a vice president. I liked the work and saw the opportunity to make a career. Banking was a good fit for me."

Career Outlook

Banking employment is expected to grow more slowly than average through 2012. There should be plenty of job openings for tellers. There will be many jobs in management and customer service.

What obstacles have you overcome?

"I'm constantly overcoming people's perception of me. People see what you cannot do instead of what you can do. I'm 3 foot 11 inches, so people think because I'm short that there are things I can't do. I was told I was too short to be a bank teller. I became the bank teller who stood on a stool."

Learn More About It

Take a group field trip to a bank in your community. Call the bank first to make arrangements. Ask a worker in the bank to discuss the different jobs in banking. Prepare by making a list of questions to ask. Write a thank-you note after you visit the bank.

What advice do you have for students?

"Get an education. When you go on job interviews, look and act professional. Be yourself and be confident. Be prepared. Have a good résumé. Take with you to job interviews all the information you will need to fill out the job application."

For help with this activity, visit **ewow.glencoe.com/tips**.

Glencoe Online

Test your knowledge with the online games and activities at **ewow.glencoe.com**.

Key Term Review

job opening (p. 128)
job lead (p. 128)
job listing (p. 129)
employment agency (p. 129)
temp job (p. 130)
temp-to-hire job (p. 130)
classified ad (p. 132)

job board (p. 134)
contact (p. 138)
networking (p. 139)
referral (p. 139)
contact list (p. 140)
contact information (p. 140)
cold-calling (p. 144)

Check Your Understanding

1. Name three good sources of job leads.
2. Explain how to find job listings on the Internet.
3. Define contacts, networking, and referrals.
4. Explain why networking can be your best job-search tool.
5. List the four steps in networking.

Write About It

6. **Write a Letter**   Write a letter to a contact. Choose a person you do not know well. In the first paragraph, remind the contact how you know each other. In the second paragraph, explain why you are writing the letter. In the third paragraph, list your year in school, the job you want, your work experience, and your skills. In the fourth paragraph, thank the contact and ask him or her to write or call you with any information.

Role-Play

7. **Practice Networking**   Write an introduction to use in networking. Include your year in school, the job you want, your work experience, and your skills. With a partner, pretend that you are talking to a referral. Introduce yourself. Explain where you got the person's name. Ask for job leads and referrals. Switch roles with your partner.

Teamwork Challenge

8. **Cold-Call Employers**   Find a local phone book. With a partner, look in the yellow pages. Choose two businesses where you might like to work. Call or visit those businesses. Introduce yourselves and ask if there are any job openings for workers with your skills. If there are no job openings, ask for referrals. Write a paragraph describing your experiences.

Computer Lab

Write a Job Posting   Find a large job board on the Internet. Find and read three different job postings. Then write a job posting for a job you would like to have. Make sure your job posting is realistic. Use a word processor to type, format, and print your job posting.

Personal Career Portfolio

Make a Contact List   Write a contact list. Format your list like the one in **Figure 6.3** on page 141. List the names and contact information of at least 10 people. Add your contact list to your Personal Career Portfolio.

Go to **ewow.glencoe.com** for help.

Chapter 7

Applying for a Job

You Already Know...

- employers want to know about you before they hire you
- you need to show employers that you have skills
- it is important to make a good first impression
- many employers ask for a written job application

You Will Learn...

- how to ask for a job application form
- personal facts you will need to list on a job application form
- the difference between a chronological résumé and a skills résumé
- the five parts of a chronological résumé
- the purpose of a cover letter

Personal Career Portfolio *Preview*

For your portfolio, you will make a personal fact sheet. As you read, think about what information you will include on your sheet.

Preview Find the four figures in this chapter. Read the title and caption of each figure. Then use your own words to describe what each figure shows.

Preparing Job Application Forms

Ready, Set, Read

Key Terms

job application form

job applicant

standard English

online job application form

accurate

personal fact sheet

reference

Main Idea

A job application form is a form you fill out to apply for a job. A job application form asks for facts about you, your work experience, and your education.

Thought Organizer

Copy the list below. As you read, write facts to include on your personal fact sheet.

Personal Fact Sheet

- <u>date of birth</u>
- _____
- _____
- _____

- _____
- _____
- _____
- _____

Fill Out a Job Application Form to Apply for a Job

job application form ■ A printed sheet with blanks that you fill in to apply for a job.

job applicant ■ A person applying for a job.

What do you do after you find a job opening? You apply for the job. One way to apply is to fill out a job application form. A **job application form** is a printed sheet with blanks that you fill in to apply for a job. A person who is applying for a job is called a **job applicant**.

Some employers ask you to fill out the job application form at the place of work. Other employers let you take the form with you.

It is best to take the form home. This gives you more time to fill it out. It also gives you the chance to get help from a teacher or working adult.

Job Application Forms Ask for Facts About You

Each job application form is a little different. Most job application forms ask the same kinds of questions, however. Most job applications start with:

- your name, home address, and phone number
- your social security number (SSN)
- job for which you are applying
- date you can start work
- days and hours you can work
- pay you want
- whether or not you have been convicted of a crime

Figure 7.1 on the next page shows a sample job application form. Read it carefully.

All About You
Employers want to know about you before they hire you. They will only hire you if you prove that you can do a good job. What should you do if you do not understand something on a job application form?

Figure 7.1

Job Application

Fill out all fields completely and return to Dave Ko, Human Resources Manager.

Position Applied for: _____ Date of Application: _____

Name: _____
　　　　　　LAST　　　　　　　　　　　FIRST　　　　　　　　　MIDDLE INITIAL

Address: _____
　　　　　　STREET　　　　　　　CITY　　　　　　　STATE　　　　　ZIP CODE

Date available to start work: _____ Days/Hours available: _____

Type of employment desired:　　　　❏ Full-Time　　❏ Part-Time　　❏ Temporary

Are you legally eligible to work in this country?　　❏ Yes　　❏ No

If you are under 18, do you have a work permit?　　❏ Yes　　❏ No

Have you ever been convicted of a felony?　　❏ Yes　　❏ No

If yes, explain: _____

Education

Name and Location of School	Dates Attended	Degree Received/Date
1.		
2.		
3.		

Work Experience
List all jobs you have held over the past 10 years.

From	To	Employer	Phone
Job Title			
Supervisor		Nature of the Work and Responsiblities	
Supervisor's Phone			
Salary (Hourly)		Reason for Leaving	

From	To	Employer	Phone
Job Title			

Employment Application Job applications can be very detailed. Applications may ask about your education, military service, work experience, previous addresses, and more. Why would an employer ask if you have been convicted of a felony, or serious crime?

You Can Get Job Application Forms in Person

How do you get a job application form? You can visit businesses in person and ask for a form.

Some job listings ask you to come to the business to pick up a job application form. Visit the business. Say that you would like to fill out a job application form.

"May I Have an Application Form?" You can ask for a job application from most retail businesses. Stores, restaurants, and coffee shops are retail businesses. Walk in and ask if they are accepting applications. If they are, ask for a job application form.

You can also ask for a job application form if you see a "help wanted" sign. James du Lac saw a "help wanted" sign in a café window. He went in and said, "Hello, my name is James du Lac. I would like to apply for the job you have available. May I have an application form?" He got a form and took it home to fill it out.

Make a Good First Impression It is important to make a good first impression when you visit a business. Be polite. Dress neatly. Speak in standard English. Standard English is the form of English taught in school. It is the form of English you see in the newspaper. It is formal English. Use correct grammar. Avoid slang words.

Do you speak with an accent? Do not worry. Many people speak standard English with an accent.

You Can Get Job Application Forms by Calling Employers

You may need to call an employer to get a job application form. You will need to call first if you have a job lead from a contact. You will also need to call if a job ad gives a phone number. If a contact person is listed in the ad, call and ask for that person.

While You Read

Question Where can you ask for a job application form?

standard English ■ The form of English taught in school.

"I Am Calling About the Job Advertisement..."

When you call, say your name and tell why you are calling. Explain how you heard about the job. Ask if the job is still open.

If the job is open, ask how you can apply for the job. You might need to go to the business and pick up a job application.

Lilly Washington saw an ad for a bank teller job. She called the number in the ad. She said, "Hello, my name is Lilly Washington. I am calling about the job advertisement in today's *Times* for a bank teller." Lilly learned that the job was still available. She was told to pick up a job application at the bank. She wrote down the address and hours of the bank, said, "Thank you," and hung up.

While You Read

Question What are two ways to show good phone manners?

Use Good Phone Manners Use good phone manners when you call. Speak clearly and in standard English. Speak loudly enough to be heard. Speak at a medium speed, not too fast. Be polite. Know what you are going to say before you call. It helps to make notes ahead of time.

If you have to leave a recorded message, make it short. Speak clearly and slowly. Give your name and phone number. Say why you are calling.

The Phone is a Job-Search Tool
Be polite and confident over the phone. Practice what you are going to say ahead of time. Take notes. End every call by thanking the person. Why is it important to use good phone manners?

Online Job Application Form

Northern Star
Online Application for Employment

Position Desired: [Choose a position: ▼]   Date Available: [ ]

Personal Data:

First Name: [ ]   Last Name: [ ]
Email Address: [ ]   Local Address: [ ]
Local Phone: [ ]   Permanent Addr: [ ]
Perm. Phone: [ ]   Major/Minor: [ ]
Year in school: [Please choose a year: ▼]   GPA: [ ]
Graduation Date: [ ]

Education:

List any courses that you have taken which pertain to this position. Please specify if taken in high school, junior college, or four year university:
[ ]

Experience:

Employer	Phone #	Position	Began? Left?	Reason for leaving?
[ ]	[ ]	[ ]	[ ]	[ ]
[ ]	[ ]	[ ]	[ ]	[ ]
[ ]	[ ]	[ ]	[ ]	[ ]

Do you have any special skills such as knowledge of computers, photography, etc.?
[ ]

Please list 3 business references including name, phone # and relationship:
[ ]
[ ]
[ ]

Why would you like to work at the Star, and how did you find out about this position?
[ ]

What days and times would you be available to work?
[ ]

I certify that all the above statements are true and I agree that deliberate statement of misinformation is grounds for termination without notice.

I agree☐

[Submit Application]

THE NORTHERN STAR IS AN EQUAL OPPORTUNITY EMPLOYER

Online Job Application Form
You can apply for jobs online (over the Internet). Instead of using a pen, you type your answers into each field of an online form. What do you think is good about applying for a job online? What is not so good? Explain.

You Can Get Job Application Forms on the Internet

Today, many businesses offer job application forms on the Internet. Job postings often instruct you to fill out an online job application form. An **online job application form** is a job application form on the Internet.

Online job application forms ask the same questions as printed job application forms. You type in each answer in a separate field. You then click a button to submit the application over the Internet.

online job application form ■ A job application form on the Internet.

Fill Out Job Application Forms Neatly and Accurately

Take your time filling out job application forms. Make sure every answer is neat, complete, and accurate. **Accurate** means truthful and without errors.

Employers want workers who pay attention to detail. They want workers who are dependable. Use the job application form to show that you pay attention to detail and are dependable. Fill the form out neatly. Fill it out completely. Make sure all your answers are accurate.

accurate ■ Truthful and without errors.

While You Read

Question Why should you make a personal fact sheet?

personal fact sheet ■ A list of all the information about yourself that you will need for a job application form.

Make a Personal Fact Sheet

You can make sure that your answers are accurate by preparing a personal fact sheet. A **personal fact sheet** is a list of all the information about yourself that you will need for a job application form. A personal fact sheet makes it easy to fill out a job application form.

Start your personal fact sheet by listing the information on the bulleted list on page 153. Then list these facts:

- your date of birth
- your driver's license number, if you have one
- your interests and hobbies
- awards you have won

List the Work You Have Done Write about your work experience next. List all of these things for each job you have done:

- name, address, and phone number of the place you worked
- name and telephone number of your supervisor
- job title
- job tasks
- starting and ending dates
- starting and ending pay
- reason for leaving the job

List the Schools You Have Attended   Employers also want to know where you have gone to school. List the name, address, and phone number of each high school you have attended. List the dates you went there. List what classes and vocational courses you have taken.

List Places You Have Lived   Some job application forms ask about places you have lived. Write down your current address. If you rent your home, write the name and phone number of the manager. Also write down your previous addresses.

List Job Accommodations You Might Need   Will you need job accommodations for certain tasks? Maybe you need help lifting heavy things. Maybe you do not see well enough to drive. Write these things on your fact sheet. If the employer knows these things, it is easier to decide which job you can do best.

While You Read

Connect Think about a job that interests you. Will you need job accommodations to do this job?

Making Good Choices

Telling "White Lies"

Ana reads an ad for a job in a nursery. The ad says that experience in a nursery is required. Ana is a delivery person for a flower shop. She does not have experience working in a nursery. She took a gardening class at the local arboretum. She takes care of several house plants.

Ana is thinking of telling a "white lie" on her job application. She plans to say that she works with plants at her current job. She just will not mention that she only delivers them.

You Make the Call What do you advise Ana to do? Do you think telling a "white lie" will hurt or help her?

For help in answering this question, visit **ewow.glencoe.com/tips** and select the *Smart Tip* for the Chapter 7 *Making Good Choices*.

reference ■ A person who will tell an employer that you will do a good job.

Choose Your References Some job application forms ask for references. A **reference** is a person who will tell an employer that you will do a good job.

Your references should be adults who know you well. Adult friends, teachers, counselors, and past employers who like you make good references. Do not use relatives or students as references.

Talk to your references before you apply for a job. Ask permission to give out their contact information.

Real-World Connection

Using Electronic Résumés

A résumé that you put online or send by e-mail is called an *electronic résumé*. Many Web sites let you post your résumé online for free. Employers can search these online résumés.

You need to register on a career Web site to put your résumé online. Click on "log in," "register," or "create account." Type in your name and any other information. Cut and paste the text of your résumé into the field. Click on the "submit" button.

How do you create a good electronic résumé? Think about what keywords an employer might search for. For example, an employer might look for employees who know how to use a specific kind of technology. Mention all your skills. Mention all the technology you can use.

Think like an employer. Who would you want to hire if you had a job opening?

Take the Next Step Visit an electronic résumé guide. Read about how to post an electronic résumé on the Internet. Summarize the information in one paragraph.

For help doing this activity, go to **ewow.glencoe.com/tips** and find the *Smart Tip* for the Chapter 7 *Real-World Connection*.

List Your References   Create a list of your references. Write down their names, job titles, and contact information.

Employers will call your references. They will ask about you. They might ask whether you get along well with others. They might ask whether you have a positive attitude. Are you responsible and honest? Will you do well in the new job?

Make Sure Your Job Application Form Is Perfect

The way your job application looks is as important as what it says. Would you hire someone who turned in a sloppy job application form? No.

Read the Directions First   Read the directions before you start to fill out the form. Read the form from beginning to end. Make sure you understand every question.

Take the form home if you can. If you need help, ask a teacher, counselor, or family member. If you cannot take the form home, ask the person who gave it to you to define words you do not understand.

Write Slowly and Carefully   Fill out the form slowly and carefully. Use a black or dark blue pen. Print carefully. Do not use cursive handwriting. Make sure there are no cross-out marks or fingerprints.

Spell correctly. Refer to your personal fact sheet. If you are not sure how to spell a word, use a dictionary.

Your application form should look neat. Make sure the form stays clean and unwrinkled. It helps to keep it in a folder.

Answer Every Question   Work line by line. Answer every question. Do not leave any blanks. If a question does not apply to you, draw a short line in the space. This shows that you did not skip over it.

When you sign your name on the form, use your full name. Do not use a nickname. Sign your name in cursive writing.

While You Read

Connect How neat is your handwriting? Can other people read it?

Check your answers online by visiting **ewow.glencoe.com/review** and selecting the Section 7.1 Review.

After You Read

Retell

1. Describe two ways to get job application forms. Give a good example of each way.

2. Reread the section on page 161 titled "List Your References." Summarize this section in your own words.

Think Critically

3. What do you think is more important—the way a job application form looks or what it says? Give your reasons.

Math Practice

Answer the multiple-choice math questions at **ewow.glencoe.com/math**.

Working With Percentages

You apply for a sales job at a clothing boutique. You fill out the job application form. Then you are given a test. On the test, you are asked to calculate the cost of a sweater that is on sale. The original price of the sweater was $150. It is on sale for $100. By what percentage was it reduced?

Step 1	Calculate the difference between the original price and the sale price. **$150 − $100 = $50**
Step 2	Calculate the percentage by dividing the difference by the original price. **$50 ÷ $150 = 0.33**
Result	The sweater was reduced by 33%.

Figure It Out

You buy a lamp at a flea market for $8.00. You sell the lamp at an online auction for $15.00. What percentage profit do you make on the lamp?

Writing Your Résumé

Ready, Set, Read

Key Terms

résumé
chronological
    résumé
job objective
skills résumé
spell check
cover letter

Main Idea

A résumé is a one-page summary of your skills, work experience, and education. You send a résumé and a cover letter to apply for a job.

Thought Organizer

Copy the chart below. As you read, fill in the five parts of a chronological résumé.

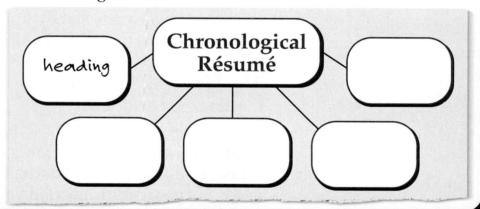

A Résumé Is a Summary of Your Qualifications

One way to apply for a job is to fill out a job application form. Another way to apply for a job is to hand in a résumé. A **résumé** is a one-page summary of your skills, work experience, and education. It tells employers what you have to offer.

Every worker needs a résumé. Many employers will ask for your résumé when you apply for a job. Some employers will ask you to attach your résumé to your job application form. Many online job application forms have a blank field where you paste your résumé.

résumé ■ A one-page summary of your skills, work experience, and education.

A Chronological Résumé Lists Your Experience in Time Order

The most common format is the chronological résumé. A **chronological résumé** is a résumé that lists your achievements in time order. It lists your work experience and education separately.

A Chronological Résumé Has Five Parts

A good chronological résumé has five parts:

1. heading
2. job objective
3. skills summary
4. work experience
5. education

Find these five parts in the chronological résumé in **Figure 7.2** on the next page for Melissa Cantos.

The Heading Lists Your Name and Contact Information

The first part of the résumé is the heading. The heading contains your name and contact information.

List your first name and last name. Use your given name, not your nickname. Add your middle name or initial if you like.

Write your street address, city, state, and zip code. Write your home phone number below the address. List your e-mail address if you have one.

The Job Objective Describes the Type of Job You Want

The second part of the résumé is the job objective. A **job objective** is the type of job you want. Your job objective should be specific. It should match the job for which you are applying.

Here are some specific job objectives:

• Salesperson at small family-owned hardware store.

• Receptionist at fast-paced real estate firm.

Figure 7.2

Chronological Résumé

24 Branford Circle #115 • Hastings, MO 48002 • (269) 555-0189
MCantos@emails.com

Melissa Cantos

Job Objective   Full-time administrative assistant position in law office.

Skills Summary
- Dependable, responsible, and hard-working.
- Strong interpersonal and communication skills.
- Able to maintain confidentiality working with legal documents.
- Knowledge of word-processing and database software including Microsoft Excel and Microsoft Word.
- Bilingual English/Spanish.
- Type 65 wpm.

Work Experience

Nov. 2005–present   Englander, Watanabe & Raskin
                          Bremerton, MO

Administrative Assistant (part-time)
- Perform essential administrative tasks such as scheduling, filing, managing correspondence, and answering busy phones.
- Transcribe case files and notes.

Feb. 2004–Oct. 2005   Centerton Assisted Living Facility
                          Centerton, MO

Staff Assistant (part-time)
- Performed administrative and managerial duties such as handling phone calls, keeping patient logs, filing, and answering questions from prospective residents and family members.
- Coordinated activities for elderly adults.

Education

2005   Springfield High School   Springfield, MO
High School Diploma
- Course work in criminal justice and introduction to law.
- Participant in statewide Law Honors Project.
- Three semesters of computer applications courses.

Be Brief Be brief on a résumé. Use bullet points to describe your skills and experiences. Would you hire Melissa Cantos as an administrative assistant? Why or why not?

Study Tip

Improve your writing skills by learning to spot your mistakes. Ask a teacher or counselor to explain the mistakes in your writing. Ask how you can avoid these mistakes next time.

The Skills Summary Highlights Your Skills

The third part of the résumé is the skills summary. The skills summary highlights the education, experience, and skills relevant to the job you want.

Include job-specific skills such as typing, speaking another language, and using computer programs. Include transferable skills such as being dependable and paying attention to detail. List all the skills that relate to the job you want.

Work Experience Lists the Jobs You Have Done

The work experience section lists all the jobs you have done. Write your most recent job first. Then write your next most recent job. List your first job last. Include the name and location of each employer. List even small jobs. Jobs such as baby-sitting and gardening show that you are dependable and hardworking.

While You Read

Connect Think of three action verbs that describe work activities you have done.

Use Action Verbs Write two or three bullet points for each job. Describe your accomplishments at each job. Be positive. Show that you did your job well. Show that you helped the company. Show that you proved your skills.

Start each bullet point with an action verb. An *action verb* is a verb that describes doing something active. It helps an employer visualize what you did at your job. Examples of action verbs are *manage, help,* and *create.*

Use the past tense for actions you did in the past. Use the present tense for actions you are still doing. Look at Melissa's résumé on page 165 to see how she wrote her bullet points.

Education Lists Your School Experience

The education section lists your secondary and postsecondary education. List the name and location of each school. List the date you finished or the date you will finish. List your vocational classes. List other classes or projects that might help you on the job.

In Action You have many different skills and talents. Include the strongest ones on your résumé. What skills is this worker showing here?

A Skills Résumé Lists Groups of Skills

The second résumé format is the skills résumé. A **skills résumé** is a résumé that lists your achievements by type of skill. Skills résumés are sometimes called functional résumés.

Each person has a different mix of skills. One person might have child care skills, dependability, and computer skills. Another person might have skills such as athletics, leadership, and attention to detail. Your skills are unique. Your skills résumé will be unique, too.

Look at Melissa Cantos's skills résumé in **Figure 7.3** on page 168. How would your skills résumé differ from hers?

skills résumé ■ A résumé that lists your achievements by type of skill.

Figure 7.3

Skills Resume

24 Branford Circle #115 • Hastings, MO 48002 • (269) 555-0189
MCantos@emails.com

Melissa Cantos

Job Objective	Full-time administrative assistant position in law office.
Communication Skills	• Handle client correspondence in English and Spanish at law firm. • Motivated fellow students to donate canned food for Springfield High School food drive. • Counseled clients and their families at assisted living facility.
Computer Skills	• Create and update expense account worksheets in Excel. • Transcribed case files and notes using Dictaphone and word-processing software. • Desktop-published poster for dance at Springfield High School. • Type 65 wpm.
Attention to Detail	• Manage computerized records for four attorneys. • Spent 100 hours preparing legal brief for Law Honors Project. • Wrote and distributed over 50 phone messages per day at law firm.
Experience	Nov. 2005–present *Administrative Assistant* (part-time), Englander, Watanabe & Raskin, Bremerton, MO Feb. 2004–Oct. 2005 *Staff Assistant* (part-time), Centerton Assisted Living Facility, Bremerton, MO
Education	2005 High School Diploma, Springfield High School, Springfield, MO

Show Your Skills Melissa Cantos wants a job as an administrative assistant. Communication skills, computer skills, and attention to detail are important for this job. Compare this résumé to the résumé on page 165. Which one do you prefer? Why?

Identify Your Strongest Skills

Start your skills résumé by listing what you do well. What do you know how to do? What do you know a lot about? What kind of experience do you have? Make a list.

Group Your Skills into Categories

While You Read

Connect What are your three strongest skills?

Group your skills and experiences into two or three categories. Your categories should be broad. You might use categories such as:

- attention to detail
- dependability
- responsiblity
- initiative
- communication skills
- problem-solving skills
- sales skills
- customer service skills
- computer skills
- management skills

Create Bullet Points   Write three or four bullet points for each skill. Start each bullet point with an action verb. Use the past tense for actions you did in the past. Use the present tense for actions you are still doing.

Be sure that you use the correct tense. For example, let's say that you work at a clothing store. You are in charge of customer service. Since you are still responsible for this, your verb should be in present tense. Your bullet point might look like this.

- Manage customer service for Marina Clothing store.

Let's say that last month, you made a filing system for the store. Since this action took place in the past, your verb should be in past tense. Your bullet point might look like this:

- Created filing system for Marina Clothing store.

Always use the past tense when you are talking about jobs or projects that have ended.

List Your Work Experience and Education

List your work experience and education at the bottom of the skills résumé.

Be brief. List the dates of each job, the name and place of the employer, and your title. List the dates of each school and the name and place of the school. List your diploma or degree.

Which Résumé Format Should You Use?

Experienced workers usually use chronological résumés. Many employers prefer to receive chronological résumés. Chronological résumés show what a worker has done every year.

Younger workers often use skills résumés. A skills résumé is a good choice if you have little work experience. A skills résumé is also a good choice if you have done several short-term jobs.

Make Sure Your Résumé Is Perfect

It takes time to write a good résumé. Make sure all the information is correct. Make sure you have included the best information.

Ask a teacher, family member, or adult worker to read your résumé. Then read it one more time to be sure everything is right.

Use a Spell-Check Program   Make sure that there are no errors in spelling or grammar on your résumé. A spell-check program can help you do this. A spell check is a computer tool that finds misspelled words and suggests correct spellings.

spell check ■ A computer tool that finds misspelled words and suggests correct spellings.

While You Read

Visualize Imagine what your résumé will look like when it is finished.

Your Résumé Should Look Good   Make sure your résumé looks good, too. Print your résumé in black ink on white paper. Make sure that it is easy to read. Make sure that the page is not crowded with type.

Print several copies of your résumé. Keep them in a folder so they stay clean and unwrinkled. Take your résumé with you when you visit contacts or employers.

Sell Your Skills in a Cover Letter

You need to send a cover letter with your résumé. A **cover letter** is a letter of application that says why you are a good match for the job.

The purpose of a cover letter is to "sell" yourself to the employer. A good cover letter can convince an employer to hire you.

cover letter ■ A letter of application that says why you are a good match for the job.

Point of View

Getting Your Résumé Right

Noah Sternberg of New York City wanted a career in banking. He kept that career goal in mind when writing his résumé. "I decided to write a chronological résumé," Noah says. "I had experience with two different after-school jobs. With both jobs, I worked with the public and handled people's money. Both jobs were good experience to be a bank teller."

"I spent several days writing my résumé. For the job objective, I said I wanted to be a bank teller. I made sure my skills matched those needed for a bank teller."

Noah had his mother and his math teacher read his résumé. "My mom found two spelling errors," Noah says. "My math teacher thought it was good because I talked about my skills. The time I spent writing my résumé paid off. I got a job as a bank teller!"

It's Your Turn Noah thought about what he wanted before he wrote his résumé. Write the names of two different jobs you might like. Write a skills summary for each one. How does skills summary change as the job changes?

For help completing this activity, visit **ewow.glencoe.com/tips** and go to the *Smart Tip* for the Chapter 7 *Point of View*.

Begin With the Heading and the Greeting

Begin your letter with the heading. The heading is your name and contact information. Then move down two lines and write the date you are sending the letter. Move down at least two more lines and write the name, business, and address of the person you are writing.

Now add a greeting. Your greeting will say:

Dear Mr. _____ :

or it will say:

Dear Ms. _____ :

When you do not know the name of the person who will read your letter, use a greeting such as "Dear Sir or Madam." The greeting should be followed by a colon.

The First Paragraph Says Why You Are Writing

Explain why you are writing in the first paragraph of your letter. Explain that you want to apply for a job.

Give the title of the job that interests you. Say where you learned about the job opening. If you are answering a newspaper ad for an assembler, you might write, "I am writing in response to your advertisement in the *Times* for an assembler."

Keon Williams heard about a job opening for a mail clerk. He got the job lead from his contact Shanya Brown. Read what he wrote in the first paragraph of his cover letter in **Figure 7.4**.

While You Read

Question What is the purpose of the second paragraph of a cover letter?

The Second Paragraph Talks About Your Skills

Describe your skills in the second paragraph of your cover letter. The purpose of this paragraph is to show the employer that you are a great choice for the job. It should convince the employer to look at your résumé.

Keon Williams is applying for a job as a mail clerk. He used his second paragraph to write about skills that a mail clerk needs. Read what he wrote.

Figure 7.4

KEON J. WILLIAMS
1236 S. Ailona Ave. • San Francisco, CA 98567
(415) 555-0101 • kjwill@emailcentral.net

November 30, 2006

Samuel Katz
United Merchants, Inc.
300 Commerce Center Plaza
San Francisco, CA 98007

Dear Mr. Katz:

Shanya Brown suggested that I write to you about a job as a mail clerk in your office.

Why hire me? I am personable, efficient, and dependable. I pay attention to detail and have excellent communication and organizational skills.

I have three years of experience in an office environment. I have handled incoming and outgoing mail, answered busy phones, and provided customer service. I am completing the computer career pathway at Martin Luther King, Jr. High School. Please see my enclosed résumé to learn more about me.

Thank you very much for considering me for this opportunity. I look forward to speaking with you and telling you more about what makes me a good match for the job.

Sincerely,

Keon J. Williams

Keon J. Williams

Sell Your Skills A good cover letter is brief and interesting. It describes your job skills. It also shows your writing skills. Why would an employer want to hire someone who has good writing skills?

The Third Paragraph Talks About Your Education and Experience

The third paragraph of your cover letter talks about your education and experience. Describe jobs you have done that are similar to the job you want. If you have not had a paying job, do not say so. Write about the classes you have had. Write about experiences you have had.

Keon Williams worked in his father's business for three years. He did not receive pay. However, he got a lot of work experience. Read what he wrote in the third paragraph of his cover letter.

A Positive Self-Image Your résumé and cover letter reflect you. They should show your positive self-image. Why is it important to make a good first impression on an employer?

The Fourth Paragraph Thanks the Employer and Asks for an Interview

In the last paragraph, thank the employer for considering you for the position. Say that you would like to speak to the employer. You can even ask for an interview at the employer's convenience.

End Your Cover Letter With the Closing

Your closing should be typed two spaces down from the last sentence. Your closing shuld leave enough room for a signature. Write "Sincerely," for a closing. Type down four lines and type your name. It should look like this:

Sincerely,

Your Name

After you print the letter, sign your letter in the space above your name. Use blue or black ink.

Make Sure Your Cover Letter Is Perfect

Your cover letter should make a good first impression. Make sure your letter sounds positive and confident. Make sure it sounds professional and not too casual. Use good manners in your writing. Use good grammar and punctuation too. Use a spell-check program to check your spelling. Ask a teacher and an adult friend to read your letter.

Your letter should look professional. Check a reference book to see how a business letter should look. For example, check *The Gregg Reference Manual*. Look in the Index under *Letters* or *Application letters*. Many word-processing programs can also help you write a professional letter.

Write one really good letter. Then use it as a guide when you write other letters. Of course, you will have to change the letter to fit the job.

While You Read

Connect Who could help you write a perfect cover letter?

Check your answers online by visiting ewow.glencoe.com/review and selecting the Section 7.2 Review.

After You Read

Retell

1. Describe a job objective. Explain why you might need to change your job objective from time to time.

2. List four ways to make sure your résumé is perfect. Use your own words.

Think Critically

3. The purpose of a cover letter is to "sell" yourself to an employer. Do you feel comfortable "selling" yourself? Why or why not?

Math Practice

Answer the multiple-choice math questions at ewow.glencoe.com/math.

Calculating Percentages

Groceryland has built a new store in your town. You are about to start a job as a cashier in the new store. Your employer tells you that the tax on your weekly earnings will be 15% of your pay. Your pay is $80 a week. How much will you pay in taxes each month?

Step 1 Multiply your total earnings ($80) by the tax rate.
$80 × .15 = $12

Step 2 Multiply the tax each week by the number of weeks in a month (4).
$12 × 4 = $48

Result You will pay $48 each month in taxes.

Figure It Out

Your employer asks you if you want to pay $60 of your total monthly earnings to a charity. You earn $125 per week. What percentage of your salary will go to charity each month?

Insurance Pool Governing Board Analyst

Diane C. Nelson
Oregon

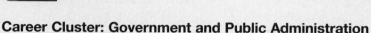

Career Cluster: Government and Public Administration

What does an insurance pool governing board analyst do?

"I analyze insurance premiums for the State of Oregon. It's like balancing one giant checkbook."

Why did you choose a career in government?

"I chose a career in math. I love math. The job in government came by good fortune. I excelled in math in school. I also have a degree in math."

What obstacles have you overcome?

"I have bipolar disease. You have to change medication frequently with a mental illness. I'm affected when we are adjusting the medication. It affects how I process math and how I am socially. I have to work harder to stay focused."

What advice do you have for students?

"You may think you are feeling differently from other people, but you really are a lot like the people around you. Many people have problems and obstacles to overcome. Stop focusing on how different you are. You're really not."

Insurance Pool Governing Board Analyst

Training
Jobs with state and local governments require different levels of education depending on the job. Jobs in math and accounting require an associate or four-year degree.

Skills and Talents
To work in insurance in a state government requires good math and communication skills.

Career Outlook
Employment in state and local government is expected to increase through 2012.

Learn More About It
Many government jobs require you to take a civil service exam. Go online to learn more about the civil service exam for your state. Write a one-page summary about what you learned.

For help with this activity, visit **ewow.glencoe.com/tips**.

Key Term Review

job application form (p. 152)

job applicant (p. 152)

standard English (p. 155)

online job application form (p. 157)

accurate (p. 158)

personal fact sheet (p. 158)

reference (p. 160)

résumé (p. 163)

chronological résumé (p. 164)

job objective (p. 164)

skills résumé (p. 167)

spell check (p. 170)

cover letter (p. 171)

Check Your Understanding

1. Describe how to ask an employer for a job application form when calling on the phone.

2. Name six facts you will need to list on a job application form.

3. Explain the difference between a chronological résumé and a skills résumé.

4. List and define the five parts of a chronological résumé.

5. Explain the purpose of a cover letter.

Write About It

6. **Write a Cover Letter**   Look on the Internet or in your local newspaper for a job opening that interests you. Write a cover letter to the employer. Talk about your skills and experience. Show how they would help you do the job well. Make sure your letter is positive and enthusiastic. Follow the format described on pages 171–175.

Role Play

7. **Ask for a Job Application**   Work with a partner. Pretend that you are asking an employer for a job application. One person is the employer and the other person is the job applicant. As the job applicant, introduce yourself. Say what kind of work you would like. Ask if the employer is accepting job applications. If so, ask for a job application form. Ask if you may take it home. Switch roles with your partner.

Teamwork Challenge

8. **Talk to Employers**   What is the right way to fill out an application form? With a partner, talk to an employer who uses job application forms. Ask for advice on how to fill out a job application form. What makes a good impression? What does not make a good impression? Why? Write a short report about what you learned.

Computer Lab

Read a Résumé Makeover   Many career Web sites offer résumé makeovers. A résumé makeover shows how to change a weak résumé into a strong résumé. Use an Internet search engine to find a résumé makeover. Write a paragraph about the makeover. Describe how the résumé changed.

Personal Career Portfolio

Make a Personal Fact Sheet   Make a personal fact sheet. Use the guidelines on pages 158–159. Finish with a list of at least three references.

   Go to **ewow.glencoe.com/portfolio** for help.

Chapter 8

Interview Success

You Already Know...

- finding a job takes time and preparation
- employers want to meet you in person before they hire you
- it is important to make a good impression on an employer
- speaking and writing skills help you make a good impression

You Will Learn...

- the purpose of a job interview
- how to prepare for a job interview
- which types of questions are often asked in interviews
- how to make a good impression on an employer
- what to say in a thank-you letter after an interview

Personal Career Portfolio *Preview*

For your portfolio, you will prepare answers to seven common interview questions. As you read, think about how you will answer the interview questions in the text.

Draw From Your Own Background What do you know about job interviews? Write the phrase "job interviews" on a piece of paper. Brainstorm with a partner. Write down every word you think of that relates to job interviews. Share your results with another group.

Preparing for the Interview

Key Terms

job interview
interviewer
ethics
conflict
body language

Main Idea

A job interview is an opportunity for you and the employer to get to know each other. Prepare for the interview by practicing what you will say to the interviewer.

Thought Organizer

Draw the chart below. As you read, write one reason to do each of the things listed.

Step	Why Do It?
Research the company.	To show you are interested in the job.
Prepare answers to interview questions.	
Prepare questions to ask the interviewer.	
Practice your interview skills.	

An Interview Is a Conversation With an Employer About a Job

You have found job openings. You have filled out job applications. You have sent your résumé and cover letter. Now it is time for job interviews.

A **job interview** is a meeting between an employer and a job applicant about a job. Some interviews last just a few minutes. Others may last an hour or longer.

job interview ■ A meeting between an employer and a job applicant about a job.

An Interview Helps the Employer and You

Employers use job interviews to decide who to hire. That is why doing well in an interview is important.

The interview is also helpful to you. You have a chance to see if you really want the job.

Employers Pick a Few Applicants to Interview

Most employers interview just a few applicants for every job. Employers read the applications they receive. They pick several people who seem right for the job. They call each of these people for an interview.

You will not get an interview every time you apply for a job. No one does.

Be Ready to Receive a Call   Be ready to receive a call for an interview. The employer will call and ask when you can come for an interview. Know what days and times you will be free. Make sure you can get to the interview on time. Allow at least two hours for your interview.

Write down all the facts you will need. Write the time of the interview. Write the exact address. Also ask if there is anything special you should bring with you.

Write the name of the interviewer. The **interviewer** is the person who will interview you. Ask how to spell and say the interviewer's name.

While You Read

Connect How would you feel if you got a call for an interview? Excited? Nervous?

interviewer ■ The person who interviews you.

Be Ready What makes the difference between a great interview and an okay interview? Preparation. Make sure you know where to go, when to be there, and who you are meeting. How much time should you allow for an interview?

183

Prepare for Interview Success

A job interview is a chance to show your skills and abilities. It is a chance to show an employer that you are right for the job.

The employer will ask you many questions. He or she will want to learn about you. What are your skills and abilities? What kind of experience do you have? Can you do the job? Can you get along with others? Can you think well?

You will do well in an interview if you prepare. How do you prepare? Do these things:

- Research the company.
- Prepare answers to common interview questions.
- Prepare questions to ask the interviewer.
- Practice your interview skills.

Figure 8.1 shows how these four strategies can lead to interview success.

Figure 8.1 Steps to Interview Success

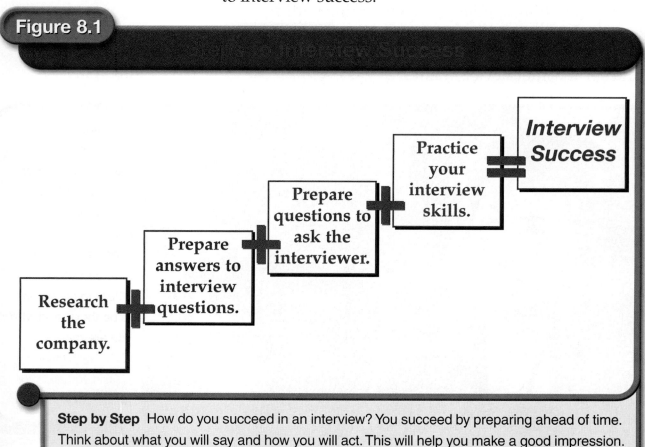

Step by Step How do you succeed in an interview? You succeed by preparing ahead of time. Think about what you will say and how you will act. This will help you make a good impression. Why do you think it is important to prepare questions to ask at the interview?

Research the Company

Find out about the company where you will interview.

Knowing about the company shows the interviewer that you are really interested in the job. It helps you decide whether you want to work for that company. It also helps you predict what the interviewer will ask.

Find Out As Much As You Can   Find out as much as you can about the company. Find answers to these questions:

- What kind of products or services does the company make or have?
- Who are the company's customers?
- Who are the company's competitors?
- How many people work at the company?
- How does the company treat its employees?
- How long has the company been in business?
- Is the company facing any problems? What are they?

Use as many sources as you can for your research. Good sources include the Internet, books and magazines, and your contacts.

Use an Internet Search Engine   Use an Internet search engine to research the company. Type the name of the company into the search field. Explore the results. Read any articles in magazines or newspapers.

Visit the Company's Web Site   You can learn a lot about a company from its Web site. You can learn what the company does. You can learn about the size of the company.

Look at all the areas of the Web site. Many companies have a Web page titled "About Us" or "Company Information." Read that page to learn about the company. It might give you company history and policy.

Look for the company's mission statement. A *mission statement* is a description of the company's goals and values.

While You Read

Question What should you find out about a company before the interview?

You can find a *site map* on many Web sites. A site map is like an index. It lists all the pages on a Web site. If you cannot find what you want on a Web site, use the site map.

Visit Business Web Sites   Some Web sites collect facts about companies. These Web sites are good sources of business information.

Read Books and Magazines   A librarian can help you find helpful books and magazines. Many reference books talk about companies and industries. For example, you can learn about different industries from the *Career Guide to Industries*.

While You Read

Question What can you learn about a company through networking?

Network for Information   Networking is another good way to learn about a company. Ask your contacts whether they know anyone who works at the company.

Ask for referrals, too. You may find a person who works at the company. You may find a person who worked at the company in the past. Ask that person what it is like to work there. Is the work interesting? Is it a good place to work? Can you build a career there?

Making Good Choices

Handling Tough Questions

Ryan worked in sales for a cell phone company. Ryan asked for time off to attend a concert. His boss said no. Ryan thought his boss was unreasonable, so Ryan took the day off. As a result, he was fired. Now Ryan is trying to get a job with another cell phone company. He had one interview. He was asked why he left his job. Ryan admitted he was fired, but he explained that his boss was unreasonable. Ryan was never called back.

Ryan knows he will be asked why he left his job at his next interview. He is not sure what he should say.

You Make the Call What advice would you give Ryan? For help in answering this question, visit **ewow.glencoe.com/tips** and find the *Smart Tip* for the Chapter 8 *Making Good Choices*.

Prepare Answers to Common Interview Questions

You also need to prepare answers to common interview questions. This helps you give good answers on the day of the interview.

Every interviewer asks different questions. Some interviewers will ask about your education. Other interviewers will ask about your interests and hobbies. Some interviewers might even ask about current events or the last book you read.

Some Interview Questions Are Illegal   Before you start to prepare, you should know that some questions are not allowed.

Interviewers should not ask you about your age, gender, national origin, color, race, or religion. Employers should not ask whether you are married or pregnant. Employers also should not ask about your health or disabilities.

Good interviewers know how to avoid these kinds of questions. But what do you do if an interviewer asks you a question that is illegal? Stay calm. Think about why the interviewer asked the question. He or she most likely wants to know some important information, and does not realize that asking the question is illegal.

Some questions might seem harmless. For example, an interviewer could ask, "How old are you?" or "What year were you born?" The interviewer probably wants to know if you are old enough to legally do the job. You might feel comfortable answering these questions, but a good answer might be, "I am over the legal minimum age to do this job."

Imagine that the interviewer asks, "How do your disabilities affect your daily life?" Why would the interviewer ask this? He or she probably wants to know if you can perform all the duties of the job. You do not need to talk directly about your disabilities. Instead, you might reply, "Are you concerned that I might not be able to do this job? What are the duties of the job?"

Visualize Imagine that an interviewer asks you an illegal question. How do you feel?

What Kind of Worker Are You? The interviewer will want to know what kind of worker you are. He or she will want to know whether you will do a good job.

The interviewer might say, "Tell me about yourself." Speak briefly about your skills, work experience, and education. Show the interviewer that you can do the job.

Do not give personal information. For example, do not talk about your friends. Focus on your job skills.

What Kind of Work Do You Want? Think about this question before your interview. Some young people just say, "anything." Employers do not like this answer. They want you to know what jobs you would like.

Look over your career plan. Review your values, interests, and talents. Pick work that is a good match.

Visualize Imagine yourself five years in the future. What do you see?

What Are Your Goals? Most interviewers want to know about your goals for the future. An interviewer might ask, "Where do you see yourself in five years?"

Describe your career goal. Show how the job fits into your career plan. For example, you might say, "My goal is to open my own business. This job would be a great chance to learn more about sales and marketing."

What Are Your Strengths and Weaknesses? The interviewer may ask about your strengths and weaknesses. The interviewer wants to see whether you are self-aware. The interviewer also wants to see whether you fit the job.

Name three of your best skills or personal qualities. Explain how you have showed these skills or qualities. For example, you might say, "I have excellent creative thinking skills. At my last job, I designed window displays that brought in new customers."

Do not tell the interviewer about major faults. Name one skill or personal quality you would like to improve. Say what you are doing to improve it.

For example, you might say, "Public speaking is a challenge for me. I am improving this skill by taking a debate class at school."

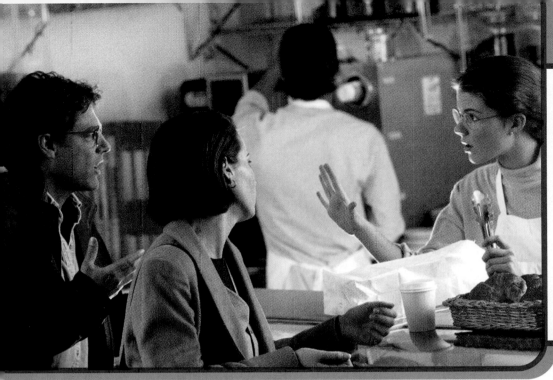

Show Your Skills
How you handle difficult situations says a lot about you. It shows your ethics, your people skills, and your communication skills. Why would an interviewer want to know about your ethics?

Do You Show Ethics?　Many interviewers want to know about your ethics. **Ethics** means knowing right from wrong.

For example, the interviewer might ask, "What would you do if you caught a coworker stealing?" Show the interviewer that you will act ethically. Show that you will do the right thing. If you are not sure what to answer, say that you would ask your supervisor for advice.

ethics ■ Knowing right from wrong.

Do You Handle Conflict Well?　The interviewer might also ask how you handle difficult situations such as conflicts. A **conflict** is a strong disagreement.

For example, the interviewer might say, "Give an example of a time when you had a conflict with another person. How did you solve it?" Tell how you used your communication skills to solve the conflict.

conflict ■ A strong disagreement.

What Kind of Pay Do You Expect?　Prepare for this question by doing research. Find out what others are paid for this type of work. Mention this in your answer.

For example, you might say, "The average pay for entry-level drivers is $12.00 an hour." This shows the employer that you have a good idea of fair pay.

While You Read

Connect Why do you think an interviewer would ask a question about pay?

Prepare Questions to Ask the Interviewer

You also need to prepare questions to ask at the end of the interview. Asking questions helps you get important information. It also shows the interviewer that you prepared well for the interview.

Think about what you still want to know. For example, do you understand all the job tasks? Do you know what hours you would work?

Choose two or three of these questions to ask.

- What is a normal day like in this job?
- Could you describe the work environment?
- What would my responsibilities be?
- Would I work alone or with a team?
- Who would be my supervisor?
- What are the chances to move up in the company?
- Do you offer training?
- What can you tell me about the people who work here?
- Is there anything else I should know about this job or this company?

You can also write two or three of your own questions. Write all your questions down on a piece of paper. That way you will not forget them.

While You Read

Question Why should you practice answering interview questions?

Practice Your Interview Skills

You are not quite ready for your interview—you need to practice. Practicing your interview skills helps you remember your answers. It helps you sound confident.

Write out your answers to common interview questions. Read them out loud several times. Then work with a friend, family member, or teacher. Ask that person to play the role of the interviewer.

Practice answering the interviewer's questions. Speak clearly in standard English. Look at your notes if you need to. Practice so that you will not need your notes in the interview.

Use Positive Body Language Practice positive body language before your interview. <mark>Body language</mark> means the messages that your movements send. Body language includes posture and expressions.

It is important to practice positive body language before the interview. When you give your answers, smile. Look the interviewer in the eye. Lean slightly forward to show interest.

Ask for advice each time you practice. Did you look and sound confident? You will get better each time.

body language ■ The messages that your movements send.

Real-World Connection

Why Wasn't I Hired?

There are a few common reasons people are not hired.

Appearance is one reason. Some applicants look sloppy. They are not dressed well or groomed.

Poor body language is another reason. Some applicants do not look the interviewer in the eye. They lean back in their chair, bored.

Poor manners are another reason. Some applicants are late to the interview. They chew gum or eat during the interview. They do not thank the interviewer for his or her time.

A poor attitude is the biggest reason of all that people are not hired. Many job applicants do not show interest in the job. They expect a lot of money for a little work.

Take the Next Step Find a worker who interviews job applicants. Ask him or her to explain what makes a good impression and what makes a bad impression. Ask for specific examples. Write them in a one-page report.

For help doing this activity, go to **ewow.glencoe.com/tips** and find the *Smart Tip* for the Chapter 8 *Real-World Connection*.

Check your answers online by visiting ewow.glencoe.com/review and selecting the Section 8.1 Review.

After You Read

Retell

1. Define body language. Give four examples of positive body language to use during an interview.

2. Reread the section titled "Some Interview Questions are Illegal." List the questions that interviewers are not allowed to ask. In your own words, explain how to handle illegal questions.

Think Critically

3. Imagine that you have an interview with a soda company. You do research. You learn that the company has been paying some workers unfair wages. Would you still want to work there? Explain.

Math Practice

Answer the multiple-choice math questions at ewow.glencoe.com/math.

Saving Money

You earn $200 a month. You save 10% of your earnings. Most people save only 3.5%. How much more do you save each month at 10% than you would save at 3.5%?

Step 1 Calculate the amount you save each month at 10%.
$0.10 \times \$200 = \$20$

Step 2 Calculate the amount you would save at 3.5%.
$0.035 \times \$200 = \$7$

Step 3 Find the difference between the two numbers.

Result You will save $13 more per month.

Figure It Out

You earn $300 a month. During the last three months, you spent $30, $36.30, and $29.55 on entertainment. What is the average percentage of your earnings that you spent on entertainment each month?

Succeeding in the Interview

Key Terms

hygiene
appropriate
positive
   attitude
enthusiasm
courtesy
follow up

Main Idea

Make a good impression on an employer with a positive appearance, attitude, and body language. Follow up after the interview by sending a thank-you letter.

Thought Organizer

Copy the chart below. As you read, write down three ways to show a positive attitude.

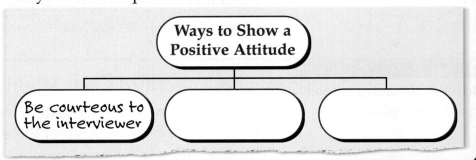

Ways to Show a Positive Attitude

Be courteous to the interviewer

Make a Good Impression

You will probably be nervous on the day of your interview. You have a lot to think about. Will the interviewer like you? Will you know what to say? Will you get the job?

Do not worry. You will be less nervous if you know how to make a good impression. Here are the things you can do to make a good impression:

- arrive early and alone
- bring everything you might need
- focus on appearance
- use positive body language
- show a positive attitude
- follow up after the interview

Arrive Early and Alone

Plan to arrive for the interview about five minutes early. If you are even one minute late, it makes a bad impression. If you arrive more than ten minutes early, wait to go inside. Arriving too early makes you look too anxious. Most interviewers cannot be ready for you if you are too early.

A day or two before the interview, find out how to get to the business. Make sure you know the way. If you are driving, allow extra time for traffic.

Go to the Interview Alone   You may want someone to come with you to help you find the business. A friend, your teacher, or a parent may go with you.

Do not take anyone with you into the interview. The only exception is if your teacher or parent knows the employer and plans to introduce you. Employers want to see that you can succeed on your own.

While You Read

Question What do you need to take to a job interview?

Take Everything You Might Need

Go to the interview prepared. Take everything you might need. Here are several things you need to take to the interview.

- paper and pen to make notes
- personal fact sheet
- two copies of your résumé
- list of references
- notes about the company
- prepared answers to questions
- list of questions to ask the interviewer

Keep all the papers in a folder so they stay neat.

While You Read

Connect Do you feel more self-confident when you are well-dressed?

Focus on Appearance

Your appearance will affect the interviewer's first impression of you. It is the first thing the employer will notice. Give thought to how you look. Make sure you are clean and well-dressed.

Pay Attention to Hygiene **Hygiene** is the care you give your health and cleanliness. Make sure your hygiene is perfect for the interview.

Take a bath or shower before you dress for an interview. Brush your teeth. Use deodorant. Some people forget to do this. Their body odor may lose them the job. It sounds simple, but it makes a big difference.

The smell of cigarettes loses jobs, too. The smell of cigarettes bothers many people. Wear very little perfume, cologne, or aftershave. Many people are sensitive to fragrance.

Make sure your hair and nails are clean and neat. Wear only simple jewelry. If you are a woman, use only a little makeup. If you are a man and do not wear a beard, shave before the interview.

hygiene ■ The care you give your health and cleanliness.

Look Your Best
Take your time to look your best for the interview. Iron your clothes the evening before your interview. Make sure your hair, nails, and clothes are clean and neat. What does good hygiene say to an employer?

Wear Appropriate Clothes   Choose clothes that are appropriate for the job. Appropriate means correct for the situation.

For example, if you have an interview for a job as salesperson, a suit is appropriate. Wear dress shoes. Make sure they are shined and in good condition. A T-shirt, jeans, and sneakers are not appropriate.

If you apply for an outdoor job, such as working in a recreation center, more casual clothes are appropriate. You could wear jeans and a button-down shirt.

Whatever you wear, be sure it is clean and ironed. Do not wear clothing that is worn, faded, or has stains. Do not wear shoes that have holes in them.

You may not always know what kind of clothing to wear for an interview. If you are unsure about what clothing is appropriate for your interview, ask. You can call the company and ask about the dress code. The person who interviews you will probably appreciate your attention to detail.

While You Read

Visualize Picture yourself using positive body language in an interview.

Pay Attention to Positive Body Language

Remember to use positive body language. Smile. Stand up straight. Look the interviewer in the eye.

Give a Firm Handshake   Give a firm handshake to the interviewer. A firm handshake shows self-esteem. Your handshake is an important part of your first impression.

If the interviewer does not know your name, introduce yourself. For example, you might say, "I am Lynn Fisher. I have an 11:30 appointment to interview for the job as a server." Speak clearly and loudly enough to be heard.

Sit Up Straight   Stand until the interviewer asks you to sit. If the interviewer does not ask you to sit, then stand for the interview.

When you do sit, sit up straight. Do not slouch. Lean a little bit forward in your chair. Leaning forward shows that you are interested. It shows that you are paying attention.

Positive Body Language The way you act tells the employer a lot about you. Do you have a good attitude? Are you interested in the job? What positive body language is this job applicant using?

Show a Positive Attitude

A positive attitude is an important part of doing well at an interview. A **positive attitude** is a cheerful view of life.

Be positive about yourself. Be positive about others. Do not say bad things about other companies or people. Do not criticize your former jobs or employers. Focus on the good things you have learned from past experiences.

Focus on what you can do for the employer. The employer does not owe you a job. You must show the employer that you will earn your pay. Your attitude shows in how you act in life, whether at school, with family or friends, or at work. A positive attitude can be more important to an interviewer than your experience or your education.

positive attitude ■ A cheerful view of life.

enthusiasm ■ Interest and eagerness.

Show Enthusiasm for Work It is important to show enthusiasm for work and for the job. <mark>Enthusiasm</mark> is interest and eagerness.

Show that you are interested in the work. Show that you are eager to work. Show that you are willing to learn.

Sell yourself with enthusiasm. Be honest. Give an honest answer to every question.

Be Courteous to Everyone You Meet Being courteous is another way to be positive. Being courteous means showing <mark>courtesy</mark>, or politeness and respect.

courtesy ■ Politeness and respect.

Be courteous to everyone you meet at the workplace. The employer may ask them how they liked you.

While You Read

Question How can you show courtesy to the interviewer?

Be Courteous to the Interviewer Show courtesy toward the interviewer. Be on time for the interview. Arrive a few minutes early so that you have a few moments to prepare yourself. What if you have an emergency the day of the interview? If you think that you are going to be late or that you cannot make it to the interview, you should call. The interviewer will appreciate this.

It is important to have good manners during the interview. Greet the interviewer with enthusiasm. Make sure you pronounce his or her name correctly. Do not lean on the desk or read papers on it. Sit up straight. Do not cross your arms or tap your feet. Keep your hands in your lap. Do not chew gum or smoke. Do not place anything on the interviewer's desk. Speak carefully to avoid stuttering when you speak to the interviewer.

Wait to ask your questions until the interviewer asks if you have any. Then look at your notes and ask two or three questions.

It is all right to ask about pay and benefits. But wait until the interview is almost over. You do not want to sound as if you only care about money.

Always thank the interviewer after the interview. Thank the interviewer for his or her time and effort.

Follow Up After the Interview

Do not forget to follow up after the interview. To **follow up** means to finish something or do the next step.

Make sure you know what the next step is. At the end of the interview, say to the interviewer, "I am very interested in this job. What is the next step?"

If you are told to call in a few days, wait two or three days. Then call. If you are told that you will be called, wait about a week. Then call to say that you are still interested in the job.

follow up ■ To finish something or do the next step.

Make Notes for Your Personal Career Portfolio

How did the interview go? Make notes about the interview as soon as it is over. Try to learn from your experience.

You will not be offered a job every time you are interviewed. Nobody is. Make notes for your next interview. Write down ideas to help you next time. Were you prepared for every question?

While You Read

Question When should you make notes about the interview?

Write a Thank-You Letter

Write a letter of thanks for the interview. Write your thank-you letter as soon as the interview is over. This shows you are still interested in the job. It shows you care enough to take the time to write. Read the sample thank-you letter in **Figure 8.2** on the next page.

Thank the Interviewer   First, thank the interviewer for his or her time. Say what you liked about the conversation. Say what you liked about the company. Point out something new that you learned.

Sell Yourself Again   Second, sell yourself again. Say that you are interested in the job. Say why you think you would be right for the job.

You can also add facts about yourself that you forgot to mention in the interview. You can add to any answers you gave in the interview.

Figure 8.2

Naomi Robertson

154 Franklin Ave. • El Cajon, CA 92020 • (619) 555-0106
naomirobb@travelcollege.edu

March 13, 2009

Melissa Perez
Human Resources Manager
Travel Associates, Inc.
5595 6th Ave.
San Diego, CA 92101

Dear Ms. Perez:

Thank you very much for taking the time to meet with me yesterday.
I learned a great deal about the travel industry from our conversation.

I was also inspired by your enthusiasm for your job. Travel Associates is
obviously a great place to work, and I am excited about joining your
team as a travel assistant.

The job is an excellent match for my skills and interests. I did not get a
chance to mention that I am an excellent listener, which helps me provide
excellent client service. I hope you will seriously consider me for the job.

Again, thank you. I will call you at the end of next week to see whether
you have made your decision.

Sincerely,

Naomi Robertson

Naomi Robertson

Follow Up With a Thank-You Letter Writing a thank-you letter shows the employer that you are courteous and responsible. It also shows that you want the job. Why do you think that many job applicants do not write thank-you letters?

Make Your Letter Neat and Courteous It is best to type a thank-you letter. Use a word-processing program. Make sure the thank-you letter is neat and courteous.

If the interview was very casual, you can write a thank-you letter by hand. However, the letter should be respectful. Remember that you are writing to an employer, not a friend.

Point of View

Making a Positive Impression

Mohamed Alshehri is an assistant to the publicity manager of a minor league baseball team in Dayton, Ohio. "I'm living my dream," he says.

The idea of working in sports marketing began in high school. "I like people and I know a lot about sports. I wanted to work with a professional sports team. I like the idea of promoting the team and the team's products."

Mohamed was in his second year of junior college when he applied for his job. "I was a big fan of the baseball team," he says. "I did a lot of research on the team. In my cover letter, I described all my skills and personal qualities that I knew would make me great for the job. My cover letter got me an interview. My enthusiasm got me a second interview. What got me the job was the thank-you note I wrote after the interview. No one else took the time to write one."

It's Your Turn Thank-you notes make us feel special. They let us know that someone appreciates our time and effort. Write a thank-you note to someone to let them know that you appreciate them.

For help completing this activity, visit **ewow.glencoe.com** and go to the *Smart Tip* for the Chapter 8 *Point of View*.

Check your answers online by visiting ewow.glencoe.com/review and selecting the Section 8.2 Review.

After You Read

Retell

1. Name six things you can do to have good hygiene for an interview.
2. List five ways you can show courtesy to an interviewer.

Think Critically

3. What do you think would be appropriate interview clothing for the following jobs? Why? 1) Restaurant server. 2) Businessperson. 3) Mechanic.

Math Practice

Answer the multiple-choice math questions at ewow.glencoe.com/math.

The Cost of Uniforms

You need to purchase uniforms. You buy two pairs of pants for $16 each. You buy four shirts for $10 each and two hats for $5 each. How much do the uniforms cost?

Step 1 Multiply the number of pants by the cost per item.
2 × $16 = $32

Step 2 Multiply the number of shirts by the cost per item.
4 × $10 = $40

Step 3 Multiply the number of hats by the cost per item .
2 × $5 = $10

Step 4 Add all the costs together.
$32 + $40 + $10 = $82

Result Your uniforms cost $82.

Figure It Out

Your uniforms cost $82 before sales tax. You must pay a sales tax of 5.75% on the total. How much sales tax will you pay?

Resident Companion

Pam Beilak

Texas

Career Cluster: Health Science

What does a resident companion do?

"I work in a nursing home. I provide care and companionship for the residents. I get their meals and supplies. I talk to them and spend time with them."

Why did you choose a career as a resident companion?

"I have a brain tumor. I had surgery and lived for a while in an assisted-living facility. I heard about the job and thought it would be perfect for me."

What obstacles have you overcome?

"I used to work two jobs and play on four soccer teams. My life stopped overnight when I learned I had a brain tumor. I had radiation therapy, and it affected my ability to learn. I can't focus. I'm learning my limits. I also have to overcome other people's view of me because I have cancer."

What advice do you have for students?

"Know there are people who are willing to help you. Keep trying if the first person you ask doesn't help you. Never give up."

Resident Companion

Training
Resident companions need a high-school diploma or GED.

Skills and Talents
Resident companions need to be compassionate and caring of others.

Career Outlook
Job opportunities in health-care social assistance should be numerous through the year 2012.

Learn More About It
Find the Web site of a large health-care provider near you, such as a hospital or nursing home. Go to the human resources section of the site. Find what jobs are available. Make a list of the jobs. Write a short description of each job. Post your job list in the classroom.

For help with this activity, visit **ewow.glencoe.com/tips**.

Glencoe Online

Go to **ewow.glencoe.com** to find online games and activities for Chapter 8.

Key Term Review

job interview (p. 182)
interviewer (p. 183)
ethics (p. 189)
conflict (p. 189)
body language (p. 191)
hygiene (p. 193)

appropriate (p. 196)
positive attitude (p. 197)
enthusiasm (p. 198)
courtesy (p. 198)
follow up (p. 199)

Check Your Understanding

1. What is the purpose of a job interview?
2. Name the four steps in preparing for a job interview.
3. List seven types of questions that are often asked in interviews.
4. Name six ways to make a good impression on an employer.
5. Explain what to say in a thank-you letter after an interview.

Write About It

6. **Think Creatively** Some interviewers want to see if you can think creatively. Imagine that you are in an interview. The interviewer asks, "What would you do if you had two projects due at the same time, but only enough time to finish one?" On a sheet of paper, list as many different ideas as you can. Think of creative ways to solve the problem. At the bottom of the piece of paper, write the answer you would give to the interviewer.

Role Play

7. **Practice Interviewing**   Work with a partner.
   Pretend that you are interviewing for a job. One
   person is the applicant and the other person is the
   interviewer. As the interviewer, ask the applicant
   several questions. Ask about his or her skills, work
   experience, ethics, strengths, and weaknesses.
   Switch roles with your partner.

Teamwork Challenge

8. **Learn About Positive Attitude**   A positive attitude
   can win you a job. With your team, visit a local
   company. Ask to talk to a manager who hires
   workers. Ask the manager about positive attitude.
   What is a positive attitude? How important is it
   for a job applicant to have a positive attitude?
   How can a job applicant show a positive attitude?
   Write a short report on what you learned. Share
   your report with another team.

Computer Lab

Write a Thank-You Letter   Imagine that you had an
interview for a server job at a coffee shop. Use a word
processing program to type and print a thank-you letter
to an interviewer. Use the information on pages 199–201
to help you write your letter. Be creative with your letter.

Personal Career Portfolio

Prepare Interview Answers   Prepare answers to
the seven common interview questions found on
pages 187–189. You can prepare more than one answer
to each question. Add your list to your Personal Career
Portfolio.
   Go to **ewow.glencoe.com/portfolio** for help.

Unit 2 Review

Chapter Summaries

Chapter 6 Finding Job Openings

A job opening is an available job. A job lead is information about an available job. You can find job leads at employment agencies, in the classified ads, and on career Web sites. The best way to find job leads is by networking. Networking helps you find jobs that are not advertised.

Chapter 7 Applying for a Job

Many employers ask job applicants to fill out a job application form. You can get a job application form by calling or visiting an employer. Fill out the form using a personal fact sheet. Some employers ask for a résumé and cover letter. A résumé summarizes your skills, work, experience, and education. A cover letter says why you are a good match for the job.

Chapter 8 Interview Success

A job interview is a meeting to discuss a possible job. Prepare for an interview by researching the company in advance. Prepare answers to questions you might need to answer. Also prepare questions to ask the interviewer. Practice your interview skills, such as speech and body language. Write a thank-you note after the interview to show that you are enthusiastic about the job.

These are the topics you read about in this unit. What did you learn?

Chapter 6
Finding Job Openings
- Gathering Job Leads
- Networking

Chapter 7
Applying for a Job
- Preparing Job Application Forms
- Writing Your Résumé

Chapter 8
Interview Success
- Preparing for the Interview
- Succeeding in the Interview

Unit **3**

Succeeding on the Job

Unit Preview

Unit 3 is about doing well at your job. You will learn what to expect when you start a new job. You will learn about pay and benefits, or extras that go with the job. You will find out about safety laws and rules that will protect you from getting hurt on the job. You will also improve your skills at getting along with others, communicating, and showing good character. These skills will help you move ahead in your career.

Chapter 9

Your First Days on the Job

You Already Know...

- how to find job leads
- how to apply for a job
- how to interview for a job
- how to make a good impression on an employer

You Will Learn...

- how to evaluate a job offer
- what you will do on your first day
- which forms you will fill out on your first day, and why
- the different ways workers are paid
- what benefits you can expect at your job

Personal Career Portfolio *Preview*

For your portfolio, you will describe how to prepare for your first day of work. As you read, think about everything you will do on your first day and how you will prepare.

Before You Read

Set a Purpose for Reading
Why do you need to know what will happen on your first day at a new job? Discuss this question with a classmate. Write your answer in a short paragraph.

Getting Off to a Good Start

Ready, Set, Read

Key Terms

terms
negotiate
dress code
uniform
supervisor
orientation
Form I-9
Social Security number
work permit

Main Idea

Your first day on a new job will be busy and maybe a little confusing. You will get new directions, meet new people, learn about the workplace, and fill out forms.

Thought Organizer

Copy the chart below. As you read, fill in each of the ovals with one thing you will do on your first day of work.

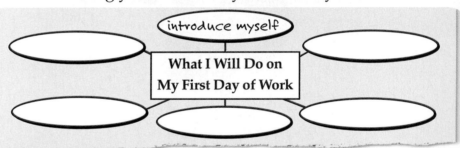

introduce myself

What I Will Do on My First Day of Work

You're Hired!

The interview is over. What happens now? If your interview went well, the employer may call you. You may receive a job offer. A *job offer* is an offer by an employer to hire you for a certain job.

The employer might say, "I would like to offer you the job," or, "Come work for us." This is great news!

Find Out the Terms of the Job Offer

terms ■ The details of an offer.

What do you do when you receive a job offer? First find out the terms of the job offer. **Terms** are the details of an offer.

Terms Include Job Title and Pay   Important terms of a job offer include job title, pay, and any extras that go with the job. Terms also include how many hours a week you will work, when you will start the job, and how long the job will last. Other terms may include the times of day you start and finish work.

Imagine that an employer offers to hire you as a teacher's aide. The terms may include that you work 40 hours per week at $12.00 per hour.

You may ask to have the terms of the job offer written down. That way you and the employer are both sure that you understand one another.

Decide Whether You Want the Job

You do not have to accept a job offer. You can reject a job offer if the job is not right for you.

Why would you reject a job offer? Maybe you think the job is not a good match for you. Maybe you have another job offer that is better. Maybe you think the terms are not good. For example, you may think the pay is too low. The job may not offer the benefits or hours you need.

If the job is not right for you, call and tell the employer. Thank the employer for his or her time and effort. Write a thank-you letter. Say positive things about the company.

You May Try to Negotiate   If you do not like one of the terms of a job offer, you could negotiate. To **negotiate** means to try to get better terms. You might try to negotiate slightly higher pay. You might ask for benefits or overtime. You might ask to work more hours per week.

For example, you might ask, "I am very interested in this job. However, I was hoping to work 30 hours per week. Is this possible?" If the employer says no, you might ask whether it is possible in the future.

Be polite when you ask. The employer does not owe you anything. The employer will not hire you if you seem unhappy with the job offer.

While You Read

Connect Would you ever turn down a job offer?

negotiate ■ To try to get better terms.

Study Tip

Being prepared is an important skill at school and at work. Gather your supplies before class. Gather your thoughts, too. Arrive ready and focused.

Your First Day of Work Will Be a Busy Day

Congratulations! It is the first day of your new job. You have done a lot of work to get this job. What do you need to do on your first day? You will do and learn many things during your first days. Here are some things to expect.

You Will Dress Appropriately for the Job

The first thing to do for your new job is to dress appropriately. Do you know what to wear to work?

Many workers follow a dress code. A **dress code** is a description of the clothes that are appropriate for work.

You might call a day ahead and ask about the dress code. For example, you could say, "Could you please tell me about the dress code?"

dress code ■ A description of the clothes that are appropriate for work.

While You Read

Question What is one safety reason for avoiding casual clothing?

Avoid Casual Clothing Most dress codes do not allow casual clothes. Casual clothes include shorts, short skirts, jeans, tank tops, and T-shirts. Casual clothes can look sloppy. Very loose clothes can even get caught in machines and cause accidents.

Many dress codes do not allow sandals or tennis shoes. These shoes might not be safe. Sandals and sneakers do not protect your feet if something heavy falls on them.

Find Out Whether You Need a Uniform

uniform ■ An outfit that shows you work for a certain company

For some jobs, you will need a uniform. A **uniform** is an outfit that shows that you work for a certain company.

Some workers wear uniforms marked with the name of their company. Will your employer require you to wear a uniform with the company name? If so, he or she must pay for the uniform.

Other workers have a very simple uniform. For example, some workers wear black pants and a white button-down shirt. They can wear pants and shirts they already have.

Learn the Dress Code Your company may have a dress code. You may need to wear a uniform. Why do you think some employers ask their employees to wear uniforms?

Workers at Clothing Stores Often Wear Clothes Their Store Sells

Workers at clothing stores often wear clothes the store sells. They get a discount to buy these clothes. They can also wear clothes that look similar to the clothes their store sells.

Some retail stores give employees money to buy clothes from the store. Workers at clothing stores are not allowed to wear clothes that show the names of other stores.

You Will Get Directions from Your Supervisor

supervisor ■ A boss or manager.

Find your supervisor as soon as you get to work. Your **supervisor** is your boss or manager. You probably met your supervisor at your job interview.

Ask your supervisor for directions. Directions tell you what do to and how to do it. Listen carefully. If you do not understand something, ask about it.

Follow your directions exactly. You may not understand why something is done. But as a beginner, just do it. After you have worked for a while, you will understand why things are done this way.

You May Start to Work Right Away   Some workers do not receive a lot of directions. They have to figure things out on their own. Do not be surprised if this happens to you.

Your new workplace may be very busy. You may have to start working right away. Look around where you work. You may see things that need to be done. Ask your boss if you should do them. Soon you will know which things you can do. Do not wait to be told that you should start working. Just start!

Learn to Do Each Task Properly   It is important to do your job well. You may want to keep your job for a long time. If you quit, you will need a recommendation from your employer. So do your very best. Learn how to do each task properly.

While You Read

Visualize Imagine that you work at a store and the cash register stops working. What do you do?

Ask for Help When You Need It   You will probably need help to learn your job. This is normal. Ask for help if you need it. If you do not know how to do something, ask your supervisor. If your supervisor is busy, ask an experienced worker. Other workers are often glad to help a beginner.

Ask questions about things you do not understand. It is better to ask than to be confused. Try not to worry. No one expects a new worker to know everything.

You Will Have an Orientation

Your supervisor will probably give you a basic orientation. **Orientation** is a program that introduces new employees to a company. You will learn how things work at your company. You will learn the company rules.

If you work for a large company, you may have a group orientation. You may get information to read. Take the information home and read it carefully.

orientation ■ A program that introduces new employees to a company.

Point of View

Be a Self-Starter

Brenna Moor moved to New York City when she graduated from high school. She found a job as an assistant to a project manager in a fashion design firm.

"Everyone was so busy my first day." Brenna says. "No one had time to train me." Brenna knew it was up to her to make herself useful. "I shadowed the project manager. I took notes. I noticed some things that I could do to help her. By the second day, I knew some things I could do to be helpful. If I had any questions, I asked."

Within six months, Brenna received a raise and words of praise from her boss. "She said she could count on me."

It's Your Turn For the next three days, look around your home and school. What needs to be done that you could do without being asked? For some things, you need to ask an adult if you can do them. Make a list of what you did in the three days.

For ideas on completing this activity, go to **ewow.glencoe.com/tips** and select the *Smart Tip* for Chapter 9 *Point of View*.

Study Tip

Listening is an important part of teamwork. Listen to other people's words. Respect their opinions. You might learn something new, even if you do not agree with them.

You Will Meet Your Coworkers

During the first days on the job you will meet some of the people in the company. You will be working together. You will want to make a good impression on them. You want to get along well.

Your boss may introduce you to your coworkers. If the boss does not introduce you, sometimes one of the other workers will. Say, "Nice to meet you" plus the person's name. Many people also shake hands.

Learn Your Coworkers' Names Your supervisor and coworkers may ask you to call them by their first names. If they do not ask you to call them by their first names, use their last names. Use "Mr." or "Ms." (pronounced *miz*) plus each person's last name.

Greet your coworkers when you see them again. Use their names. For example, say, "Hi, Rebecca" or "Hello, Mr. Farhadi." Repeating people's names helps you remember them. It also makes people feel good about you.

Greet Your Coworkers
Getting along with coworkers is very important. Your coworkers will make your job easier and more fun. Try to make a good impression on them. What should you do if no one introduces you to your coworkers?

You May Need to Introduce Yourself   Sometimes no one makes the introductions. Then you will need to introduce yourself.

Smile, say hello, and give your name. For example, you might say, "Hello. My name is Shawn. I am the new receptionist. What is your name?"

After you exchange names, you can ask a question or two. Once you start talking, you will feel more at ease.

You Will Tour Your Work Area

On your first day, you will probably tour your work area. A supervisor or a coworker may show you around.

Explore your workplace. Learn about the building. Find out where the restroom is. Find out where the elevator, stairs, and exits are. Make sure you know how to get out if there is an emergency.

Find Out Where to Put Your Things   You will also want to know where you can put your things, such as your keys and lunch. If you work in an office, you will probably have a desk where you can put your things. If you work in a store or factory, you may have a locker.

Find Out Where You Can Go During Breaks   Do you know where can you sit during your breaks? Do you know where can you eat lunch?

Some workplaces have a *lunchroom* where you can sit and eat. The lunchroom may have a water cooler, a coffee maker, a refrigerator, and a microwave. Make sure that you are allowed to use these things. Always clean up after yourself when you use the lunchroom.

You Will Do Paperwork on Your First Day

You will do some paperwork on your first day. Paperwork is work with printed forms and records. Be prepared. Bring your personal fact sheet.

You will need to fill out Form I-9. **Form I-9** is a form showing that you are allowed to work in the United States. **Figure 9.1** on page 220 shows a Form I-9.

While You Read

Question Why is it important to know where all the exits are?

Form I-9 ■ A form showing that you are allowed to work in the United States.

You Will Need a Social Security Number

Form I-9 asks for your Social Security number. A **Social Security number** is a nine-digit number that helps the government keep a record of your earnings. All workers need a Social Security number. You need a Social Security number to get a paycheck. Contact the Social Security Administration (SSA) to get a Social Security number if you do not have one.

Social Security number ■
A nine-digit number that helps the government keep a record of your earnings.

Bring Proof That You Are Allowed to Work You need to prove that you are allowed to work in the United States. Bring an identification (ID) card with a photograph and a birth certificate or a Social Security card.

If you are a U.S. citizen, bring your U.S. passport, your Certificate of Naturalization, or your Certificate of U.S. Citizenship.

If are a permanent resident of the United States, bring your green card. A green card is an identification card that shows that you are allowed to live and work in the United States.

Figure 9.1

Form I-9

U.S. Department of Justice	OMB No. 1115-0136
Immigration and Naturalization Service	**Employment Eligibility Verification**

Please read instructions carefully before completing this form. The instructions must be available during completion of this form. **ANTI-DISCRIMINATION NOTICE:** It is illegal to discriminate against work eligible individuals. Employers CANNOT specify which document(s) they will accept from an employee. The refusal to hire an individual because of a future expiration date may also constitute illegal discrimination.

Section 1. Employee Information and Verification. To be completed and signed by employee at the time employment begins.

Print Name: Last Agvado	First Marc	Middle Initial	Maiden Name N/A
Address (Street Name and Number) 113 Sutter Pl.		Apt. #	Date of Birth (month/day/year) 03/09/92
City Somerville	State NJ	Zip Code 08876	Social Security # 899-00-2987

I am aware that federal law provides for imprisonment and/or fines for false statements or use of false documents in connection with the completion of this form.	I attest, under penalty of perjury, that I am (check one of the following): ☒ A citizen or national of the United States ☐ A Lawful Permanent Resident (Alien # A ☐ An alien authorized to work until ___/___/___ (Alien # or Admission #)
Employee's Signature *Marc Agvado*	Date (month/day/year) 6/19/2008

Form I-9 Form I-9 shows that you are allowed to work in the United States. What is the purpose of a Social Security number?

Making Good Choices

Standing Up for Your Rights

You and your coworkers work at a small printing office. You spend a lot of time talking to customers on the phone or taking orders. None of you have scheduled breaks. You know that state law says that every employee gets two 10-minute breaks and a half-hour for lunch each day. Sometimes, however, a lot of customer calls come in at once. There is more work than people can handle. No one is allowed to take a break or a lunch when this happens. Workers who do take breaks are told they are not working hard enough. They lose some of their tasks and responsibilities. How do you bring this up with your supervisor?

You Make the Call Do you think it is okay for supervisors to expect employees to work without a break or without taking a lunch? Work with another student. One of you take the side of the employees. The other take the side of the employer. Discuss the issue. Switch sides and have the same discussion.

For help in answering this question, visit **ewow.glencoe.com/tips** and find the *Smart Tip* for the Chapter 9 *Making Good Choices*.

Bring Your Work Permit If you are not a U.S. citizen or a permanent resident, you will need to bring your work permit on your first day. A **work permit** is a card showing that you are allowed to work in the United States.

You also need a work permit if you are below legal working age. This is a different kind of work permit. Most states only allow people 16 and over to work. If you are under 16, you need a work permit. You can usually obtain a work permit through your school. Ask a teacher or counselor for help.

work permit ■ A card showing that you are allowed to work in the United States.

Check your answers online by visiting **ewow.glencoe.com/review** and selecting the Section 9.1 Review.

After You Read

Recall

1. Summarize the section titled "You May Start to Work Right Away." Use your own words.

2. Explain what to call your supervisor and coworkers. Should you call them by their first name or last name? Why?

Think Critically

3. Your work dress code says that jeans are not allowed. However, many of your coworkers wear jeans. Do you think it is okay for you to wear jeans, too? Why or why not?

Math Practice

Answer the multiple-choice math questions at **ewow.glencoe.com/math**.

Working at a Clothing Store

You are offered two jobs. One pays $6.00 an hour for 30 hours a week. Another pays $4.50 an hour for 37 hours, plus $50.00 a month for a clothing allowance. Which terms are better? Use 1 month = 4 weeks to calculate your answer.

Step 1 Calculate your monthly wage for the first job.
$6.00 \times 30 \times 4 = $720

Step 2 Calculate your monthly wage for the second job.
$4.50 \times 37 \times 4 = $666

Step 3 Add $50 to the monthly wages for the second job.
$666 + $50 = $716

Result The terms for the first job are better.

Figure It Out

You take a job that pays $5.00 per hour for a one-week, 20-hour orientation. Upon completion, you will earn $6.00 an hour for 20 hours each week. You will also receive a monthly clothing allowance of $50.00 a month. What is your total yearly compensation?

Your Pay and Benefits

Ready, Set, Read

Key Terms

wages
overtime
salary
tip
commission
benefits

Main Idea

You can receive pay in several ways: wages, salary, tips, and commissions. You may also receive benefits, or extras.

Thought Organizer

Copy the chart below. As you read, make a list of all the benefits you would like to get on a job.

Benefits I Would Like to Have on a Job

health insurance

Get Ready for Your First Payday

You have started your job. Your first payday is coming soon. Do you know how you will be paid?

Different workers are paid in different ways. You may receive an hourly wage or a salary. You may also receive tips or a commission.

Wages Are for Pay Each Hour You Work

Wages are an amount of money you receive for every hour you work. Most part-time jobs and entry-level jobs also pay hourly wages.

Some companies pay wages every week. Some companies pay wages every two weeks.

Your pay equals your wage times the number of hours worked. Let's say that you earn $7.50 an hour. You are paid each week. Last week you worked 24 hours. Your total pay will be $7.50 × 24, or $180.00.

wages ■ An amount of money you receive for every hour you work.

overtime ■ Extra pay that you get when you work more than 40 hours in a week.

Question What is the difference between wages and a salary?

salary ■ An amount of pay for each month or year you work.

tip ■ Money that a worker receives from a customer for doing a good job.

Employers Must Pay at Least the Minimum Wage

Your employer must pay you at least the minimum wage. The *minimum wage* is the least an employer is allowed to pay a worker per hour.

The U.S. government sets the minimum wage. In 2003 the minimum wage was $5.15. Some states and cities have higher minimum wages. If you work in Illinois, for example, your employer must pay you at least $6.00 an hour.

Overtime Is Extra Pay for Working More Than 40 Hours in a Week

If you earn wages and work over 40 hours in a week, you receive overtime pay. **Overtime** is extra pay that you get when you work more than 40 hours in a week. You may also receive extra pay if you work on holidays, such as New Year's Day.

Overtime pay is usually one and one-half times your regular wage. Let's say that you make $8.00 per hour. Your overtime is one and one-half times your normal pay. Your overtime pay will be $8.00 times 1.5, or $12.00 per hour.

A Salary is Monthly or Yearly Pay

Many full-time jobs pay a salary. A **salary** is an amount of pay for each month or year you work.

If you earn a salary, you will probably get paid twice a month. You receive the same amount of money each time. You will not receive overtime pay, even if you work more than 40 hours.

Imagine that your salary is $24,000 per year. You are paid twice a month. Each time you are paid, you will get $1,000.

Tips Are a Reward for Good Service

Some workers receive tips. A **tip** is money that a worker receives from a customer for doing a good job.

Many service workers receive tips. You will probably get tips if you work as a server or food delivery worker. You will get tips if you work as a bellhop, a hairstylist, valet parker, or washroom attendant.

Wages and Tips Must Add Up to the Minimum Wage

If you receive tips, you may get a low wage. Some workers make more in tips than they do in wages.

The law says that your wages and tips must add up to at least the minimum wage. Let's say that your hourly wage is $2.15, for example. The minimum wage is $5.15. You earn $3.00 less than the minimum wage. That means you must earn at least $3.00 in tips each hour. What if you do not get at least $3.00 in tips? Then your employer must give you a higher wage.

Commissions Are a Portion of Sales

If you work in sales, you may get a commission. A **commission** is pay based on how much you sell. You may earn wages plus commission or a salary plus commission.

Imagine that you work in a clothing store. You receive a 10 percent commission. If a customer spends $200 on clothing, you will receive a $20 commission.

commission ■ Pay based on how much you sell.

Tips Reward Good Service Customers give workers tips when they give good service. A positive attitude is part of good service. What is good delivery service? What is poor delivery service? Explain.

You May Need to Fill Out a Time Sheet

Your employer may pay you by the hour. You may need to record how much you worked each day.

Some employers ask workers to write their hours on time sheets. A *time sheet* is a form that shows how many hours you worked each day. You may need to fill out a time sheet each week. **Figure 9.2** shows a time sheet.

Most employees are not paid for their lunch break. However, most employees are paid for two 15-minute breaks each eight-hour day.

Figure 9.2

Time Sheet

Weekly Time Sheet

Employee: Natalie Kim

Department: sales   Supervisor: Todd Reyes

Day	Morning		Afternoon		Overtime		Totals	
	In	Out	In	Out	In	Out	Regular	Overtime
Monday	7:45	11:00	12:00	5:45			8	0
Tuesday	8:00	11:00	12:00	6:00	6:00	7:00	8	1
Wednesday								
Thursday								
Friday								
Saturday								
Sunday								

Approved by: _____ Date: _____

Day by Day You will need a supervisor to sign and approve your time sheet. Your company will add up the hours you worked and figure out your pay. Why do you think this time sheet has different areas for morning and afternoon hours?

Clocking In A time clock makes it easy to keep track of your hours. You must remember to clock in when you start work and clock out when you leave. Why would employers use a time clock instead of a time sheet?

You May Need to Use a Time Clock

Some employers use time clocks instead of time sheets. A *time clock* is a clock that stamps the time onto a card, called a *time card*. You put your time card in the clock to get a time stamp.

You "clock in" when you come to work. You "clock out" when you leave work. You clock in and out at lunch, too. You are paid for the amount of hours on your time card. For example, say that you clock in to work at 8:00. You clock out for lunch at 11:00. You clock back in at 12:00. You clock out for the day at 5:00. You will be paid for eight hours.

Benefits Are Extras That Go With a Job

Benefits are extras that workers receive on a job. The most common benefits are:

- paid health insurance
- paid holiday days
- paid sick days
- paid vacation days

Benefits can be worth a lot of money. Imagine that your company pays for your health insurance. This will save you hundreds of dollars each month.

Each Company Offers Different Benefits

There are many different kinds of benefits. Not all companies offer the same benefits. Some workers get a discount on goods their company sells. Some workers get money to help pay for postsecondary education.

Some workers have a *pension*, or a savings plan for retirement. *Retirement* is when you stop working, usually around age 65. When workers put money in their pension, the company puts money in, too.

Will You Receive Benefits?

Most full-time salaried workers receive benefits. However, most part-time workers do not receive benefits. Most temporary workers do not receive benefits. Most workers who earn wages get only a few benefits.

Will you receive benefits? Ask your supervisor before you accept a job offer.

Some Benefits Start on Your First Day of Work   If you get benefits, when do they start? Some benefits start right away. For example, paid sick time and paid holidays usually start on your first day. Imagine that there is a holiday during your first week. A holiday is a major day such as Thanksgiving, New Year's Day, or Labor Day. You will be paid for a day of work, but you will not have to work.

Some Benefits Start After a Few Months   Some benefits do not start right away. They start after you have been on the job for a while. For example, paid health insurance and paid vacation often start after about three months.

You Will Learn the Details of Your Benefits at Orientation   You will learn all about your benefits at your orientation. Make sure you understand your benefits. If you do not understand, ask. It is better to know than to guess.

Real-World Connection

Taking Time Off

Always ask your supervisor for time off several weeks in advance. Write down the dates you need to be gone. Add a second and third choice. Give your supervisor the dates. Remember that you may not get your first choice.

Ask your supervisor about company policies for vacation time and personal time. A policy is a rule or guideline. You must usually work at a new job for several weeks before you can take time off. You may need to find a coworker who can cover for you while you are gone. Some companies have forms you must fill out to ask for time off.

Take the Next Step Partner with another student. One of you be the supervisor. The other person be the employee who wants time off. Together write a short role play where the employee asks the supervisor for time off.

For help doing this activity, go to **ewow.glencoe.com/tips** and find the *Smart Tip* for the Chapter 9 *Real-World Connection*.

Check your answers online by visiting **ewow.glencoe.com/review** and selecting the Section 9.2 Review.

After You Read

Retell

1. List six different types of benefits that workers can receive.

2. Explain why workers who receive tips may make a low hourly wage.

Think Critically

3. Name two types of benefits that start after a few months on the job. Why do you think these benefits do not start on the first day?

Math Practice

Answer the multiple-choice math questions at **ewow.glencoe.com/math**.

Hourly Wages vs. Salary

One employer offers you an hourly wage of $8.00 an hour for 40 hours a week. A second offers a weekly salary of $300.00 for 40 hours. Which is the better rate of pay? Use 1 month = 4 weeks to calculate your answer.

Step 1 Figure out how much you would earn per month for the first job.
$8 \times 40 \times 4 = $1,280$

Step 2 Figure out how much you would earn per month for the second job.
$300 \times 4 = $1,200$

Result The hourly wage is the better rate of pay.

Figure It Out

Alpha Messenger Service offers you a weekly salary of $250.00 for 30 hours. Speedy Couriers will pay you a wage of $5.00 per hour for 40 hours a week. Which job offers the better rate of pay?

Hotel Employee

Dan Pineda
Oregon

**Career Cluster:
Hospitality and Tourism**

What does a hotel worker do?

"I work at a hotel in Grande Ronde, Oregon. I work with customers."

Why did you choose a career in hotel services?

"I applied for a job in the hotel, but I was turned down because I'm deaf. I did get a job at the hotel as a valet. I worked as a valet for a year. The hotel gave me a chance to take the classes to work at the different jobs. I took them and passed."

What obstacles have you overcome?

"I have to prove myself to people. People don't think I can do things because I'm deaf. I have to navigate through the communication barrier."

What advice do you have for students?

"It's important to be assertive, to learn how to communicate, and get out there. Face your fears. Be good in school so you have the ability to deal with different situations."

Hotel Employee

Training
Hotel workers need a high school diploma. Some hotels provide specific training.

Skills and Talents
Hospitality and tourism workers need excellent people skills, communication skills, and customer service skills.

Career Outlook
Employment in hospitality and tourism should grow faster than average through 2012.

Learn More About It
Work with one or more students. Make a book of hospitality and tourism. Brainstorm to make a list of at least 12 different categories of hospitality and tourism. You could include such areas as hotels or travel. Make a page for each category. Include a description of each category and an illustration. Arrange the pages in alphabetical order. Add a cover for your book, and fasten the pages together. Display the books around the room.

For help with this activity, visit **ewow.glencoe.com/tips**.

 ewow.glencoe.com/tips

Key Term Review

terms (p. 212)
negotiate (p. 213)
dress code (p. 214)
uniform (p. 214)
supervisor (p. 216)
orientation (p. 217)
Form I-9 (p. 219)
Social Security number (p. 220)

work permit (p. 221)
wages (p. 223)
overtime (p. 224)
salary (p. 224)
tip (p. 224)
commission (p. 225)
benefits (p. 228)

Check Your Understanding

1. Explain what to do when you receive a job offer.

2. List six things you will do on your first day at a new job.

3. Name the two forms you will fill out on your first day of a new job. Explain the purpose of each.

4. Describe four different ways that workers are paid.

5. Define benefits and list four benefits that a full-time worker might receive.

Write About It

6. **Comment on Benefits**   Most part-time workers do not receive benefits. For example, they do not receive health insurance. Many workers who are paid by the hour also do not receive benefits. Why do you think this is so? Do you think that employers should have to give all workers benefits? Why or why not? Write a page with your ideas. Present your arguments to the class.

Role Play

7. **Meet Your Coworkers**   Work with a partner. One person is a new employee. The other person is a coworker. As the new employee, introduce yourself to the coworker. Ask two or three polite questions. Switch roles with your partner.

Teamwork Challenge

8. **Interview Workers About Benefits**   Each member of your team will interview two workers about their job benefits. Interview some workers who earn wages and some workers who earn a salary. Write down all the benefits that each worker receives. Collect your results. Make a bar graph of your information. For example, your graph could show the amount of workers that receive health insurance.

Computer Lab

Fill Out a Form I-9 Online   Visit the Web site of the U.S. Citizenship and Immigration Services and find the online I-9. Read the instructions and fill out the I-9 online. Print the form, sign it, and date it. Write a short paragraph describing the process.

Personal Career Portfolio

Make a To-Do List   Describe what you can do to prepare for your first day of work. First make a list of everything you will do. Write one sentence saying how you can prepare. For example, you can prepare for filling out Form I-9 by locating your passport, a photo ID card, or your birth certificate.

Go to **ewow.glencoe.com/portfolio** for help.

Chapter 10

Job Safety

You Already Know...

- some jobs can be dangerous
- the government has laws to protect workers
- it is important to follow safety signs and rules
- accidents can happen at any time

You Will Learn...

- about injuries and illnesses that can be common on the job
- about your safety rights
- how to protect yourself from workplace hazards
- how to read safety signs and labels
- what to do in an emergency

Personal Career Portfolio *Preview*

For your portfolio, you will make a profile of the working conditions in an occupation that interests you. As you read, think about what occupation you will choose and what the working conditions might be like.

Predict How do you think a job could be dangerous? Write down several things that you think could cause an injury or illness at work. Also write down how you think you could protect yourself from these things.

Safety Basics

Ready, Set, Read

Key Terms

working
  conditions
equipment
right
hazard
OSHA
workers'
  compensation

Main Idea

Many workers become ill or get injured each year. You have the right to work in safe conditions and to know about hazards in your workplace.

Thought Organizer

Copy the chart below. As you read, write down one hazard that each worker might face at his or her job.

Worker	Hazard
restaurant server	burn from hot food
construction worker	
secretary	

Safety Is an Important Work Issue

Did you know that work can sometimes be dangerous? Workers can get injuries from their work. For example, they can fall or get burned. Workers can also get illnesses from their work. For example, they can get breathing problems from chemicals.

Learning about safety helps you avoid injuries at work. It helps you do your job better. It helps you enjoy life more.

Working Conditions Are Part of Safety

To work safely, you need good working conditions. Working conditions are the conditions in which you spend your workday. Poor working conditions can cause stress and injuries.

working conditions ■
The conditions in which you spend your workday.

Working Conditions Include Places, Tasks, and Hours

Working conditions include the place you work. Is it indoors or outdoors? Quiet or noisy? Bright or dark? Warm or cool?

Working conditions include the tasks you do. Do you sit or do you move around a lot? Do you lift heavy objects? Do you use big machines?

Working conditions also include the hours you work. Do you work long hours? Do you work on the weekends? Do you get time off to rest?

Working Conditions Include Equipment

Working conditions also include the equipment at your workplace. **Equipment** is all the objects, such as machines and tools, that you need to do a job. You need safe equipment to have good working conditions.

In an office you would use equipment such as file cabinets and computers. In a store you would use equipment such as ladders and cash registers. In a school you would use equipment such as copy machines and projectors. On a construction site you would use tools such as hammers and saws.

equipment ■ All the objects, such as machines and tools, that you need to do a job.

Working Conditions
Working conditions are different at each job. Equipment is different at each job, too. Describe the equipment you see here. Would you like to work in these conditions? Why or why not?

Some Workplaces Are More Dangerous Than Others

Some workplaces are riskier than others. Farms, construction sites, factories, and highways can be dangerous places to work.

These workplaces are dangerous because they have a lot of chemicals or heavy equipment. On farms, for example, tractors and harvesting machines can cause accidents.

On construction sites workers lift heavy pieces of steel and lumber. They climb high onto scaffolds. They hammer nails and use welding equipment.

Factories can be dangerous, too. Workers in textile plants use giant machines that weave fabric. Print workers work with huge printing presses. Canning workers work with sharp blades.

Jobs that involve driving are also dangerous. If you drive a lot for your job, you could get into an accident.

The graph in **Figure 10.1** shows how many workers get hurt on the job each year. It shows the percentages for six different industries.

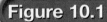

Figure 10.1

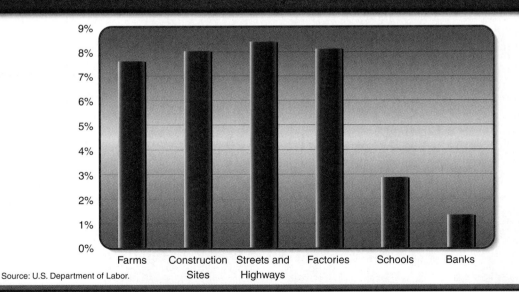

Workers' Rates of Injuries and Illnesses

Source: U.S. Department of Labor.

Risky Work On average, 6 percent of workers are hurt on the job each year. Which workplace has the highest rate of injuries and illnesses? What do you think explains this?

Injuries and Illnesses Can Happen at Any Job

Most workplaces in the United States have safe working conditions. But accidents can still happen at any time. Think of all the ways injuries can happen. You could fall, cut yourself, or breathe a chemical.

Injuries Include Sprains and Strains Sprains and strains are the most common injuries on the job. A sprain is torn tissue in a joint. A strain is a pulled or overused muscle. Bruises, cuts, fractures, and burns can also happen at work.

Illnesses Include Hearing Loss and Carpal Tunnel Syndrome There are many job-related illnesses, too. Some workers lose their hearing from working in noisy workplaces. Some workers develop carpal tunnel syndrome from working on an assembly line. *Carpal tunnel syndrome* happens when a nerve in the wrist is pinched. It causes pain in the hand and arm.

While You Read

Question What is the difference between a sprain and a strain?

You Have the Right to Safe Working Conditions

right ■ Something the law says you should have.

The law gives you specific rights. A **right** is something that the law says you should have.

You have the right to safe working conditions. You have the right to say no to unsafe tasks. You have the right to know about injuries that have happened at your workplace.

You Have the Right to Know About Hazards

hazard ■ Anything that might harm someone.

You have a right to know about any hazards at your workplace. A **hazard** is anything that might harm someone. Your employer must tell you about hazards in the workplace.

Hazards Come in Many Forms There are many different types of hazards. Uneven or slippery floors are a hazard because they can cause falls. Very high temperatures are a hazard because they can cause burns. Very loud noise is a hazard because it can damage your hearing. Even the weather can be a hazard. For example, rain, snow, and fog can cause car accidents.

While You Read

Connect What kind of safety training would you need for the career that interests you?

You Have the Right to Safety Training

You have the right to safety training at work. If your employer does not offer you training, you have the right to ask for it.

Imagine that you are a construction worker. Your employer must show you how to use tools safely. Your employer must train you in fire safety.

You Have the Right to Ask Your Employer to Fix Hazards

You have the right to ask your employer to fix hazards in the workplace. For example, imagine that there is a leaky sink in the lunch room. There is water on the floor. Someone could slip and fall. You have the right to ask your employer to fix the hazard. Your employer must fix the hazard.

You Have the Right to Contact OSHA

What do you do if your employer does not fix a safety problem? You can file a complaint with OSHA. **OSHA** is the part of the government that sets safety rules and inspects workplaces. OSHA stands for the *Occupational Safety and Health Administration.* It is a part of the U.S. Department of Labor.

You can file a complaint with OSHA over the Internet, by mail, or over the telephone. You can tell OSHA not to use your name. An OSHA inspector may come to inspect your workplace.

OSHA ■ The part of the government that sets safety rules and inspects workplaces.

Read the OSHA Poster Every employer must put up an OSHA poster. Turn the page to read the OSHA poster in **Figure 10.2.** Read the list of your rights. Are there any you do not understand?

While You Read

Connect Have you ever seen an OSHA poster at a job?

Real-World Connection

Communicating Assertively

Your safety in the workplace is important. Speak up when you see a hazard.

Tell your supervisor that there is a hazard that needs to be fixed. Speak in a calm voice. Tell your supervisor what the hazard is and where the hazard is.

What can you do if no one fixes the hazard? Remind your supervisor. What if nothing is done? Report the hazard to OSHA. Use the OSHA poster at your workplace to help you.

Take the Next Step Visit the OSHA Web site for information about hazards. Make a poster that shows how to be safe from hazards. Display the posters in class.

For help doing this activity, go to **ewow.glencoe.com/tips** and find the *Smart Tip* for the Chapter 10 *Real-World Connection*.

Figure 10.2

OSHA Poster

You Have a Right to a Safe and Healthful Workplace.

IT'S THE LAW!

- You have the right to notify your employer or OSHA about workplace hazards. You may ask OSHA to keep your name confidential.

- You have the right to request an OSHA inspection if you believe that there are unsafe and unhealthful conditions in your workplace. You or your representative may participate in the inspection.

- You can file a complaint with OSHA within 30 days of discrimination by your employer for making safety and health complaints or for exercising your rights under the *OSH Act*.

- You have a right to see OSHA citations issued to your employer. Your employer must post the citations at or near the place of the alleged violation.

- Your employer must correct workplace hazards by the date indicated on the citation and must certify that these hazards have been reduced or eliminated.

- You have the right to copies of your medical records or records of your exposure to toxic and harmful substances or conditions.

- Your employer must post this notice in your workplace.

The *Occupational Safety and Health Act of 1970 (OSH Act)*, P.L. 91-596, assures safe and healthful working conditions for working men and women throughout the Nation. The Occupational Safety and Health Administration, in the U.S. Department of Labor, has the primary responsibility for administering the *OSH Act*. The rights listed here may vary depending on the particular circumstances. To file a complaint, report an emergency, or seek OSHA advice, assistance, or products, call 1-800-321-OSHA or your nearest OSHA office: • Atlanta (404) 562-2300 • Boston (617) 565-9860 • Chicago (312) 353-2220 • Dallas (214) 767-4731 • Denver (303) 844-1600 • Kansas City (816) 426-5861 • New York (212) 337-2378 • Philadelphia (215) 861-4900 • San Francisco (415) 975-4310 • Seattle (206) 553-5930. Teletypewriter (TTY) number is 1-877-889-5627. To file a complaint online or obtain more information on OSHA federal and state programs, visit OSHA's website at **www.osha.gov**. If your workplace is in a state operating under an OSHA-approved plan, your employer must post the required state equivalent of this poster.

1-800-321-OSHA
www.osha.gov

U.S. Department of Labor • Occupational Safety and Health Administration • OSHA 3165

You Have Rights The OSHA poster tells employees about their rights in the workplace. What is an OSHA citation?

You Have the Right to Workers' Compensation

What happens if you are injured at work? You will need health care. You may not be able to go back to work for a while. You will need money to pay the bills.

This is where workers' compensation comes in. **Workers' compensation** is an insurance program that helps you if you are hurt at work. It also pays about two-thirds of your wages if you have to miss work for a week or more.

workers' compensation ■
An insurance program that helps you if you are hurt at work.

Tell Your Doctor   What happens if you are injured at work? Go to the doctor right away if you need help. You may need to go to a company doctor who treats work injuries.

Tell the doctor that your injury is related to work. The doctor will send your medical information to the workers' compensation program.

Follow your doctor's advice. Go back to work only if your doctor says it is okay. If you need to miss work, tell your employer. Make sure your supervisor knows what is happening.

While You Read

Question What is the first thing you should do after a work injury?

Tell Your Employer   Tell your employer that you were injured on the job. Explain what happened. Explain how the injury or illness happened. The employer must send a report to the workers' compensation office if you need to go to the doctor or if you miss more than one day of work.

Tell Your Workers' Compensation Program   Call the workers' compensation program in your state. Report the accident. Ask what you should do next. You may have to fill out more forms. The insurance will pay for your medical bills.

The insurance may also pay some of your lost wages. You will receive wages if you have to miss work for several days. You will receive around two-thirds of your regular pay. You will also receive pay if you have a permanent injury.

Check your answers online by visiting **ewow.glencoe.com/review** and selecting the Section 10.1 Review.

Retell

1. What should you do if you see a hazard at your workplace? Explain in your own words.
2. What three things should you do if you are injured at work? Use your own words.

Think Critically

3. How important is safety in your choice of occupation? Would you take a dangerous job? Why or why not?

Math Practice

Answer the multiple-choice math questions at **ewow.glencoe.com/math**.

Workers' Compensation

You are hurt at work at your job. You are eligible for workers' compensation. You will be off work for six weeks. If you normally earn $500 a week and workers' compensation will pay 2/3 of these wages, how much money will you receive over the 6-week pay period?

Step 1 Convert 2/3 to a decimal. (Round to the nearest .01.)
$2 \div 3 = 0.67$

Step 2 Figure out your weekly earnings with worker's compensation.
$0.67 \times \$500 = \$335$

Step 3 Calculate the money earned in your pay period.
$\$335 \times 6 = \$2,010$

Result Your total compensation will be $2,010.

Figure It Out

You normally earn $2,000 a month. You are hurt and receive workers' compensation for three months in the amount of $1,320. How much will you lose in total earnings during your recovery period?

Working Safely

Key Terms

high voltage

fire extinguisher

personal protective equipment

flammable

ventilation

material safety data sheet (MSDS)

RTK label

emergency first aid

Main Idea

As a worker, you need to learn how to use work equipment properly and safely. You also need to learn how to protect yourself against job hazards and how to handle emergencies.

Thought Organizer

Copy the chart below. As you read, write down different ways to protect yourself on the job. Write each idea at the end of a line. Add as many lines and ideas as you can.

Protect Yourself

wear proper shoes

You Have the Responsibility to Protect Yourself

Work safety is not only your employer's responsibility. It is also your responsibility. You are responsible for being a safe worker.

One way to be a safe worker is to get training. You need to learn how to: 1) use equipment correctly 2) use safety wear 3) prevent fire 4) read safety signs 5) work safely with chemicals 6) prevent muscle strains 7) handle an emergency

To be a safe worker you also need to know your limits. Never do anything that seems unsafe. Ask for help if need it. Ask for job accommodations if you need them to do your job safely.

Prevent Injuries
Learn to use all your work equipment. Do not do anything you think is unsafe. What kind of equipment is this worker using?

Learn to Use Equipment Safely

There is a right way and a wrong way to use even the simplest equipment. Make sure you learn how to use equipment the right way.

Make sure you know how to care for your equipment, too. Equipment should be checked and fixed regularly. Put equipment away when not in use. If you think something is wrong with a piece of equipment, tell your supervisor.

Learn to Work Safely Around Electricity

Be careful around electricity. Look for signs labeled "high voltage." **High voltage** means a large and dangerous amount of electricity. There is a high voltage sign in **Figure 10.4** on page 249.

Be careful around plugs and cords, too. Make sure that plugs and cords are in good condition. If a cord is worn or cut, ask for a new one. Use long cords safely. Do not put cords, tools, or other items where someone might trip over them. Do not plug too many tools into one outlet.

Unplug tools the right way. Put your thumb and fingers on the plug. Then pull it from the outlet. Do not pull the cord.

high voltage ■ A large and dangerous amount of electricity.

Learn to Prevent Fire

Fires can happen at almost any time. Fires can happen when machine parts rub together. Fires can happen when wires are unsafe. Fires can happen when surfaces become too hot.

Follow all the fire safety rules at your work. Keep your work area clean and tidy. Report any fire hazards. Report a smell of smoke or gas right away.

Know what to do in case of a fire. Know how to get to the exits. Know how to turn on the fire alarm. Also learn to use the fire extinguisher. A **fire extinguisher** is a container of chemicals that will put out a small fire.

fire extinguisher ■ A container of chemicals that will put out a small fire.

Point of View

Handling Emergencies

Jabari Johanasan works after school at a fast-food restaurant in Dallas, Texas. "The manager talked about fire safety during training. I paid attention. I'm glad I did."

Jabari was at the register when a fire broke out in one of the ovens. "At first I wasn't scared," Jabari says. But the fire quickly spread.

"My manager called 911. I went through the front of the restaurant and told everyone to leave. We held the door open so everyone could see how to get out. Smoke was coming at us fast then. I was scared, but I knew we were doing the right thing. Everyone got out and was safe."

It's Your Turn Work with a partner. Create a fire-safety plan for your classroom. Explain what everyone should do if there is a fire. Explain how to get out of the building and where to go.

For help completing this activity, visit **ewow.glencoe.com/tips** and go to the *Smart Tip* for the Chapter 10 *Point of View*.

Learn to Use Personal Protective Equipment

In your training you should learn about personal protective equipment. **Personal protective equipment** is safety wear that protects you from hazards. Injuries usually happen when workers are not using the right protective equipment.

Your employer must give you the personal protective equipment that you need. You need to know:

- what type of personal protective equipment to use
- when to use the equipment
- how to use the equipment correctly
- how to take care of the equipment
- how long to use a piece of equipment before you have to replace it

personal protective equipment ■ Safety wear that protects you from hazards.

While You Read

Connect What kinds of workers have you seen wearing personal protective equipment?

There are many different kinds of personal protective equipment. Several different types of equipment are shown in **Figure 10.3.** This equipment will let you do your job safely.

Figure 10.3

Personal Protective Equipment

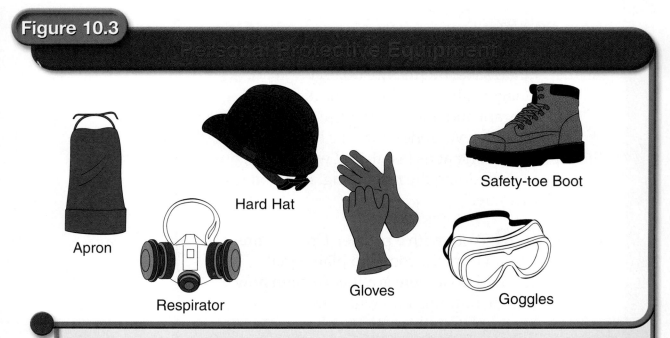

Apron

Hard Hat

Respirator

Gloves

Safety-toe Boot

Goggles

Protect Yourself There is personal protective equipment for every part of the body. Make sure your employer gives you all the equipment you need. What kinds of injuries does a hard hat help to prevent? What about a respirator?

Figure 10.4

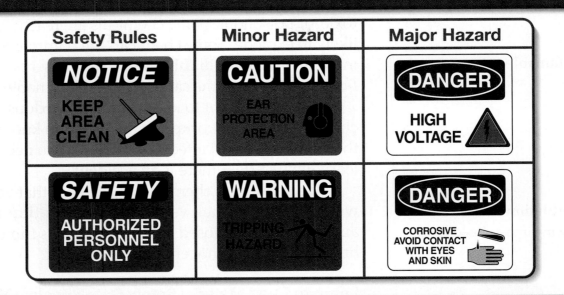

Safety Rules	Minor Hazard	Major Hazard
NOTICE KEEP AREA CLEAN	**CAUTION** EAR PROTECTION AREA	**DANGER** HIGH VOLTAGE
SAFETY AUTHORIZED PERSONNEL ONLY	**WARNING** TRIPPING HAZARD	**DANGER** CORROSIVE AVOID CONTACT WITH EYES AND SKIN

Look Out! Safety signs can prevent injuries. Always read them and follow what they say. What does the sign at the bottom right mean? Where might you find this sign?

Learn to Read Safety Signs

You also need to learn how to read safety signs. If you do not understand what a sign means, ask your supervisor. **Figure 10.4** shows several safety signs.

Blue and Green Mean Safety Blue and green signs tell you about safety rules. A notice sign might tell you to keep out. A safety sign might say no smoking.

Yellow and Orange Mean Caution Yellow and orange signs tell you about possible hazards. They warn you about situations that could cause an injury. A caution sign might tell you to put on a hard hat. A warning sign might tell you that there is a hidden step.

Red Means Danger Signs marked "Danger" in red tell you about active hazards. They warn you about situations that could cause serious injury or even death. A danger sign might tell you about poison gas.

While You Read

Connect Are there any caution or danger signs at your work or school?

Learn to Work Safely With Chemicals

Hazardous chemicals affect millions of workers. Some chemicals can damage your lungs. Some chemicals are toxic, or poisonous. Some chemicals are reactive, or likely to explode. Some chemicals are flammable or inflammable. **Flammable** means easy to set on fire. *Inflammable* means the same thing as flammable.

flammable ■ Easy to set on fire.

You have the right to know about hazardous chemicals in your workplace. You need to know how the chemicals could affect your health. You need to learn what to do if there is an accident.

If you work with chemicals, make sure that your work area has enough ventilation. **Ventilation** is fresh air flowing into a closed space. Hazardous fumes can build up if there is not enough ventilation.

ventilation ■ Fresh air flowing into a closed space.

Learn to Read Material Safety Data Sheets   You need a material safety data sheet for each chemical you use. A **material safety data sheet (MSDS)** is a document that describes a chemical and tells how to handle it. A MSDS is very detailed. It may have several pages. Take time to read it. Make sure you understand what it says.

material safety data sheet (MSDS) ■ A document that describes a chemical and how to handle it.

Learn to Read RTK Labels   Hazardous chemicals must each have a Right-to-Know label, or RTK label. An **RTK label** is a chemical safety label. It tells you:

RTK label ■ A chemical safety label.

- what the hazardous chemical is
- whether the chemical is a minor hazard ("caution") or a major hazard ("danger" or "poison")
- what body parts the chemical can harm

While You Read

Question Why are chemical labels called "right-to-know" labels?

Look at the RTK Label in **Figure 10.5** on page 251. It tells you the name of the chemical. It tells you the health and organ hazards. It tells you what to do if you come in contact with the chemical.

This RTK label has a blue, red, yellow, and white diamond. Each square has a number from zero to four. Zero means no risk. Four means highest risk.

Figure 10.5

METHANOL

CAS #67561

CAUTION

HEALTH HAZARDS: Combustible, Do not sewer, Flammable, Poison, Store below 212° F
ORGANS HAZARDS: Blood, Eyes, Intestines, Stomach

FLAMMABLE! No smoking, matches or open flames!
FIRST AID: Immediately flush eyes w/ water for 15 minutes. Ingestion: Do not induce vomiting—give warm milk or water—call 911.

CONSULT MATERIAL SAFETY DATA SHEET FOR FURTHER INFORMATION ON HAZARDS

FIRE HAZARD
HEALTH HAZARD
SPECIFIC HAZARD
REACTIVITY

HAZARD RATINGS
4 – Severe
3 – Serious
2 – Moderate
1 – Slight
0 – Minimal

You Have a Right to Know This label has a "hazard diamond" with red, blue, yellow, and white boxes. It also has symbols that tell you how to handle the chemical. What personal protective equipment should you put on before you touch this chemical?

Learn How to Prevent Strains

Another thing to learn about job safety is how to prevent common strains. Three ways to do this are to lift objects correctly, to arrange your work space, and to take regular breaks.

Lift Objects Correctly A lot of jobs involve lifting. For example, you may need to lift a box of paper or a tray of food. It is easy to pull a muscle this way.

When you lift, bend your knees and keep your back upright. Hold the object close to your body. Push your chest forward as you walk. This helps prevent back injury. Do not twist your body. Keep your shoulders in line with your hips.

Get help if an object is too heavy or awkward to lift correctly. If you feel any unusual pain, stop.

While You Read

Connect Do you know anyone with a back injury? How did the injury happen?

Arrange Your Work Space   Organize your work space to prevent injury. Put the tools you use the most closest to you. Make sure you do not have to reach above your head. Also make sure you do not have to twist your neck.

Many workers work at a computer desk for most of the day. If you use a computer, make sure you work the right way. **Figure 10.6** shows a good computer setup. Place your monitor at eye level and at arm's length. Keep your wrists straight when you type. Using a wrist rest can help.

Your chair should support your lower back. Putting a small pillow or rolled-up towel against your chair can help.

Put your feet on the floor or on a footrest. You can lean back a little, but do not let your head roll forward.

Figure 10.6

Good Work Posture

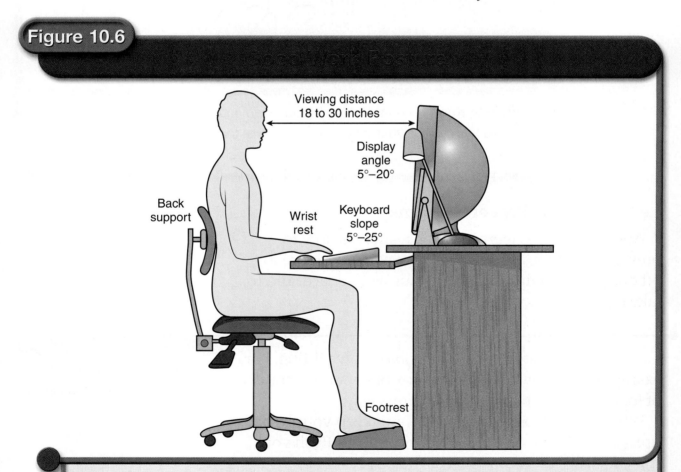

Viewing distance 18 to 30 inches

Display angle 5°–20°

Keyboard slope 5°–25°

Back support

Wrist rest

Footrest

Work Smart You need the right equipment to do your job. A good chair, a wrist rest, and a footrest can help prevent illnesses such as carpal tunnel syndrome. What should you do if you feel unusual pain while you work?

Take Regular Breaks   Many workers sit for most of the day. Sitting puts pressure on your back. Sitting also makes blood collect in your legs and feet. Get up for at least five minutes each hour. Do not sit and type for more than 40 minutes at a time.

Some jobs involve doing the same task again and again. This is hard on your body. You can damage your muscles and nerves. Try to vary your job tasks. Make sure to take breaks to stretch and rest. If you feel pain when you work, stop.

Learn What to Do in an Emergency

You need to do everything you can to stay safe. But what if something goes wrong anyway? What if there is an emergency? An **emergency** is a serious and sudden event that calls for quick action. Fires, car accidents, and explosions are emergencies.

What do you do in an emergency? Follow these steps that are recommended by the American Red Cross: check—call—care.

emergency ■ A serious and sudden event that calls for quick action.

Check   First check the scene. Make sure it is safe to go closer. Then check the victim. Find out what is wrong.

Call   Second, call for help. Dial 911 or your local emergency number. Your company may have a special emergency number. Describe the problem and give your location.

Care   Third, care for the victim. Stay with him or her until help arrives. Do not move the victim. Wait with the victim until help arrives.

While You Read

Question What should you do first before you do anything in an emergency?

Learn Where to Get First Aid

First aid is medical help that a person needs right away after an injury. You should know where to get first aid at your workplace. Is there a medical office? Is there a first aid kit? A *first aid kit* is a box with bandages, painkillers, and more. You may need first aid if there is an emergency.

first aid ■ Medical help that a person needs right away after an injury.

Check your answers online by visiting ewow.glencoe.com/review and selecting the Section 10.2 Review.

After You Read

Retell

1. Look at Figure 10.3. Name the six objects and explain when you would use them.
2. Sketch a person lifting a heavy object the right way. Sketch a person lifting a heavy object the wrong way.

Think Critically

3. Look at Figure 10.6. What job accommodations might a wheelchair user need to have a safe computer setup? Why?

Math Practice

Answer the multiple-choice math questions at ewow.glencoe.com/math.

Insurance

You have a health insurance policy that covers 80% of expenses related to injuries on the job. Your total medical expenses for an injury cost $3,500. How much of the bill will your insurance company pay?

Step 1 Convert 80% to a decimal.
80% = 80 × 1% = 80 × 0.01 = 0.80

Step 2 Multiply 0.80 by the amount of the medical expenses.
0.80 × $3,500 = $2,800

Result Your insurance will pay $2,800 towards your bill.

Figure It Out

Your insurance plan benefit pays 60% of medical costs associated with injuries, after you pay the first $150.00 of the bill. If you have medical expenses that cost $5,000, how much will you pay and how much will your insurance cover?

Human Services Director

Mark Crenshaw

Georgia

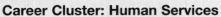

Career Cluster: Human Services

What does a human services director do?

"I manage the Interfaith Network of the Atlanta Alliance on Developmental Disabilities (AADD.) I work with churches, synagogues, and mosques to help disabled people find resources. I plan programs that educate people."

Why did you choose a career in human services?

"I saw a need to provide hospitality to people with disabilities. I have a master's degree in theological studies. This career brings together these two passions."

What obstacles have you overcome?

"I have cerebral palsy. I see a lack of understanding from other people. A few times people have crossed the street to avoid walking by me. My family is supportive. They have helped me find my voice and remove obstacles in my environment."

What advice do you have for students?

"Highlight the gifts you have instead of focusing on what society tells you that you lack. You are much more than the label someone else gave you. Resist that label and focus on educating the people around you."

Human Services Director

Training
Directors of human services organizations usually have a master's degree.

Skills and Talents
Managers in human services need to be good speakers, listeners, and leaders. They need to help people get along.

Career Outlook
Human services will be one of the fastest-growing career areas through 2012.

Learn More About It
Work with a partner. Make a list of all the careers you can think of in human services. Use the Internet or library for research. Add to your list from your research. Check your lists against the lists of your classmates.

For help with this activity, visit **ewow.glencoe.com/tips**.

 ewow.glencoe.com/tips

Key Term Review

working conditions (p. 236)
equipment (p. 237)
right (p. 240)
hazard (p. 240)
OSHA (p. 241)
workers' compensation (p. 243)
high voltage (p. 246)
fire extinguisher (p. 247)

personal protective equipment (p. 248)
flammable (p. 250)
ventilation (p. 250)
material safety data sheet (MSDS) (p. 250)
RTK label (p. 250)
emergency (p. 253)
first aid (p. 253)

Check Your Understanding

1. Name six injuries and illnesses that are common on the job.
2. List workers' safety rights.
3. Explain how to protect yourself from electricity and fire.
4. Describe the three different types of safety signs and what they mean.
5. Explain the three steps you should take in an emergency.

Write About It

6. **Find Safety Solutions** Injuries often happen when workers are not using the right protective equipment. Why might a worker not have the right protective equipment? List as many reasons as you can. For each reason, write a sentence that explains how to fix the problem.

Role Play

7. **Report Hazards**   Work with a partner. One person is a worker and the other person is a supervisor. As the worker, pretend that you see a hazard at your workplace. Tell your supervisor about the hazard. Describe the hazard and ask for it to be fixed. Explain what could happen if the hazard is not fixed. If the supervisor does not agree to fix it, explain your rights. Switch roles with your partner.

Teamwork Challenge

8. **Check School Safety**   Work with a small team to check your school for hazards. Brainstorm a list of hazards. For example, a blocked exit is a safety hazard. A wet floor is a slipping hazard. Make a safety checklist. Then work together to check your classroom and school for hazards.

Computer Lab

Learn About Safety and Health   Visit the OSHA Web site. Find the section of the site on Safety and Health Topics. Read as much as you can about one topic. Use a word-processing program to create a report about the topic. Use images, such as photographs and figures. Share what you learned with a group of classmates.

Personal Career Portfolio

Profile Working Conditions   Write a profile about the working conditions of an occupation that interests you. Look for information about working conditions in the Occupational Outlook Handbook and on the Web site of the Bureau of Labor Statistics.

Go to **ewow.glencoe.com/portfolio** for help.

Chapter 11

Getting Along With Others

You Already Know...

- it is important to get along with other people
- everyone has a different personality
- many workers work in teams
- it is important to have a positive attitude
- you will work with coworkers, supervisors, and customers

You Will Learn...

- several ways to get along with others
- how to be a strong team worker
- ways to speak well at work
- how to be a good listener
- how to deal with conflict

Personal Career Portfolio *Preview*

For your portfolio, you will make a list of work situations that require good communication skills. As you read, think about situations where communication skills would be useful.

Draw From Your Own Background Think about someone you know who gets along well with other people. What does this person do to get along so well with others? Write down everything you notice.

Working Well With Others

Key Terms

tolerance
prejudice
empathy
gossip
respect
cooperate
leadership

Main Idea

To get along at work, it is important to be positive and to treat others with respect. Cooperation and leadership skills can also help you work well in a team.

Thought Organizer

Copy the chart below. As you read, fill in each shape with one way to get along with others.

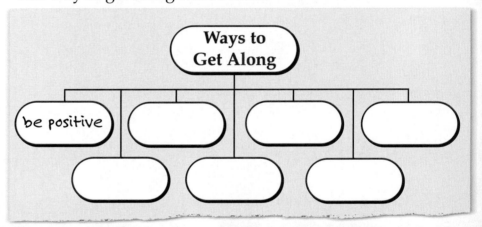

Ways to Get Along

be positive

Learn Skills for Getting Along

You will not work alone on a job. You will work with others. You will need to get along with supervisors, coworkers, and customers.

Getting along with people is very important. In fact, the main reason young workers lose their jobs is that they do not get along with people.

Getting along with people is a skill anyone can learn. It just takes some effort. You need to treat others the way you want to be treated.

Tolerate Differences

You do not choose your coworkers. Your boss does. Your coworkers may be very different from you. To get along, you will need to tolerate differences. **Tolerance** means treating everyone fairly and equally.

Be tolerant of your coworkers and others. Be tolerant of what they say and do. Do not judge. Remember that everyone is different. Find things you have in common. This will help you get along.

tolerance ■ Treating everyone fairly and equally.

Avoid Prejudice If you are tolerant, you do not judge others. You do not have prejudices. A **prejudice** is a negative attitude toward a group of people. For example, *racism* is the prejudice that people of some races are better than others. *Sexism* is the prejudice that one gender, or sex, is better than the other.

Do not judge people by their race, their gender, their age, their language, or what job they do. Get to know each person as an individual.

While You Read

Question How can you show others that you care about them?

prejudice ■ A negative attitude toward a group of people.

Take an Interest in Others

One great way to get people to like you is to be interested in them. Showing interest in others helps you get along. People like it when you care about their lives.

Show your interest by asking about things that interest them. Ask about their hobbies and interests. You might find things in common.

Show Interest Through Body Language Body language is another way to show your interest in other people. You show how you feel by how you sit, stand, or move.

Body language tells a person how interested you are in what he or she is saying. People who are bored may show it by tapping a foot or staring blankly. People who are interested often show it by looking in the eyes of the person talking. They also sit on the edge of a chair and lean toward the person talking. They smile. A smile is like saying, "I like you."

Lend a Hand One way to show that you care about others is to lend a hand. If you see that a coworker needs help, pitch in. Do not wait to be asked. What else can you do to be friendly to your coworkers?

empathy ■ The ability to imagine yourself in another person's shoes.

Show Empathy

A person who cares about other people understands them and has empathy. **Empathy** is the ability to imagine yourself in another person's shoes.

When you have empathy, you can sense what the other person is feeling. You may not feel the same way. However, you can accept their feelings. You can understand them better.

When someone shares a problem, listen. Show your interest and concern. Listening tells the other person that you care.

Be Positive

We all have worries. We all have bad days sometimes. However, it is important to have a positive attitude as much as you can. A cheerful personality will help you get along with others. People feel more comfortable around positive people.

Avoid Gossip   Avoid gossip. Gossip is saying bad things about people behind their backs. People usually gossip to make themselves feel important. Gossip can make it hard to get along with people.

A positive person usually says good things about other people. A negative person often gossips. Can you think of some other differences between a positive person and a negative person? **Figure 11.1** shows several differences between positive people and negative people.

While You Read

Connect Think of someone you know who is negative. Do you like to be around that person?

gossip ■ Saying bad things about people behind their backs.

Figure 11.1

Be a Positive Person

Positive People	Negative People
smile often	smile rarely
like others	dislike others
complain rarely	complain often
admit mistakes	blame others
cooperate	argue or avoid work
like to learn new things	do not like to learn new things

Positive and Negative Having a positive attitude will help you get along well with your coworkers, your boss, and others. Do you like to learn new things? Why or why not?

Show Respect

respect ■ High esteem.

Another way to get along is to show respect. **Respect** is high esteem.

Everyone has value. Everyone deserves respect. Treat everyone at work with respect. It does not matter how old a person is. It does not matter how much power or money the person has. Treat everyone as important.

While You Read

Visualize Imagine that you have your hands full and are trying to open a door. Someone runs up to help you. How do you feel?

Be Respectful in Your Actions Be respectful of others in what you do. Think about how your actions will affect others.

Be honest. Show others that they can believe what you say. Be dependable. Do what you say you will do. Do your fair share of work.

Remember that even small actions affect others. For example, make sure that your things do not get in anyone's way. Knock before you open a person's office door. Clean up after yourself in the break room.

Do nice things for others. Open a door for someone who has his or her arms full. Get help if a piece of equipment stops working. Do not leave it for someone else to handle.

Be Respectful in Your Words Be respectful in what you say. Think before you speak. Think about how your words will affect others. Be courteous. Remember to say "please," "thank you," and "you're welcome."

Tell your coworkers when you like their work. For example, you might say, "You did a great job, Eliza!"

Refer to others as equals. For example, do not call women "girls." Learn to pronounce and spell your coworkers' names. Use standard English so that everyone can understand you.

Be kind in your words. Do not use words that might hurt someone or make someone feel uncomfortable. Never make fun of another person. Never tell jokes about a person's culture or gender. Remember to respect differences.

Laugh a Little

It is easy to be ar... ...nd a person who has a good sense
of humor. A sen... ...umor is the ability to see the funny
side of thin... ...eople can laugh when the joke is
on some... ...ple with a truly good sense of
humo... ...n when the joke is on them.
...side of life is relaxing. A sense of
...easier to get along with others.

...on Each Day

...g the same person even when
...le person acts pretty much the
...ay. Other people can predict how
...y.

...ly one day and grouchy the next?
...ot know what to expect from you. Always
...ne person. That way others will know how to
...ong with you.

While You Read

Question Why is it hard to get along with people who are moody or act different each day?

Making Good Choices

Dealing With a Difficult Boss

One day your boss at the store is friendly. The next day he snaps at you. You find it hard to work for your boss. You like your job. You want to stay, but it is stressful. You want to tell your boss how you feel, but you are not sure how.

You Make the Call What should you do in this situation? Work with another student. Write a skit about the situation. One of you play the employee. One of you play the boss. Show how the employee could approach the boss. Show the outcome that you think will happen.

For help in answering this question, visit **ewow.glencoe.com/tips** and select the *Smart Tip* for the Chapter 11 *Making Good Choices.*

Build Your Teamwork Sk[i]lls

At work you may be assigned to [a] group of people who have the same [goal. A team] might be large or small. You might be [on a] team for years. You might be part of a d[ifferent] each day.

There are two good ways to be a strong [team member.] One is to cooperate. The other is to show le[adership.]

Cooperation is the Key to Teamwork

Teamwork depends on cooperation. To **coope[rate]** means to work well with others to reach a goal. It means putting the goals of your team goal first.

cooperate ■ To work well with others to reach a goal.

Each Team Member Has a Role Each team member should do what he or she does best.

Imagine that you work at a clothing store. You and two other employees, Norah and Jason, need to fold a shipment of clothes. What will happen if you each do your own thing? You might forget to do a task. You might do a task twice.

You need to divide up the tasks. This will make the work go faster. Each person will know exactly what to do.

While You Read

Question Why is it a good idea for team members to divide up the work?

Cooperation Is Key Each team member has a role to play. Cooperation helps the team get all the work done. What roles do you think each worker is performing here?

Do Your Part   Make sure that your tasks are completed correctly. Make sure that the work is done on time. You are important to your team. Do your part. Think about how you can help the team.

Offer to do tasks that you do well. There may be tasks that no one wants to do. Volunteer to help with these tasks. Always do your fair share of work. Make sure that your tasks are completed correctly. Make sure that your work is done on time.

If you have a good idea, share it. Listen to what everyone else has to say, too. Someone might have a great idea. Someone might know how to do something better than you can. Listening to your team will show them that you respect them. Respect the other members of your team. The more respect you give to others, the more respect they will give you.

Be a Leader

Leadership is important in teamwork, too. Leadership is not telling people what to do. **Leadership** is motivating others to work toward a goal.

One way to lead is to set a positive example. Another way to lead is to help your team solve problems. Think of ways to solve problems. Ask others to share their ideas.

leadership ■ Motivating others to work toward a goal.

Motivate Others   Some people are not strong team players. Some people think, "I don't have to help. It is not my problem." Some people think, "Someone else can do this better than I can." Other people think, "I am the only one who does anything right."

How can you work with people like this? Use your leadership skills. Motivate them to help the team.

Imagine that your coworker Norah is not interested in helping fold clothes. You could lead by example. You might say, "I volunteer to fold these shirts. Norah, could you help me?" You might suggest ways to share the work. You might say, "Norah, you are talented at organizing. Maybe you could help me sort these pairs of pants." Show your teammates that you know they can do good work. They will be more willing to help.

While You Read

Connect What is wrong with the attitude, "I am the only one who can do anything right"?

Check your answers online by visiting ewow.glencoe.com/review and selecting the Section 11.1 Review.

After You Read

Retell

1. Name four differences between a positive person and a negative person.
2. Describe five things you can do to show respect for other people. Use your own ideas.

Think Critically

3. Everyone is equal in a team. Yet leadership skills help you be a good team member. Does this make sense? Explain.

Math Practice

Answer the multiple-choice math questions at ewow.glencoe.com/math.

Commission Sales

You earn $6.50 an hour at a shoe store. You also earn a 10% commission on everything you sell. If you worked 160 hours in a month and sold $10,000 worth of shoes, what is your total monthly compensation?

Step 1 Figure out your total monthly wages.
$6.50 × 160 = $1,040

Step 2 Multiply your commission rate by the amount of shoe sales.
0.10 × $10,000 = $1,000

Step 3 Add your monthly wages and your commission.
$1,040 + $1,000 = $2,040

Result Your total monthly compensation is $2,040.

Figure It Out

Your salary at a clothing store is $300 per week. You earn a commission of 16% on your total sales for the month. If on average you sold $4,000 worth of clothing each week for a month, what are your total earnings for that month?

Communicating Well

Ready, Set, Read

Key Terms

communication
enunciate
assertive
active
   listening
conflict
compromise
emotions

Main Idea

Communication skills help you get along with others. Learn to speak well, listen actively, and solve conflicts.

Thought Organizer

Copy the chart below. As you read, fill in each rectangle with one way to speak well at work.

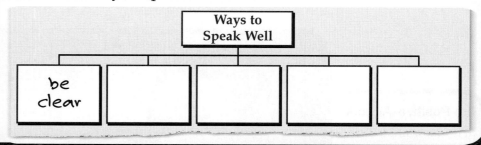

Ways to Speak Well

be clear

Good Communication Helps You Get Along

Communication is sharing thoughts and feelings. Speaking, listening, reading, and writing are all parts of communication.

People with good communication skills get along well with others. This helps them succeed at their jobs.

communication ■ Sharing thoughts and feelings.

Speak Well at Work

You will talk to a lot of people on the job. You will talk to your coworkers and your supervisor. You may also talk to customers.

Customers see you as part of the company. If you speak well, they will have a good image of the company. If you speak poorly, they will not have a good image of the company.

To improve your speech, watch people who are good speakers. Listen to how they enunciate. Note the words they use. Copy what you like.

enunciate ■ To speak each syllable clearly.

Be Clear Speak clearly. Make sure people can follow what you say. Do your words run together? Do your sentences go all over the place? Do people have to make a big effort to understand you?

Remember to use standard English. Avoid words that do not mean anything, such as "sort of," "like," and "um."

Try to **enunciate**, or speak each syllable clearly. Practice enunciating. Make it a habit.

Use Positive Words Show a positive attitude by using positive words. Always look for the most positive way to say what you want to say.

Try to use positive words instead of negative words. Show people that you value them. Say something nice when a coworker or your boss does something helpful.

Be Positive At work it is important to be positive. Being positive shows that you respect others. Recall a time when a person asked you to do a task. Describe how the person spoke. Describe why you did or did not like it.

Show Respect   You speak differently to different people. You use different words. You use a different tone of voice.

At work you will talk to coworkers, supervisors, and customers. Remember that these people are not casual friends. Show respect. Be polite.

Always show respect for your supervisor. It is okay to ask your supervisor questions. It is not okay to argue. It is not okay to talk to your supervisor the way you would talk to your best friend.

Say What You Mean   Everyone has thoughts and feelings. Your thoughts and feelings are important. You have a right to say them.

Practice being assertive. Assertive is direct, honest, and polite. Assertive is different from aggressive. *Aggressive* is direct, honest, and rude.

assertive ■ Direct, honest, and polite.

Imagine that a coworker has an idea you do not like. An assertive person might say, "That's a good idea, but I disagree because…." An aggressive person might say, "You're wrong."

Ask for What You Need   If you need something, ask for it. No one can read your mind. Be direct but polite.

Here are some assertive ways to ask for things:

- "Ms. Chang, I need to go to the dentist next week. May I leave an hour early on Wednesday?"

- "Sidney, could you please show me how to put ink in the printer?"

- "Mr. Fratelli, would you have ten minutes this afternoon to talk to me about my report?"

While You Read

Connect What is the difference between asking for something and demanding something?

Be a Good Listener

Everyone wants to be understood. That is why active listening is so important. Active listening is paying attention and responding to what someone says.

active listening ■ Paying attention and responding to what someone says.

An active listener pays attention and understands. An active listener tries to see things from your point of view.

Using Proper Speech at Work

You and your friends have a special language. You use words that other people may not understand. These words are called slang. It is okay to talk with your friends in slang, but most of the time, you should not use slang at work. Customers and coworkers may not understand you. Your supervisor may not understand you. You might have poor communication with others in the workplace.

What if you work with a friend who speaks the same slang as you? Can the two of you talk together at work? If other people are around, the answer is no. Employers want you to speak so all of your customers and coworkers can understand what you are saying.

Take the Next Step Work with a partner. Make a list of all the slang words you know. Use this list of slang words to write a hip-hop song. Perform your song for your classmates.

For help doing this activity, go to **ewow.glencoe.com/tips** and find the *Smart Tip* for the Chapter 11 *Real-World Connection*.

Pay Attention

The first part of active listening is paying attention. Listen closely when people talk to you. Stay focused. Try not to think about other things. Try not to let your mind wander.

Show the person that you are interested. Make eye contact. Lean forward.

Let the other person finish every sentence. In a pause you could say, "go on," or "uh huh" to encourage that person to finish his or her thought.

Pay Attention to Body Language   Look at the person's body language, too. Body language can tell you a lot about how a person really feels. Does the person look nervous? Relaxed? Angry? Pay attention to more than just words. Try to imagine the person's feelings.

Respond

The second part of good listening is responding. Responding shows the other person that you are paying attention.

Responding helps you to understand the other person. Responding helps you remember what you heard.

Repeat what you heard. You can use your own words. Ask whether you understood correctly.

It is very important to respond to directions. You can make sure you understand exactly what you need to do.

- "Let me make sure I understand. You would like to meet with Laura and me in your office at 12:30?"
- "Let me repeat that. I need to deliver these letters to Mr. Marks in room 305?"

While You Read

Connect How do you feel when you tell someone something important and they do not respond?

Pay Attention and Respond Use body language to show that you are a good listener. Make eye contact and lean forward slightly. Why is responding an important part of active listening?

Learn to Deal With Conflicts

Good communication helps people get along at work. People talk about problems before they become big. People show empathy and respect.

Sometimes conflict happens anyway. A conflict is a strong disagreement. Conflict can happen when people have different needs or ideas. Conflicts can happen at home or school. Conflicts can happen between friends. Conflicts can also happen at work. You might find yourself in a conflict with a coworker or customer.

Avoid Arguments

Sometimes people disagree. That is okay. Arguments are not helpful, however. An *argument* is an angry conflict. Arguments cause bad feelings. Arguments make it hard to work together. People who argue on the job are often fired.

Avoid arguments. Stay calm when another person is angry. Give your opinion calmly. Do not yell.

Question Why is a compromise sometimes called a "win-win situation"?

compromise ■ An agreement where both sides give in a little.

emotions ■ Strong feelings.

Communicate and Compromise

Arguing never helps. But ignoring a conflict does not help either. Ignoring a conflict usually makes it worse.

The best way to handle a conflict is to communicate and compromise. A compromise is an agreement where both sides give in a little. Each side wins a little, too.

Control Your Emotions Emotions are strong feelings. Everyone has emotions. Love and anger are emotions. Strong emotions can be hard to handle.

Things will happen that make you angry. You have no control over events. You do have control over your reactions. Do not take your anger out on coworkers.

If something really bothers you, take a timeout. Calm down first. Talk later.

Share your thoughts and feelings. Explain your reasons so the other person will understand. Try not to hurt the other person's feelings. Do not say things you do not mean. This will make it hard to work together.

Listen to the Other Person   You will not get your way just by talking. You must listen to the other person. Try to understand how he or she sees things. Think about the situation. Maybe the other person is right.

What do you do if someone is rude to you? Do not be rude back. Respond to the other person the way you would like the person to respond to you.

While You Read

Think of Solutions   Both people must have a chance to say how they feel. Both people must think about how the other person feels. Then they must find a solution.

Look for a solution that can help both people. You could say, "What can we do about this problem? What are your ideas?" Work together to solve the problem.

Visualize Imagine that you and another person find a solution to a big personal conflict. How do you feel?

Point of View

Solving Conflict

Kiona Jones plans to be a lawyer. Kiona took a summer job as a clerk for the city council. Bebe, Kiona's coworker, believes the way to get people to listen is by being aggressive. Kiona believes in more peaceful ways. Bebe is often rude to Kiona.

Kiona invited Bebe to have lunch. "I told her my way was just different. I promised to listen to her to see her point of view. She said she'd listen to me too. We haven't become best friends, but we get along."

It's Your Turn   Write an essay about a time when someone made you angry. Write how you handled the situation. Then write how you would handle the person and situation using communication and compromise.

For help completing this activity, visit **ewow.glencoe.com/tips** and go to the *Smart Tip* for the Chapter 11 *Point of View*.

Check your answers online by visiting ewow.glencoe.com/review and selecting the Section 11.2 Review.

After You Read

Recall

1. Explain why it is important to speak well at work. Use your own words.
2. Define *compromise*. Explain how to reach a compromise. Use your own words.

Think Critically

3. Do you agree that you can control your reactions? Explain.

Math Practice

Answer the multiple-choice math questions at ewow.glencoe.com/math.

Teamwork

You bake cookies for a team-building exercise. Each batch makes 24 cookies. You have enough ingredients for 3 batches. Your cookie sheet only fits 6 rows of cookies and 3 across. How many times will you use the sheet?

Step 1 Figure out the total number of cookies you will make.
$24 \times 3 = 72$

Step 2 Calculate how many cookies can fit on the sheet.
6 rows $\times$ 3 cookies across = 18

Step 3 Divide the total number of cookies by the number of cookies that can fit on the sheet at one time.
72 cookies $\div$ 18 = 4

Result You will use the cookie sheet 4 times.

Figure It Out

You and other team members attend a seminar on conflict. The seminar costs $150 per person. You will need to drive two cars to the seminar, and make a 100-mile round trip from your office. If two drivers are reimbursed 37.5 cents per mile, what is the cost for the seminar?

Computer Room Operator

Anne Rindfleisch
Wisconsin

Career Cluster: Information Technology

What does a computer room operator do?

"I process the orders for the day for Burlington Coat Factory. I also take Internet orders."

Why did you choose a career in computer technology?

"There was a good opportunity for jobs in that field."

What obstacles have you overcome?

"I was born with no arms and no legs. To work with computers, I had to learn to use a mouth stick to type and to push buttons. I have to leave early to make sure I get to work on time because I drive my wheelchair to work. I use my shoulder to drive the wheelchair. When I was younger, there were no wheelchair curbs. I got into trouble with the police because I had to get off the sidewalk and into the street to cross a street."

What advice do you have for students?

"Get an education no matter what it is. Knowledge will help you in life. Accept everyone for the way they are."

Computer Room Operator

Training
Computer room operators need at least a high school diploma.

Skills and Talents
Computer room operators need computer training, basic math skills, and good reading and typing skills.

Career Outlook
Employment for computer operators is expected to decline through 2012. Opportunities will be best for operators who have postsecondary education and keep up with the latest technology.

Learn More About It
Play a trivia game. Organize into two teams. Each team should write down 12 information technology terms. Add a definition for each term. One team gives the other a definition of a term. The other team must guess the correct term. The team that guesses the most terms correctly is the winner.

For help with this activity, visit **ewow.glencoe.com/tips**.

Glencoe Online

Go to **ewow.glencoe.com** to find online games and activities for Chapter 11.

Key Term Review

tolerance (p. 261)
prejudice (p. 261)
empathy (p. 262)
gossip (p. 263)
respect (p. 264)
cooperate (p. 266)
leadership (p. 267)

communication (p. 269)
enunciate (p. 270)
assertive (p. 271)
active listening (p. 271)
compromise (p. 274)
emotions (p. 274)

Check Your Understanding

1. Name seven ways to get along with others.
2. List and define two skills that will help you be a strong team worker.
3. List five habits that can help you speak well at work.
4. Explain how to be an active listener.
5. Describe the right way to deal with conflict.

Write About It

6. **Tolerating Differences**   Make a list of all the ways that the students in your class are different from each other. For example, people may speak different languages. Write a paragraph saying how you feel about these differences. Do people tolerate each other's differences well? Are some differences hard for you to tolerate? Explain. Give examples.

Role Play

7. **Communicate and Compromise**   Work with a partner. Pretend that you are coworkers. You have a conflict. For example, one of you plays a radio loudly. The other talks on the phone a lot. Choose a partner to go first. This partner explains his or her thoughts and feelings. The other partner responds. Together, find a solution.

Teamwork Challenge

8. **Practice Active Listening**   Work in a team of three. Choose roles: speaker, listener, and observer. The speaker talks about a problem he or she is having. The problem can be real or made up. The listener pays attention and responds. The observer watches the listener. The speaker and listener talk for three or four minutes. Then the observer says what he or she saw. Did the listener respond well? Did the listener use positive body language? Discuss. Change roles and start again.

Computer Lab

Make a Chart   Use the computer to make a chart of habits that can help you get along with others. Make a chart with two columns and seven rows. Use the Thought Organizer you made in Section 11.1. In the left column, write one good habit on each row. In the right column, write one thing you could do to show this habit. For example, describe one way to show respect for others. Print your chart and share it with another student.

Personal Career Portfolio

Describe Communication Skills   Describe three work scenes that require skills at speaking and listening. For example, helping a customer requires these skills. Taking directions from a supervisor requires these skills. Describe each scene in two or three sentences. Then explain how you could use speaking and listening skills in each scene.

   Go to **ewow.glencoe.com/portfolio** for help.

Chapter 12

Being a Valuable Employee

You Already Know...

- employers like employees who do a good job
- if you do a good job, you may earn more money
- it is important to have a good relationship with your supervisor
- work experience helps you become a better worker
- listening skills are important on the job

You Will Learn...

- what it means to have good character
- how to be a responsible worker
- how to show initiative and enthusiasm
- how feedback helps you improve your job skills
- how to accept constructive criticism

Personal Career Portfolio *Preview*

For your portfolio, you will make a performance evaluation. As you read, think about your behavior at school and at work.

Preview Make a list of differences between a good worker and a poor worker. Write down everything that comes to mind. Now skim the chapter. Make a list of key terms highlighted in yellow. Do your two lists have any words in common?

281

Employability Skills

Ready, Set, Read

Key Terms

employability skills
character
responsibility
work ethic
initiative
punctuality
time management
harrassment
loyalty

Main Idea

Employers want workers with good character. Good character includes positive qualities such as responsibility, punctuality, initiative, and honesty.

Thought Organizer

Copy the chart below. As you read, fill in each line with one of the qualities described in the section.

Good Character

- responsibility
- _____
- _____
- _____

- _____
- _____
- _____

Learn Employability Skills

employability skills ■
Basic skills that you need to get a job, keep a job, and do well at a job.

All employers want workers with employability skills. **Employability skills** are basic skills that you need to get a job, keep a job, and do well at a job.

Employers look for workers who can get along and communicate with others. They look for workers who know how to listen and are eager to learn. They look for workers who show respect for themselves and for others. They also look for workers who have good character. **Character** is a person's ethics and behavior.

character ■ A person's ethics and behavior.

How can you show good character? By developing skills and qualities such as responsibility, punctuality, initiative, enthusiasm, honesty, loyalty, and a strong work ethic.

Responsibility Is Working Hard and Setting High Standards for Yourself

Responsibility is one of the most important employability skills. **Responsibility** is working hard and setting high standards for yourself.

Responsible workers work hard. They take their jobs seriously. They do their share of the work.

Admit Your Mistakes Everyone makes mistakes. You will make some mistakes when you are new to a job. That is okay. No one is perfect.

Be responsible. Admit your mistakes. Do not hide your mistakes or blame others. Your boss will be impressed that you take responsibility.

Learn from your mistakes. Try not to make the same mistake more than once. Think about why the mistake happened. Think about how you could do things better next time.

Finish What You Start Some people are always starting something new. They never finish anything. Have you known anyone like this?

On the job, you must finish what you start. Work on each task until it is done. You may have to leave one task for a while to do another task that is more important. Come back and finish what you started, though. Show responsibility by finishing your tasks.

You are part of a team. Other people depend on you. Your company can only be successful if all the tasks get finished. The company will not make money if tasks are left unfinished.

Work Fast, But Do a Good Job Do your job tasks as quickly as you can. However, do not try for just speed. If you try to do things too fast, you may make mistakes. The work may be sloppy. Work as fast as you can, but do a good job.

Sometimes you may have too much to do at one time. If you cannot do something on time, tell your boss right away. Ask which task you should put first.

responsibility ■ Working hard and setting high standards for yourself.

While You Read

Question Why is it important to finish what you start?

The Work Ethic Is the Belief That Work Has Value

work ethic ■ The belief that work has value.

In Chapter 8 you learned that ethics means knowing right from wrong. The work ethic is a little different. The **work ethic** is the belief that work has value.

Some people do not have a strong work ethic. They do not take pride in what they do. They often do not do a very good job.

People with a strong work ethic know that their skills and efforts have value. They take pride in their work. They work for more than a paycheck. People who have a strong work ethic do a good job.

While You Read

Connect Do you work better if you are supervised at home, work, or school?

Work Well Without Supervision Some people work hard only when the boss is around. They do little when the boss is not looking. These workers do not last long on the job.

Not working during your work hours is like stealing from your employer. It will make your coworkers dislike you. It might cause your employer to fire you.

Valuable employees work hard all the time. Employers trust them. Employers give them more important work to do.

Always Do Your Best Always show a strong work ethic. Remember that your work matters to your team and to your company. What would you do if a coworker does not show a good work ethic?

Having a Good Work Ethic

"Lots of people want to give me a tip when I carry their groceries to the car," says grocery worker Paulo Hernandes of Columbus, Ohio. "I never take the tips. Helping people is part of my job. My parents taught me to take pride in my work," Paulo says. "They told me it doesn't matter if I'm sweeping the floors or running the place. I need to do a good job." Paulo began working at the grocery when he was 16. He's at community college now studying drafting. He still works at the store part-time.

"My manager is always telling me what a good job I do. I know he will give me a good recommendation when I look for a job in drafting."

It's Your Turn Carry a small notebook with you for one week. Take notes about the customer service you receive. Write a summary about your observations. Present it to your class.

For help completing this activity, visit **ewow.glencoe.com/tips** and go to the *Smart Tip* for the Chapter 12 *Point of View*.

Initiative Is Doing Work Without Being Told

Employers like workers who take initiative. Taking **initiative** means doing work without being told. Workers with initiative do not need as many directions. They do not need to be watched as carefully. This saves employers time and money.

Workers with initiative are sometimes called *self-starters.* You may see this word in job listings.

At work, you may see tasks that need to be done. Do them if you know how. Do not wait to be told to do them.

initiative ■ Doing work without being told.

Initiative and Enthusiasm Do you see something that needs to be done? Do it! Why would employers like employees who show initiative?

Show Enthusiasm by Being Excited About What You Do

No job is all fun. There will be some work that you do not like. Accept your work, however. Do even the hard jobs with enthusiasm. *Enthusiasm* is interest and eagerness.

Smile. Be friendly. Be quick to start tasks. Volunteer to help others.

If you show enthusiasm in your work, you will look happy. You will work quickly and well. Other workers will be happy to work with you. When you like your work, life can seem more interesting. Your boss will appreciate you more. He or she will probably give you more interesting work to do.

Punctuality Is Being on Time

Punctuality is another important work skill. **Punctuality** means being on time.

punctuality ■ Being on time.

Find out what time you need to be at work each day. If your shift starts at 8:00 a.m., be at work at 8:00 or earlier. Always be on time for work. Coming at 8:10 or 8:15 is not okay.

Call your supervisor if you cannot come to work on time. You should be late only if there is an emergency. For example, there might be a storm. You might get sick.

Come to work ready to work. Imagine that your shift starts at 8:00 a.m. You need to be ready to work right at 8:00 a.m. Remember that you will not have a break until later.

Learn when lunch and break times are. Take only the time you are allowed. Learn when quitting time is. Never quit work early unless your boss says to do so.

Making Good Choices

Being Honest About Time

Bryan works in a printing shop. He is responsible for opening his area of the shop every morning. Bryan gets to work late almost every morning. Bryan records the time he works on a time sheet. He records the time he should arrive instead of the time he does arrive. Bryan's supervisor works in another area. She does not know that Bryan comes in late every morning. If Bryan writes down the time he actually comes in, he may get fired. What should he do?

You Make the Call Have a brainstorming session with two other classmates. Discuss the different ways Bryan's behavior is right or wrong. Choose one member of your group to share your conclusions with the class.

For help in answering this question, visit **ewow.glencoe.com/tips** and select the *Smart Tip* for the Chapter 12 *Making Good Choices*.

Time Management Is Using Time to Reach Your Goals

time management ■ Using time to reach your goals.

Time is limited. Valuable employees make the most of their time through time management. **Time management** is using time to reach your goals.

Manage your time with a schedule. A *schedule* is a chart showing how you will spend each day.

Make a list of all the tasks you need to do. Write how long each job task will take. Write when each task is due. Plan when you will start and finish each task. Plan time to work on each task. For example, imagine that it is Monday and you have a project due Friday. The project will take you ten hours. You might plan to work on it for two hours each day this week. Fill in your schedule hour by hour. Plan time to finish all your tasks. Then make sure to follow your schedule each day.

A calendar or day planner can help you make a schedule. You can also keep a schedule on a computer. **Figure 12.1** shows a schedule on a computer.

Figure 12.1

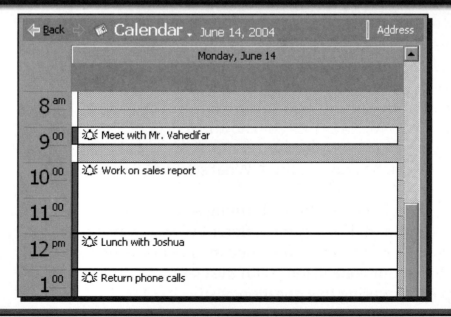

Daily Schedule

| ← Back → 📧 **Calendar .** June 14, 2004 | Address |

Monday, June 14

8 am

9 00 — 🔔 Meet with Mr. Vahedifar

10 00 — 🔔 Work on sales report

11 00

12 pm — 🔔 Lunch with Joshua

1 00 — 🔔 Return phone calls

Hour by Hour A schedule helps you stay on track. A computer can help you stay on track. You can set an alarm to go off a few minutes when you need to start something new. Would you rather make a schedule on a calendar or on a computer? Why?

Respect Laws and Company Rules

Every company has a code of conduct. A *code of conduct* is a list of rules for behavior at work. Being respectful toward others is an important part of behavior at work.

Some work behaviors are also illegal. Discrimination is illegal. For example, it is illegal to turn away a job applicant just because he or she has a disability.

Harassment is also illegal. **Harassment** is unwelcome behavior that creates a hostile environment.

Learn the Types of Harassment Harassment can take many forms. Name-calling or joking is a form of harassment. Unwanted staring or touching is a form of harassment. Bullying is a form of harassment.

There are many types of harassment. Racial harassment is words or actions against someone's skin color, language, or national origin. Religious harassment is words or actions against a person's religion.

Sexual harassment is unwelcome behavior of a sexual nature. Sexual harassment could include unwelcome behavior such as jokes, gestures, or touching. Both women and men can be victims of sexual harassment.

People with disabilities may face harassment, too. For example, a person might make unwelcome comments about another person's disability.

Report Harassment What should you do if you are harassed? Do not stay silent. Talk to the harasser if you can. Say that you do not like the person's behavior. Tell the person to stop. For example, you might say, "I don't like your comments. I want you to stop."

You should also speak up if you see another person being harassed. Imagine someone tells a joke about a person with disabilities. You could say, "I don't think that's funny."

What if the harassment happens again? Talk to your supervisor. Explain what is happening. Your supervisor should take action. You may need to make a formal report, too.

harassment ■ Unwelcome behavior that creates a hostile environment.

Honesty Is Being Truthful

Honesty means telling the truth. An honest person does not lie, cheat, or steal. Employers can trust honest workers.

Be honest in your work. Do not steal time by working less than a full day. Do not cover up your mistakes. Speak up when something goes wrong so that it can be fixed as soon as possible.

Do not take even small items from your company without permission. That is stealing.

Deal honestly with your coworkers so they will trust you. Tell customers the truth. This will help create a good name for your company. You will build a reputation for being honest.

While You Read

Connect Are you loyal to your friends?

loyalty ■ Being on the side of something or someone.

Loyalty Is Doing What You Can for Your Company

There may be some things you do not like about the company you work for. After all, no company is perfect. As long as you work there, be loyal to the company. Show loyalty. **Loyalty** means being on the side of something or someone. It also means not doing anything that would hurt that person or thing.

Part of being loyal is keeping secrets. On some jobs, you may be told things *in confidence*. This means that you must not tell other people about them. Do not even tell your friends or family.

Do not speak badly about the company. Your employer may hear about it. You may lose your job. If you cannot be loyal to the company, look for another job.

Good Health Habits Are a Healthy Diet, Exercise, and Sleep

Another important way to be a valuable worker is to have good health habits.

Why does health matter? You are less likely to make mistakes if you are healthy and alert. You are less likely to get sick and miss work. You are less likely to cause an accident.

Eat a Healthy Diet   Take an active role in your health. Eat a healthy diet of vegetables, fruits, grains, and protein. Avoid foods high in fat, salt, and sugar. Avoid caffeine, alcohol, tobacco, and other drugs. These things are not good for your health. They can also make you tired at work.

Exercise   Exercise makes you stronger. Exercise also gives you more energy. It makes you more alert.

Try to exercise at least twenty minutes each day. Do exercise that makes your heart work. Also do exercises that strengthen your muscles. You can also benefit from exercises that make you more flexible, such as yoga.

Get Enough Sleep   Sleep is an important part of health. Most people need at least eight hours of sleep each night. Some people need nine hours or more. Sleep as much as you need. If you are tired during the day, you probably do not get enough sleep at night.

While You Read

Connect Are you often tired or sleepy during the day?

Get Moving
Staying in shape helps you enjoy life more. What is your favorite kind of physical activity? Why?

Check your answers online by visiting **ewow.glencoe.com/review** and selecting the Section 12.1 Review.

Retell

1. Explain why not working is like stealing.
2. Explain why having good health habits makes you a better worker. Use your own words.

Think Critically

3. Imagine that you know some secret information about your company. Imagine that a customer asks about this information. You want to be honest but also loyal. What do you do?

Math Practice

Answer the multiple-choice math questions at **ewow.glencoe.com/math**.

Time Management at Work

At work, you spend 20 hours per week answering phones, 15 hours writing letters, and 5 hours organizing files. What percentage of your 40-hour workweek do these tasks take? Round up to the nearest percent.

Step 1 Divide hours spent on the phone by 40.
$20 \div 40 = 0.50$ **or 50%**

Step 2 Divide hours spent writing letters by 40. Round up.
$15 \div 40 = 0.375$, **rounded to 38%**

Step 3 Divide hours spent organizing files by 40. Round up.
$5 \div 40 = 0.125$, **rounded to 12%**

Result You spend 50% of your time answering the phone, 38% on writing letters and 12% on organizing files.

Figure It Out

Your manager wants you to increase the time you spend training co-workers from 30% to 50% each month. If you currently work 160 hours each month, how many additional hours will you need to dedicate to training?

 ewow.glencoe.com

Moving Ahead in Your Career

Ready, Set, Read

Key Terms

raise
promotion
labor contract
feedback
constructive
  criticism
receptive
defensive
performance
  review

Main Idea

Raises and promotions are rewards for excellent work. You can become a better worker by learning to accept feedback and criticism.

Thought Organizer

Copy the chart below. As you read, think of things that an employer might give an employee feedback about. Write one thing at the end of each line.

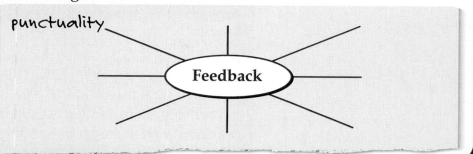

punctuality

Feedback

Employability Skills Make You a Valuable Worker

If you do your job well and show character, you will be a valuable employee. Your employer may offer you a raise or a promotion.

A **raise** is an increase in pay. A raise is a reward for doing an excellent job. You may get a raise if you help your company make money. Many companies give raises to good workers each year.

A **promotion** is a move to a job with more responsibility and higher pay. For example, a salesperson might become an assistant manager. An assistant manager might become a full manager. When you get a promotion, you usually get a raise, too.

raise ■ An increase in pay.

promotion ■ A move to a job with more responsibility and higher pay.

Union Workers Have Labor Contracts

Union workers get raises and promotions in a special way. Union workers have labor contracts. A **labor contract** is a written agreement about wages, hours, and working conditions. For example, the contract may say when you will receive a raise.

Will you be part of a union? Find out if the workers in your company belong to a union. Find out if you must join or if you have a choice. Joining a union also costs money. Union members pay to join. Union members must also pay dues each month.

Unions protect workers' needs. Union members have a right to *strike*, or stop working. Union members can strike if they are not being treated fairly.

labor contract ■ A written agreement about wages, hours, and working conditions.

Real-World Connection

Being in a Union

Many workplaces have unions. You may have to decide if you want to join the union. Union members receive many benefits, such as raises or promotions. Union members vote for the union leaders. The leaders work with the company to make labor contracts about wages.

Different career areas have different unions. There is a union for clerical workers. Another union is for auto workers. Still another union is for airline pilots. Airline mechanics have their own union. Even teachers have a union.

Take the Next Step Some unions offer apprenticeship programs. Use the Internet to learn about apprenticeship programs offered by unions. Write a one-page summary of your findings.

For help doing this activity, go to **ewow.glencoe.com/tips** and find the *Smart Tip* for the Chapter 12 *Real-World Connection*.

Earn a Raise or Promotion With a Good Work Record

Your employer may promote you or give you a raise if you have a good work record. Do you do your job well? Your employer will think you deserve a higher wage. He or she may think you can do a job with more responsibility.

Employers promote workers who have good employability skills. They promote workers who show responsibility and initiative. They promote workers who come to work on time. They promote workers who get along well with others.

Seniority Is Not Enough   Employers also promote workers who have seniority. *Seniority* means being on the job a long time. But having seniority is not the only reason an employer may promote you. You have to be an excellent worker, too.

Improve Your Knowledge and Skills

Imagine that you are only able to do one task. You do your job well. But your boss may not think about you for a raise or promotion. You may stay in your job for a long time.

Work to improve your knowledge and skills. This will help you get ready for a promotion.

Take Classes   You can build your knowledge and skills by taking classes. For example, you might take a night class. Some employers even let their workers take classes on company time.

What if you want to change jobs or careers? You can take classes that can prepare you for the job you want to have.

Learn on the Job   You can also learn on the job. Practice new tasks in your spare time. Ask your boss if you can learn to do something new. For example, ask if you can help with a new project. Ask your boss if you can get more training on the job.

While You Read

Question Why is seniority not enough to earn a promotion?

Read   You can also learn new skills by reading. Read books that could help you do your work better. Does your company have any material that could help you learn? Read that, too.

Join Groups   Meet other people who do the same type of work. You can meet people in unions and trade groups. They can help you improve your knowledge and skills. Some groups have speakers. Some groups hold classes to improve members' skills.

Feedback Helps You Do Your Job Better

feedback ■ Information about how well you are doing your job.

How do you know whether you are doing a good job? You need **feedback**, or information about how well you are doing your job.

When you start a new job, you will probably get a lot of feedback. Your boss and coworkers will watch to see how you are doing. They want to know if you can do your job. They want to know if you are following company rules. They want to know if you are using your work time fairly. They want to know if you are a team worker.

While You Read

Question What is the difference between praise and constructive criticism?

Feedback Includes Praise and Constructive Criticism

Your boss will probably have good things to say about your work or your attitude. He or she will praise what you do well. *Praise* is a comment about something you do well.

constructive criticism ■ A comment about things you can do better.

Your boss will also give you constructive criticism. **Constructive criticism** is a comment about something you can do better.

The purpose of constructive criticism is to help you do your job better. Pay attention to constructive criticism. It is useful.

Some workers do not pay attention to constructive criticism. They keep doing things the wrong way. They do not learn or improve.

Be Receptive
Criticism can be hard to hear. It can make you a better worker. Name two common defensive reactions to criticism.

Be Open to Criticism

It is important to be **receptive**, or open to other people's opinions. Coworkers and supervisors will give you criticism. They need to help you do your job. They need to tell you how to do things better.

The opposite of receptive is defensive. Being **defensive** means being closed to other people's opinions. Some defensive people get angry. Other defensive people refuse to listen.

Criticism is not the same as an insult. An insult is a comment about you as a person. Criticism is a comment about your behavior. You can change your behavior and become a better worker.

receptive ■ Open to other people's opinions.

defensive ■ Closed to other people's opinions.

Listen, Respond, Solve, and Act   Listen closely to criticism. Use your active listening skills: pay attention and respond. Repeat what you heard. Repeat key words. Make sure you understand the problem.

Then think about how you can fix the problem. Discuss ideas with your boss. Ask for advice. For example, you might say, "Do you have any ideas on how I can improve in this area?"

Once you have a solution, act on it. Use the feedback to be a better worker. Show your boss that you are trying.

You Receive Feedback During a Performance Review

At your work you may have a performance review. A performance review is a meeting where your boss tells you how well you have been doing your job. You might have a performance review once a year. You might have a performance review once every six months.

You may also get a performance evaluation. A *performance evaluation* is a written report saying how well you do your job. Your boss will show you your evaluation and talk with you about it. This will help you become a better worker.

Figure 12.2 shows a sample performance evaluation.

performance review ■
A meeting where your boss tells you how well you have been doing your job.

While You Read

Visualize How would you feel about asking your boss for feedback?

Ask for Feedback Often

One of the best ways to be a good worker is to ask for feedback often. Do not wait until your performance review. Try to improve all the time. This shows initiative, enthusiasm, and responsibility.

Ask your boss to talk about your work performance. Ask to meet for ten minutes. Ask for advice about how to do better. You might say, "Are there any suggestions you could give me?" You might say, "Is there anything I can do better?" Ask for specific advice.

Be open to what your boss says. Thank your boss. Follow through on your boss's suggestions. Show that you are trying.

Figure 12.2 Performance Evaluation

Employee Name: Bradley Washington **Date:** September 30, 2009
Job Title: Child Care Assistant **Supervisor:** Jennifer Fornari

Describe what the employee does well. Bradley has excellent skills with infants and toddlers. He does a good job leading activities and keeping the kitchen and playroom supplies clean and orderly. Bradley is a hard worker and has a generally positive attitude. He has begun to show more initiative in planning activities. He has also asked for feedback on his performance and been open to constructive criticism.

Describe what the employee needs to improve. Bradley sometimes comes to work late. On two occasions he was absent but did not call in sick until mid-morning. Bradley should also focus on building his teamwork skills. He often does not contribute to team activities.

Responsibility and Work Ethic
__X__ performs job tasks well, completely, and on time
_____ performs most job tasks adequately
_____ work is often poor, incomplete, or late

Attendance and Punctuality
_____ is almost always present and punctual
__X__ is occasionally late or absent
_____ is often late or absent

Communication and People Skills
_____ has excellent communication skills and is a solid team player
__X__ communicates adequately, does most teamwork tasks
_____ has trouble working and communicating with others

Initiative and Enthusiasm
_____ always shows initiative and enthusiasm
__X__ has a generally positive attitude and shows some initiative
_____ has a poor attitude and must be closely supervised to complete job tasks

Willingness to Learn
__X__ seeks feedback and new challenges
_____ somewhat open to feedback and new challenges
_____ shows little interest in feedback and new challenges

Written Feedback Use feedback as a tool to do your job better. Focus on improving your skills. What skills could this employee improve?

Check your answers online by visiting **ewow.glencoe.com/review** and selecting the Section 12.2 Review.

After You Read

Retell

1. Describe four ways to improve your knowledge and skills on the job. Give a specific example of each.

2. Reread the section titled "Listen, Respond, Solve, and Act." Explain what this title means. Use your own words.

Think Critically

3. Some people do not give criticism well. They do not say things in a nice way. Imagine that you have a performance review. Your boss says something that hurts your feelings. What is the best way to act? Why?

Math Practice

Answer the multiple-choice math questions at **ewow.glencoe.com/math**.

Promotions

You are promoted from a salesperson to assistant manager and will earn an additional $5,000 each year. If you earned $32,000 as a salesperson, what is the percentage increase in salary you will receive when promoted?

Step 1 Divide the increase by your former salary.
$5,000 ÷ $32,000 = 0.156

Step 2 Convert 0.156 to a percentage.
0.156 = 100 × 0.156 = 15.6%

Result Your salary will increase by 15.6%.

Figure It Out

You estimate that in order to achieve your financial goals you need to earn 20% more each year. If you currently earn $28,000 what is the total dollar amount you must earn in order to reach your goal?

Lawyer

Gene Feldman
California

Career Cluster: Law, Public Safety, and Security

What does a lawyer do?

"A lawyer gives legal advice and represents clients in court. I specialize in employment discrimination and violation of the Americans With Disabilities Act (ADA). ADA gives civil rights protection to people with disabilities. I represent people with disabilities who are discriminated against in employment."

Why did you choose a career in law?

"I have a strong sense of what is right and wrong. I'm in this area of the law to do something useful. I want to seek out justice for people with disabilities."

What obstacles have you overcome?

"I have cerebral palsy. I had to realize that I could compete with everyone else. I also have to deal with people's expectations of what someone with a disability can do. Most people don't think about people with a disability being an attorney. I'm creating possibilities where none existed before."

What advice do you have for students?

"To dream big."

Lawyer

Training
Lawyers need a bachelor's degree and a law school degree. They must pass the bar exam in the state where they want to practice law.

Skills and Talents
Lawyers need excellent skills in reading, writing, speaking, listening, and thinking.

Career Outlook
Employment of lawyers will grow at an average rate through 2012.

Learn More About It
Pick an occupation in this career cluster. Find a professional who hires people in this occupation. Ask what he or she looks for when hiring people for this job. What education is needed? What experience is needed? What type of personality is best? Write a summary of your findings.

For help with this activity, visit **ewow.glencoe.com/tips**.

Glencoe Online

Go to **ewow.glencoe.com** to find online games and activities for Chapter 12.

Key Term Review

employability skills (p. 282)
character (p. 282)
responsibility (p. 293)
work ethic (p. 284)
initiative (p. 285)
punctuality (p. p. 287)
time management (p. 288)
harassment (p. 289)
loyalty (p. 290)

raise (p. 293)
promotion (p. 293)
labor contract (p. 294)
feedback (p. 296)
constructive criticism (p. 296)
receptive (p. 297)
defensive (p. 297)
performance review (p. 298)

Check Your Understanding

1. List seven skills and qualities that show good character.

2. Define responsibility. Explain three ways to be a responsible worker.

3. Define initiative and enthusiasm. Explain how you can show these qualities. Use your own words.

4. Explain why feedback can help you do your job better.

5. Describe how to deal with criticism.

Write About It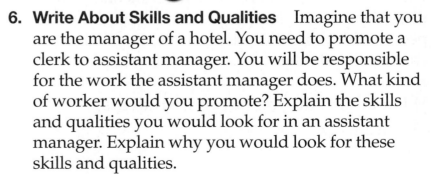

6. **Write About Skills and Qualities**   Imagine that you are the manager of a hotel. You need to promote a clerk to assistant manager. You will be responsible for the work the assistant manager does. What kind of worker would you promote? Explain the skills and qualities you would look for in an assistant manager. Explain why you would look for these skills and qualities.

Role Play

7. **Interview for a Promotion** Work in pairs. One partner pretends to be the manager of a clothing store. The other partner pretends to be a salesperson at the store. The manager interviews the salesperson about a promotion to supervisor. The employer asks the employee how he or she shows good character at work. Take turns playing each role.

Teamwork Challenge

8. **Give and Receive Feedback** Work in small groups to write two skits. Both skits should show an employer giving an employee constructive criticism. In the first skit, the employee reacts defensively. In the second skit, the employee reacts receptively. Perform both skits for the class.

Computer Lab

Create a Computer Presentation Use presentation software to create a presentation about good character at work. Define each of the character qualities described in Section 12.1. Then describe one specific way to show each quality at work or school. Share your presentation with your classmates.

Personal Career Portfolio

Evaluate Your Performance Make a performance evaluation of your work in this class. Copy the format in **Figure 12.2** or ask your teacher for a blank copy of this form. Write your name and the date at the top. Describe what you do well and what you need to improve. Then give yourself a check mark for each category. Where are your skills strong? Where do you need to improve?

Go to **ewow.glencoe.com/portfolio** for help.

Chapter Summaries

Chapter 9 Your First Days on the Job

During your first days of work you will meet your supervisor and coworkers. You will tour your work area. You will get your first job tasks. You will also fill out forms that relate to pay and taxes. During your first days you will also learn how you will be paid and what benefits you will receive.

Chapter 10 Job Safety

Safety laws and rules protect workers from injuries and illnesses. You have the right to safe working conditions. You also have the right to medical care if you are hurt on the job. You need to learn to use equipment safely, to read safety signs, and to handle emergencies.

Chapter 11 Getting Along With Others

Get along with people by taking an interest in others, being positive, showing respect, cooperating, and motivating others. Good communication skills help you get along with others. Speak clearly and assertively, and be a good listener. Work with others to solve conflicts.

Chapter 12 Being a Valuable Employee

Employers like workers who have employability skills and good character. Employability skills include responsibility, punctuality, initiative, honesty, loyalty, and good health habits. Good workers are also open to feedback, or criticism. As a valuable employee, you may receive a raise in pay or a promotion.

These are the topics you read about in this unit. What did you learn?

Chapter 9
Your First Days on the Job
- Getting Off to a Good Start
- Your Pay and Benefits

Chapter 10
Job Safety
- Safety Basics
- Working Safely

Chapter 11
Getting Along With Others
- Working Well With Others
- Communicating Well

Chapter 12
Being a Valuable Employee
- Employability Skills
- Moving Ahead in Your Career

Skills for Everyday Living

Unit Preview

Unit 4 is about skills for independent living. You will learn how to read your paycheck and how to pay taxes to the government. You will learn how to handle your money so that you can buy what you need. You will learn the basics of computer hardware and software. Then you will think about and learn how to plan for an independent future.

Chapter 13

Your Paycheck and Your Taxes

You Already Know...

- there are many kinds of taxes
- different people pay different amounts of taxes
- you need to fill out forms when you start a new job

You Will Learn...

- the types of information to look for on your paycheck
- why money is taken from your earnings
- how the government uses your tax money
- the purpose of Form W-4, Form W-2, and Form 1040EZ
- how to get help filling out tax forms

Personal Career Portfolio *Preview*

For your portfolio, you will fill out Form W-4. As you read, think about the information you will need to fill out this form.

Set a Purpose With a partner, write an end to this statement: "Learning about taxes will help me to _____ ." Write down as many things as you can.

Understanding Your Paycheck

Ready, Set, Read

Key Terms

taxes
gross pay
net pay
deduction
FICA
Social Security
income tax
Internal
    Revenue
    Service (IRS)
Form W-4
dependent

Main Idea

Your employer will take tax money out of your paycheck and send it to the government. Your paycheck shows how much you earned and how much tax you paid.

Thought Organizer

Copy the chart below. As you read, write down several things that taxes pay for.

Taxes

roads

Taxes Are Payments to the Government

Many new workers are surprised when they get their first paycheck. They know how much money per hour to expect. They know how many hours they worked. The amount on the paycheck should be the two numbers multiplied together, right? Not quite.

Why? Because money was taken from your paycheck to pay taxes. Taxes are money that you must pay to the government. Taxes keep the government running. Tax money pays for services such as education, roads, public transportation, police, prisons, and national defense. Your tax money funds government programs that provide services such as payments and health care for retired and low-income workers.

taxes ■ Money that you must pay to the government.

Organizing Your Paperwork

Amy Mokri of Cary, Illinois, works at a movie theater. "I only work part-time, but I still have a lot of financial paperwork to keep track of," Amy says. "I decided to set up a filing system for my financial records. That way when I have to file income taxes, I'll have all the information I need."

Amy bought a plastic box and six file folders. She labeled each file folder. These are the labels Amy used: pay stubs, W-2 forms, W-4 forms, insurance info, tax info, and miscellaneous info.

"When I get my paycheck, I tear off the stub and put it into the folder labeled pay stubs right away. It can easily get lost if I wait." Amy keeps her portable file box on her desk so it will be handy when she is ready to file something.

It's Your Turn Create a filing system for your financial papers. In place of file folders, you can use regular notebook paper folded in half. Use a cardboard shoebox to hold your financial records.

For help completing this activity, visit **ewow.glencoe.com/tips** and go to the *Smart Tip* for the Chapter 13 *Point of View*.

Payroll Taxes Are Withheld From Your Pay

There are many kinds of taxes. Taxes that are taken from your pay are called *payroll taxes.* Every worker has to pay payroll taxes.

The law says that your employer must withhold taxes from your pay. *Withhold* means take out for taxes. Your employer withholds tax money and sends it to the government.

Read Your Paycheck

Read your paycheck each time you are paid. Your paycheck has important information about your pay and your taxes.

Your paycheck will have two parts. The bottom part is the check itself. You can take your paycheck to a bank to exchange it for cash or put it into savings.

The top part is the pay stub. The *pay stub* shows how much you earned and how much you were paid. Read the pay stub in **Figure 13.1**.

Your Pay Stub Shows Your Gross Pay and Your Net Pay

gross pay ■ The amount of pay you earn.

net pay ■ The amount of pay you receive on your check.

Read your pay stub to find your gross pay and your net pay. **Gross pay** is the amount you earn. **Net pay** is the amount you receive. Net pay is sometimes called take-home pay.

Look at Viridiana Sanchez's pay stub. She worked 28 regular hours at a rate of $12.00 per hour. She worked 4 overtime hours at $18.00 per hour. How much is her gross pay for this week?

Figure 13.1

Pay Stub

Employee Name		Employee SSN		Pay Period Ending
Viridiana Sanchez		448-10-5453		12/15/09
Earnings	**Hours**	**Rate**	**Amount**	
Regular	28	12.00	336.00	
Overtime	4	18.00	72.00	
Gross Pay			**408.00**	
Deductions				
Federal Income Tax			25.84	
State Income Tax			18.56	
FICA (Social Security)			31.21	
Health Insurance			10.00	
Dental Insurance			5.00	
Total Deductions			**85.61**	
Net Pay			**322.39**	

Please detach and retain this statement. It is a record of earnings and deductions as reported to the federal and state governments.

Gross Pay and Net Pay Gross pay is what you earn. Net pay is what you receive. How many total hours did Viridiana Sanchez work this week?

Your Pay Stub Shows Your Deductions

Your pay stub also lists all of your deductions. A **deduction** is an amount taken from your gross pay.

Most deductions are for taxes. You may have deductions besides taxes, however. Some workers put money into savings. Some workers pay for health care. They pay some and the employer pays some. When you cash your paycheck, part of your expenses are already paid.

FICA Tax Is One Type of Payroll Tax

You will also see taxes on your pay stub. FICA tax is one type of tax you will see on your pay stub. **FICA** means Social Security tax. FICA stands for Federal Insurance Contribution Act. **Social Security** is a government program that helps disabled and retired people.

FICA tax is a little less than 8 percent of your pay. That means you pay about $8.00 for every $100.00 you earn.

deduction ■ An amount taken from your gross pay.

FICA ■ Social Security tax.

Social Security ■ A government program that helps disabled and retired people.

You Get Credits for Paying FICA Tax You and your employer both make FICA tax payments. Your employer puts in the same amount as you do. He or she sends the whole amount to the government.

The government keeps a record of the months you work and pay FICA tax. You get credit for the months you work. You must work a certain number of months before you can get Social Security benefits.

Social Security Helps Disabled and Retired People
The Social Security program gives four main types of benefits. Disability benefits help injured workers who will not be able to work for a year or more. Survivor benefits help the families of workers who have died. Retirement benefits help older people who no longer work.

Medical benefits help elderly people, people with disabilities, and people with kidney disease. These benefits are called *Medicare* and *Medicaid*.

While You Read

Question Why does the government keep track of how long you have paid FICA tax?

Income Tax Is Another Kind of Payroll Tax

income tax ■ Tax on the money you earn.

Another type of tax is income tax. **Income tax** is tax on the money you earn, or your *income*. The U.S. government has an income tax. Most states have an income tax. Some large cities have an income tax, too.

Internal Revenue Service (IRS) ■ The part of the federal government that collects taxes.

Federal income tax goes to the Internal Revenue Service, or IRS. The **Internal Revenue Service (IRS)** is the part of the federal government that collects taxes. State and local income tax goes to your state and local tax offices.

Look at **Figure 13.1** again. How much did Viridiana Sanchez pay in federal income tax? How much did she pay in state income tax?

While You Read

Question What things make your income tax rate go up or down?

Income Tax Rates Vary The amount of income tax you must pay is known as your income tax rate. Your tax rate depends on how much money you earn. The more you earn, the higher your tax rate will probably be.

Your tax rate depends on other things too. For example, your tax rate changes if you get married. Your tax rate changes if you have children.

Tax Rates Getting married affects your taxes. Having or adopting a child also affects your taxes. Why do you think that people who have children pay less tax than people who do not have children?

314

Figure 13.2

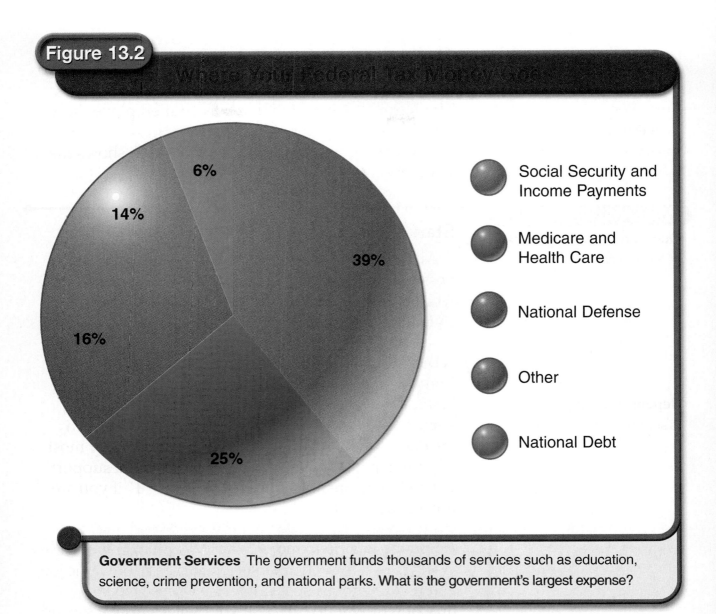

Where Your Federal Tax Money Goes

6%

14%

39%

16%

25%

- Social Security and Income Payments
- Medicare and Health Care
- National Defense
- Other
- National Debt

Government Services The government funds thousands of services such as education, science, crime prevention, and national parks. What is the government's largest expense?

Income Taxes Pay for Government Services What happens to the income tax you pay? The government spends this money on hundreds of services. For example, state income taxes pay for schools, state roads, libraries, courts, police, and prisons. State income taxes also pay for welfare programs, job services, and health services.

Federal taxes pay for programs across the country. For example, the federal government pays for Congress, national parks, national roads, the military, and health care for the poor and elderly.

Figure 13.2 shows where your federal tax money goes.

Form W-4 Affects Your Income Taxes

How does your employer know how much money to take from your pay? Your employer uses Form W-4. The **Form W-4** is a form that tells your employer how much money to withhold for taxes.

Look at **Figure 13.3** on the facing page. It shows the Form W-4 of William Yi, a young worker.

Form W-4 ■ A form that tells your employer how much money to withhold for taxes.

While You Read

Question What is the top half of the W-4 called?

Start With the Worksheet

All new employees must fill out a Form W-4. Your boss will ask you to fill out the form when you start work. Start with the top half of the form. This half is called the "Personal Allowances Worksheet."

A Dependent Is a Person Who Is Supported by Someone Else   Start with line A. Leave the line blank if you are a dependent. A **dependent** is a person who is supported by someone else. Children are dependents. If your parents or guardians pay most of your expenses, you are a dependent. If you support yourself, you are not a dependent. Write "1" if you are not a dependent.

dependent ■ A person who is supported by someone else.

A Spouse Is a Husband or Wife   Go on to line B of the W-4. Write "1" if you are married and have only one job and if your spouse does not work. Spouse means husband or wife. Write "1" if your wages from a second job or your husband's or wife's wages are $1,000 or less. Leave line B blank if these things are not true for you.

Are you married? If so, enter "1" on line C.

Line D asks you how many dependents you have. Write the number. If you have no dependents, leave lines D through G blank.

Add Up Lines A Through G   Add up all the numbers on lines A through G of your W-4. Write the total on line H. The higher the number, the less tax will be taken from your paycheck.

Figure 13.3

Personal Allowances Worksheet (Keep for your records.)

A Enter "1" for **yourself** if no one else can claim you as a dependent . . . . **A** ___1___

B Enter "1" if:
- You are single and have only one job; or
- You are married, have only one job, and your spouse does not work; or
- Your wages from a second job or your spouse's wages (or the total of both) are $1,000 or less.

. . **B** ___1___

C Enter "1" for your **spouse**. But, you may choose to enter "-0-" if you are married and have either a working spouse or more than one job. (Entering "-0-" may help you avoid having too little tax withheld.) . . . . **C** _____

D Enter number of **dependents** (other than your spouse or yourself) you will claim on your tax return . . . . **D** _____

E Enter "1" if you will file as **head of household** on your tax return (see conditions under **Head of household** above) . **E** _____

F Enter "1" if you have at least $1,500 of **child or dependent care expenses** for which you plan to claim a credit . . **F** _____
(**Note:** Do **not** include child support payments. See **Pub. 503**, Child and Dependent Care Expenses, for details.)

G **Child Tax Credit** (including additional child tax credit):
- If your total income will be between $15,000 and $42,000 ($20,000 and $65,000 if married), enter "1" for each eligible child plus **1 additional** if you have three to five eligible children or **2 additional** if you have six or more eligible children.
- If your total income will be between $42,000 and $80,000 ($65,000 and $115,000 if married), enter "1" if you have one or two eligible children, "2" if you have three eligible children, "3" if you have four eligible children, or "4" if you have five or more eligible children. **G** ___2___

H Add lines A through G and enter total here. **Note:** This may be different from the number of exemptions you claim on your tax return. ▶ **H** ___2___

For accuracy, complete all worksheets that apply.	• If you plan to **itemize or claim adjustments to income** and want to reduce your withholding, see the **Deductions and Adjustments Worksheet** on page 2. • If you have **more than one job** or are **married and you and your spouse both work** and the combined earnings from all jobs exceed $35,000, see the **Two-Earner/Two-Job Worksheet** on page 2 to avoid having too little tax withheld. • If **neither** of the above situations applies, **stop here** and enter the number from line H on line 5 of Form W-4 below.

- - - - - - - - - - - - **Cut here and give Form W-4 to your employer. Keep the top part for your records.** - - - - - - - - - - - -

Form **W-4**	**Employee's Withholding Allowance Certificate**	OMB No. 1545-0010
Department of the Treasury Internal Revenue Service	▶ **For Privacy Act and Paperwork Reduction Act Notice, see page 2.**	

1 Type or print your first name and middle initial William T.	Last name Yi	**2** Your social security number 899 51 1636

Home address (number and street or rural route) 432 S. Elm Street	**3** ☒ Single ☐ Married ☐ Married, but withhold at higher Single rate. Note: If married, but legally separated, or spouse is a nonresident alien, check the "Single" box.
City or town, state, and ZIP code San Ramon, CA 94580	**4** If your last name differs from that shown on your social security card, check here. You must call 1-800-772-1213 for a new card. ▶ ☐

5 Total number of allowances you are claiming (from line **H** above **or** from the applicable worksheet on page 2) **5** | 2

6 Additional amount, if any, you want withheld from each paycheck . . . . **6** $

7 I claim exemption from withholding for 2003, and I certify that I meet **both** of the following conditions for exemption:
- Last year I had a right to a refund of **all** Federal income tax withheld because I had **no** tax liability **and**
- This year I expect a refund of **all** Federal income tax withheld because I expect to have **no** tax liability.
If you meet both conditions, write "Exempt" here . . . . ▶ **7**

Under penalties of perjury, I certify that I am entitled to the number of withholding allowances claimed on this certificate, or I am entitled to claim exempt status.

Employee's signature
(Form is not valid unless you sign it.) ▶ *William Yi*

Date ▶ September 6, 2007

8 Employer's name and address (Employer: Complete lines 8 and 10 only if sending to the IRS.)	**9** Office code (optional)	**10** Employer identification number

Cat. No. 10220Q

Form W-4 Form W-4 has directions to help you. If you are not sure what to write, ask for help. What is the purpose of the W-4?

Fill Out the Certificate

Now fill out the bottom half of Form W-4. This half is called the "Employee's Withholding Allowance Certificate." Items 1 and 2 ask for your name, address, and Social Security number. Item 3 asks whether you are single or married.

Copy the number from line H into the box for item 5. On line 6 you can ask to have extra money taken from your paycheck.

Low-income workers may have no tax money held back at all. They are exempt from taxes. *Exempt* means free from a duty. Ask your boss if this might be true for you. If you are exempt, write EXEMPT on line 7.

Finally, sign and date the form. Your employer will fill out items 8, 9, and 10. You are done with your W-4.

Making Good Choices

To Cheat or Not to Cheat?

Melissa Peters volunteers at an animal shelter. She sometimes uses her own car to transport animals. The mileage between shelters is tax-deductible. This means that the government will take the amount of mileage and use it to reduce her taxable income. Melissa will then pay less tax. Melissa is preparing her income tax. She is thinking about reporting more miles than she actually drove.

Every year the Internal Revenue Services (IRS) examines some income tax reports. This is called an *audit*. If Melissa is caught cheating on her taxes, she could be fined or even arrested. It is illegal to cheat on your taxes.

You Make the Call Do you think it is okay to cheat on your income tax return? Why do you think people cheat even if it is illegal?

For help in answering this question, visit **ewow.glencoe.com/tips** and select the *Smart Tip* for the Chapter 13 *Making Good Choices*.

After You Read

Retell

1. Define *deduction* and list five types of deductions that you might see on your pay stub.

2. Explain who benefits from Social Security.

Think Critically

3. Your employer has to withhold tax money from your pay and send it to the government. Why do you think the government does not let you take all your pay and send your tax money on your own?

Math Practice

Deductions

Each week your gross pay is $280. Each week $10 is withheld from your paycheck to help pay for health insurance. Other deductions including taxes and FICA total 20% of your gross pay minus health insurance. What is your weekly net pay?

Step 1 Subtract the insurance deduction from your gross pay.
$280 − $10 = $270

Step 2 Calculate your other deductions.
0.20 × $270 = $54

Step 3 Subtract the adjusted pay by the total dollar amount of other deductions.
$270 − $54 = $216

Result Your net pay is $216 each week.

Figure It Out

You are promoted and move into a different tax rate. Your new salary pays $1,000 a week, gross. What is your new income tax rate if each week $280.00 is deducted? What will your net pay be each month?

Filing Your Taxes

Key Terms

income tax
return
tax liability
Form W-2
tax preparer
Form 1040EZ
refund

Main Idea

Each year you must fill out an income tax form to figure out how much tax you owe. There are several ways to get help filling out your income tax forms.

Thought Organizer

Copy the chart below. As you read, list the facts you need to know in order to fill out your income tax return.

my income

Facts I
Need to
Know

You Need to File an Income Tax Return

income tax return ■ A form that you fill out to show how much income tax you owe.

Every year you must file an income tax return. An **income tax return** is a form that you fill out to show how much income tax you owe. To *file* a tax return means to fill out the form and send it in. Your tax return reports your income for the year that has just ended.

You must file your tax return each year by April 15. You will pay a fine if you do not file a tax return. You will also pay a fine if you file your tax return late.

Your Tax Liability Is the Amount You Owe

tax liability ■ The amount of tax you owe.

The purpose of the income tax return is to figure out your tax liability. **Tax liability** means the amount of tax you owe. The W-4 form helps your employer guess your tax liability. You do not know your exact tax liability until you fill out your return.

You Need a Completed Form W-2 to File Your Return

The first step to fill out your return is to get your completed Form W-2. **Form W-2** is a form that shows how much you earned and how much your employer withheld for taxes. You need this information to fill out your tax return.

Your employer must fill out your Form W-2 and have it ready by January 31. You may get it in the mail or you may need to pick it up. You will get three copies of your W-2. You send one to the IRS. You send one to your state tax office. You keep one for your records.

Figure 13.4 shows the Form W-2 that William Yi received from his employer.

Form W-2 ■ A form that shows how much you earned and how much your employer withheld for taxes.

Figure 13.4

Form W-2

a Control number	22222	Void ☐	For Official Use Only ▶ OMB No. 1545-0008		
b Employer identification number 09-X12X0X0			1 Wages, tips, other compensation $	2 Federal income tax withheld $ 2,792
c Employer's name, address, and ZIP code Bayview Health Systems 300 Commerce Park San Ramon CA 94583			3 Social security wages $ 23,475	4 Social security tax withheld $ 1455.45
			5 Medicare wages and tips $ 23,475	6 Medicare tax withheld $ 340.39
			7 Social security tips $ 23,475	8 Allocated tips $
d Employee's social security number 899-51-1636			9 Advance EIC payment $	10 Dependent care benefits $
e Employee's first name and initial William T. Last name Yi			11 Nonqualified plans $	12a See instructions for box 12 $
			13 Statutory employee ☐ Retirement plan ☐ Third-party sick pay ☐	12b $
			14 Other	12c $
432 S. Elm Street San Ramon, CA 94580				12d $
f Employee's address and ZIP code				
15 State Employer's state ID number CA 11-X1X0X1X	16 State wages, tips, etc. $ 23,475	17 State income tax $ 1200.85	18 Local wages, tips, etc. $ 23,475	19 Local income tax $ 135	20 Locality name San Ramon
	$	$	$	$	

Form **W-2** Wage and Tax Statement (99)

Department of the Treasury—Internal Revenue Service

For Privacy Act and Paperwork Reduction Act Notice, see separate instructions.

Wage and Tax Statement You need Form W-2 to fill out your income tax return. Which part of the W-2 gives information about state income tax?

You Need a Federal Income Tax Form to File Your Federal Return

The second thing you need is a federal income tax form. The IRS has several tax forms. Form 1040 is an income tax form that all taxpayers can use.

Make sure you have an up-to-date tax form. You can get tax forms at many post offices and libraries. You can order forms from the IRS by calling 1-800-TAX-FORM.

You can also get tax forms at the Web site of the Internal Revenue Service. Find the form you want and print it. Forms are also available in Braille and in spoken format.

While You Read

Connect Does your state have income tax?

You Need a State Income Tax Form to File Your State Return   You may need a state income tax form too. You will need to file a state income tax return if you paid state income tax.

Get a state income tax form from your state tax office. Look in the blue pages of your phone book for your state's tax board or department of revenue.

You Can Get Help Filing Your Taxes

Tax forms can be complicated. Luckily, you can get help filling them out.

Tax Preparers Provide Tax Help for a Fee   Many people hire tax preparers to fill out their tax forms. A **tax preparer** is a person you can pay to fill out your tax forms.

tax preparer ■ A person you can pay to fill out your tax forms.

The IRS Offers Free Tax Help   You can also get free help with your taxes. You can call the IRS at 1-800-829-1040. You can ask questions about how to file your taxes. You can get help in English or Spanish. You can get help over a TDD machine. *TDD* stands for Telephone Device for the Deaf.

The IRS has Taxpayer Assistance Centers that offer help. Find the address and phone number of your local Taxpayer Assistance Center in the blue pages of your phone book.

Getting Tax Help
The IRS offers free tax help. Call the IRS to find out where you can get help in your community. Would you pay a tax preparer to fill out your tax forms? Why or why not?

You Can Learn to File Your Taxes Yourself

You can also file your taxes yourself. It just takes some time and practice.

Every tax form comes with directions. The directions tell you how to fill out the form. Read the directions before you fill out the form. Fill out the form slowly. Work line by line. Make sure you fill in every line.

The 1040EZ Is the Easiest Income Tax Form

One easy way to file your taxes is to use Form 1040EZ. Form 1040EZ is the simplest federal income tax form. It is only one page. You can use the 1040EZ if:

- you are single or you and your spouse are filing your return together
- you have no dependents
- you are not blind
- you make less than $50,000 a year
- you received $1,500 or less in interest (money from savings) that year

Are these things true for you? They are true for William Yi. He used the 1040EZ. Turn to page 325 to see his 1040EZ in **Figure 13.5.**

While You Read

Question How long is Form 1040EZ?

Form 1040EZ ■ The simplest federal income tax form

Study Tip

Being punctual is an important skill. Plan how much time you will need for a form or project. Then work backwards from the due date. Write down exactly what you must do each day so that you finish on time.

Fill Out Your Form 1040EZ Line by Line

Fill out Form 1040EZ line by line. Start with the top of the 1040EZ. Print or type your name, address, and Social Security number.

You can also use the address label on the outside of your tax form. The label has your name and address. You will have an address label if your form came to you in the mail.

Add Up Your Income

Write your earnings on line 1. Find your earnings on your W-2. You will have more than one W-2 if you have more than one job.

Did you receive any income from interest payments? Write the amount on line 2. Did your receive payments from the government for being unemployed? Write the amount you received on line 3. Line 4 asks you to add lines 1, 2, and 3. What is William Yi's total for line 4?

Are You a Dependent? Line 5 asks whether you are a dependent. You are not a dependent if you support yourself. Check "yes" if you are a dependent. Turn the 1040EZ form over. The worksheet on the back tells you what to do.

Check "no" on line 5 if you are not a dependent. Enter the number for whether you are single or married. Subtract line 5 from line 4. This is your taxable income. Enter the number on line 6.

While You Read

Connect Will you pay income tax this year?

Figure Out How Much Tax You Paid

Write how much federal income tax you paid on line 7. Copy the number from line 2 of your W-2.

Line 8 asks about the Earned Income Credit. The *Earned Income Credit* allows low-income workers to pay little or no tax. The 1040EZ directions tell you whether you can get the Earned Income Credit.

Line 9 asks you to add lines 7 and 8. This number is the amount of tax you have paid. How much income tax did William Yi pay last year?

Figure 13.5

Form **1040EZ** — Department of the Treasury—Internal Revenue Service — Income Tax Return for Single and Joint Filers With No Dependents (99) — OMB No. 1545-0675

Label (See page 12.) Use the IRS label. Otherwise, please print or type.

Your first name and initial: William T. Last name: Yi
Your social security number: 899 51 1636

If a joint return, spouse's first name and initial — Last name — Spouse's social security number

Home address (number and street). If you have a P.O. box, see page 12. — 432 S. Elm St. — Apt. no.

▲ **Important!** ▲ You **must** enter your SSN(s) above.

City, town or post office, state, and ZIP code. If you have a foreign address, see page 12. — San Ramon, CA 94580

Presidential Election Campaign (page 12) ▶ Note. Checking "Yes" will not change your tax or reduce your refund. Do you, or your spouse if a joint return, want $3 to go to this fund? ▶

You: ☐ Yes ☒ No   Spouse: ☐ Yes ☐ No

Income

Attach Form(s) W-2 here. Enclose, but do not attach, any payment.

1 Wages, salaries, and tips. This should be shown in box 1 of your Form(s) W-2. Attach your Form(s) W-2. — 1 — $23,475

2 Taxable interest. If the total is over $1,500, you cannot use Form 1040EZ. — 2 — 0

3 Unemployment compensation and Alaska Permanent Fund dividends (see page 14). — 3 — 0

4 Add lines 1, 2, and 3. This is your **adjusted gross income.** — 4 — $23,475

Note. You must check Yes or No. }

5 Can your parents (or someone else) claim you on their return?
Yes. Enter amount from worksheet on back. ☐
No. ☒ If **single,** enter $7,800. If **married filing jointly,** enter $15,600. See back for explanation. — 5 — $7,800

6 Subtract line 5 from line 4. If line 5 is larger than line 4, enter -0-. This is your **taxable income.** ▶ 6 — $15,675

Payments and tax

7 Federal income tax withheld from box 2 of your Form(s) W-2. — 7 — $2,792

8 **Earned income credit (EIC).** — 8 — 0

9 Add lines 7 and 8. These are your **total payments.** ▶ 9 — $2,792

10 **Tax.** Use the amount on **line 6 above** to find your tax in the tax table on pages 24–28 of the booklet. Then, enter the tax from the table on this line. — 10 — $2,001

Refund Have it directly deposited! See page 19 and fill in 11b, 11c, and 11d.

11a If line 9 is larger than line 10, subtract line 10 from line 9. This is your **refund.** ▶ 11a — $701

▶ b Routing number — ▶ c Type: ☐ Checking ☐ Savings

▶ d Account number

Amount you owe

12 If line 10 is larger than line 9, subtract line 9 from line 10. This is the **amount you owe.** For details on how to pay, see page 20. ▶ 12

Third party designee Do you want to allow another person to discuss this return with the IRS (see page 20)? ☐ **Yes.** Complete the following. ☐ **No**

Designee's name ▶ — Phone no. ▶ ( ) — Personal identification number (PIN)

Sign here Joint return? See page 11. Keep a copy for your records.

Under penalties of perjury, I declare that I have examined this return, and to the best of my knowledge and belief, it is true, correct, and accurately lists all amounts and sources of income I received during the tax year. Declaration of preparer (other than the taxpayer) is based on all information of which the preparer has any knowledge.

Your signature: William Yi — Date: 4/15/08 — Your occupation: Home Health Care Aide — Daytime phone number: (415)555-6702

Spouse's signature. If a joint return, **both** must sign. — Date — Spouse's occupation

Paid preparer's use only

Preparer's signature ▶ — Date — Check if self-employed ☐ — Preparer's SSN or PTIN

Firm's name (or yours if self-employed), address, and ZIP code ▶ — EIN — Phone no. ( )

For Disclosure, Privacy Act, and Paperwork Reduction Act Notice, see page 23. — Cat. No. 11329W — Form **1040EZ** (2003)

The Simplest Tax Form Doing your taxes is easy if you use the 1040EZ. It is only one page long. What were William Yi's total payments to the IRS this year?

Look Up Your Tax Liability in the Tax Tables

You know how much you have paid. Now you need to find out how much you owe. Find the tax tables in the 1040EZ direction booklet. Tax tables are a list of tax liability. Go to the line that has your taxable income. Find the number to the right of your income. This is the amount of tax you owe. **Figure 13.6** shows a tax table with the amount of money William Yi owes.

While You Read

Question Why would you get an income tax refund?

refund ■ A return of money.

You May Get a Tax Refund

Have you paid more tax than you owe? If so, you will get a tax refund. A **refund** is a return of money. Write your refund amount on line 11 of the 1040EZ. You will get a check from the government after you file your return.

Have you paid less tax than you owe? If so, you will owe more tax. Write the amount you owe on line 12 of the 1040EZ. Send this money with your return.

Figure 13.6

Tax Tables

If Form 1040EZ, line 6, is—		And you are—		If Form 1040EZ, line 6, is—		And you are—		If Form 1040EZ, line 6, is—		And you are—		If Form 1040EZ, line 6, is—		And you are—	
At least	But less than	Single	Married filing jointly	At least	But less than	Single	Married filing jointly	At least	But less than	Single	Married filing jointly	At least	But less than	Single	Married filing jointly
		Your tax is—				Your tax is—				Your tax is—				Your tax is—	
9,000				**12,000**				**15,000**				**18,000**			
9,000	9,050	1,004	903	12,000	12,050	1,454	1,203	15,000	15,050	1,904	1,554	18,000	18,050	2,354	2,004
9,050	9,100	1,011	908	12,050	12,100	1,461	1,208	15,050	15,100	1,911	1,561	18,050	18,100	2,361	2,011
9,100	9,150	1,019	913	12,100	12,150	1,469	1,213	15,100	15,150	1,919	1,569	18,100	18,150	2,369	2,019
9,150	9,200	1,026	918	12,150	12,200	1,476	1,218	15,150	15,200	1,926	1,576	18,150	18,200	2,376	2,026
9,200	9,250	1,034	923	12,200	12,250	1,484	1,223	15,200	15,250	1,934	1,584	18,200	18,250	2,384	2,034
9,250	9,300	1,041	928	12,250	12,300	1,491	1,228	15,250	15,300	1,941	1,591	18,250	18,300	2,391	2,041
9,300	9,350	1,049	933	12,300	12,350	1,499	1,233	15,300	15,350	1,949	1,599	18,300	18,350	2,399	2,049
9,350	9,400	1,056	938	12,350	12,400	1,506	1,238	15,350	15,400	1,956	1,606	18,350	18,400	2,406	2,056
9,400	9,450	1,064	943	12,400	12,450	1,514	1,243	15,400	15,450	1,964	1,614	18,400	18,450	2,414	2,064
9,450	9,500	1,071	948	12,450	12,500	1,521	1,248	15,450	15,500	1,971	1,621	18,450	18,500	2,421	2,071
9,500	9,550	1,079	953	12,500	12,550	1,529	1,253	15,500	15,550	1,979	1,629	18,500	18,550	2,429	2,079
9,550	9,600	1,086	958	12,550	12,600	1,536	1,258	15,550	15,600	1,986	1,636	18,550	18,600	2,436	2,086
9,600	9,650	1,094	963	12,600	12,650	1,544	1,263	15,600	15,650	1,994	1,644	18,600	18,650	2,444	2,094
9,650	9,700	1,101	968	12,650	12,700	1,551	1,268	15,650	15,700	2,001	1,651	18,650	18,700	2,451	2,101
9,700	9,750	1,109	973	12,700	12,750	1,559	1,273	15,700	15,750	2,001	1,659	18,700	18,750	2,459	2,109
9,750	9,800	1,116	978	12,750	12,800	1,566	1,278	15,750	15,800	2,016	1,666	18,750	18,800	2,466	2,116
9,800	9,850	1,124	983	12,800	12,850	1,574	1,283	15,800	15,850	2,024	1,674	18,800	18,850	2,474	2,124
9,850	9,900	1,131	988	12,850	12,900	1,581	1,288	15,850	15,900	2,031	1,681	18,850	18,900	2,481	2,131
9,900	9,950	1,139	993	12,900	12,950	1,589	1,293	15,900	15,950	2,039	1,689	18,900	18,950	2,489	2,139
9,950	10,000	1,146	998	12,950	13,000	1,596	1,298	15,950	16,000	2,046	1,696	18,950	19,000	2,496	2,146

Your Tax Liability William Yi has a taxable income of $15,675. He looks in the tax table to find his tax liability. He is single. How much does William owe the IRS?

Using the E-File System

Do you want to file your return electronically? The IRS Web site makes it easy. The first thing to do to file your income taxes online is to collect all your information. The IRS Web site will tell you what information you will need. The IRS also provides tax experts to answer any questions you have. Their help is free.

Some tax preparation and e-filing services have formed partnerships with the IRS. These services will help you file your tax return online.

Take the Next Step Work with a partner. Use a computer to access the IRS Web site. Read the information about using the e-filing system. Outline the information.

For help doing this activity, go to **ewow.glencoe.com/tips** and find the *Smart Tip* for the Chapter 13 *Real-World Connection*.

Send in Your Form Sign and date your 1040EZ. Write your occupation and phone number. Make two photocopies of the form. Keep one copy. Attach the other copy to your state income tax return. Then send the form to the IRS.

You Can File by Phone or Over the Internet

You do not have to fill out a paper income tax return. You can file your tax return by phone or over the Internet.

You can fill out a tax form on the computer and submit it over the Internet. The IRS calls this the *e-file* system.

Another way to file your return is to use the telephone. The IRS calls this the *TeleFile system*. You need a TeleFile tax package from the IRS to use TeleFile. Call (800) 829-1040 to ask for a TeleFile package.

Check your answers online by visiting **ewow.glencoe.com/review** and selecting the Section 13.2 Review.

After You Read

Retell

1. Explain why you need to fill out an income tax return after you have already filled out a Form W-4.

2. Explain why you need a completed Form W-2 to file your income tax return. Also explain how many copies of the W-2 you need, and why.

Think Critically

3. Good tax preparers have experience. Good tax preparers also know a lot about tax laws. List five ways you could find out whether a certain tax preparer has experience and knowledge.

Math Practice

Answer the multiple-choice math questions at **ewow.glencoe.com/math**.

Tax Liability

Your total tax liability is $4,030 for the year. You paid $5,000. By what percentage did you overpay the Internal Revenue Service?

Step 1 Subtract what you owed from what you paid.
$5,000 − $4,030 = $970

Step 2 Divide the difference by the total amount paid.
$970 divided by $4,030 = 0.24

Step 3 Convert the decimal point to a percentage.
0.24 × 100 = 24%

Result You overpaid by 24%.

Figure It Out

Your tax liability is $1,625, but you only paid $1,500. By what percentage did you underpay your taxes?

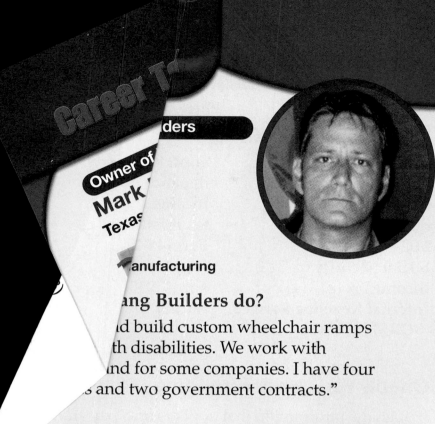

Career T-

Owner of ...ders

Mark ...

Texas...

...anufacturing

...ang Builders do?

...d build custom wheelchair ramps ...th disabilities. We work with ...nd for some companies. I have four ...s and two government contracts."

...y did you choose a career manufacturing wheelchair ramps?

"I have a spinal cord injury from an accident when I was 15. I'm a wheelchair user. I tried different jobs, but I left them because they weren't fulfilling. I did community-service work as a volunteer to build wheelchair ramps. That's how it started. I found a career I love. I have fun at work."

What obstacles have you overcome?

"At first people aren't sure I can do the work. I consider myself lucky. I'm doing better than I ever thought I would. Everything may not go well 100 percent of the time, but there's more good than bad."

What advice do you have for students?

"Find something you enjoy doing. At the end of the day—or after 40 years—it helps if you're happy."

Owner of Lang Builders

Training
Most manufacturing jobs require at least a high-school diploma or GED.

Skills and Talents
Designing and manufacturing a product requires conceptual skills. Mechanical skills and math skills also are needed. Knowledge of civil engineering may be needed. People skills also are helpful.

Career Outlook
Most manufacturing jobs are expected to decrease over the next several years through 2012.

Learn More About It
Many manufacturing jobs are now being done in other countries. Some people think this is a good idea for American workers. Some people think this is a bad idea. Research the issue. Write a one-page editorial that takes one side of the issue. Read your editorial to the class.

For help with this activity, visit **ewow.glencoe.com/tips**.

Go to **ewow.glencoe.com** to find online games and activities for Chapter 13.

Key Term Review

taxes (p. 310)
gross pay (p. 312)
net pay (p. 312)
deduction (p. 313)
FICA (p. 313)
Social Security (p. 313)
income tax (p. 314)
Internal Revenue Service (IRS) (p. 314)

Form W-4 (p.
dependent (p.
income tax retu
tax liability (p. 3
Form W-2 (p. 321)
tax preparer (p. 32,
Form 1040EZ (p. 323
refund (p. 326)

Check Your Understanding

1. List the information that appears on a pay stub.
2. Why does your employer take money from your earnings before paying you?
3. Explain how the government uses FICA and income tax money.
4. Describe the purpose of Form W-4, Form W-2, and Form 1040EZ.
5. List two ways to get help filling out tax forms.

Write About It

6. **Write About Taxes** You may be comfortable doing your own taxes. It can be a fun challenge, like a math puzzle. But should you really be doing your own taxes? Have you ever thought about hiring a tax professional to file for you? Write a paragraph describing whether you would prefer to file your taxes yourself or if you would rather hire a tax professional to do it for you. Explain your opinion.

Role Play

7. **Be a Tax Preparer**   Work in pairs. Start with two blank 1040EZ forms. One partner pretends to be a tax preparer. The other partner pretends to be a customer. As the tax preparer, explain how to file an income tax return. Explain what documents the customer needs. Help the customer fill out each line of the 1040EZ. Switch roles with your partner.

Teamwork Challenge

8. **Find Tax Help Near You**   Find out about tax help in your community. Choose either a tax preparer or a free service. Find out the name and phone number of the preparer or service. Call or visit and ask questions. For example, what tax services are offered? How much do the services cost? Prepare a report to share with your classmates.

Computer Lab

Learn About State Income Tax   Learn about your state's income tax. Visit the Web site of the income tax office for your state. Find out how much income tax your state collected last year. Then find out how your state spent this money. Make a pie chart to show how your state spent income tax last year.

Personal Career Portfolio

Fill Out Form W-4   Visit the Web site of the IRS. Find the section called "Fill-In Form W-4." Find this form by searching in Forms and Publications for "W-4." Fill out the form online. Print it out, sign and date it, and place it in your Personal Career Portfolio.

Go to **ewow.glencoe.com/portfolio** for help.

Chapter 14

Managing Your Money

You Already Know...

- earning money helps you be independent
- you will have many expenses
- it is important to save money for the future
- bank accounts can help you manage your money

You Will Learn...

- why it is important to manage your money
- how to make and follow a budget
- how to keep track of your spending
- the benefits of savings and checking accounts
- what credit is and how to use it

Personal Career Portfolio *Preview*

For your portfolio, you will make a budget on a computer spreadsheet program. As you read, think about what you will put in your budget.

Draw From Your Own Background Think about how you spend and save money. Explain whether you make a plan for your spending. Also explain whether you are happy with the way you spend and save your money. Is there anything you would like to do better?

Making a Budget

Ready, Set, Read

Key Terms

budget
expenses
savings
fixed expenses
flexible
  expenses
prioritize

Main Idea

It is important to be responsible with your money. A budget helps you spend your money wisely.

Thought Organizer

Copy the chart below. As you read, fill in the definitions of each of the terms below. Write some examples in the right-hand column.

Key Term	Definition	Examples
expenses	things you spend money on	food
savings		
fixed expenses		
flexible expenses		

Money Helps You Be Independent

It feels good to have your own money. Having your own money lets you be independent. Having your own money helps you live the lifestyle you choose.

What is money? Money is something you can exchange for goods and services.

Be Responsible With Money

Money is limited. Most people want more goods and services than they can buy. That is why you need to be responsible with your money.

Earning a paycheck is the first part of your money responsibility. Knowing what to do with this money is the second part.

Use Your Money to Reach Your Goals

Your pay may seem like a lot of money at first. Your money needs to pay for many things, however. You need to plan what you really want from your money.

Many goals cost money. Buying a car costs money. Many fun activities cost money too.

Imagine that you want to buy a car. You will need to pay for the car. You will need to pay for car insurance. You will need to pay for gas and repairs.

You will need to manage your money. You will need to watch your spending in order to save money.

Real-World Connection

Does Money Buy Happiness?

We need money for food and shelter. We need money for clothing and transportation. We also need money for extras like magazines and movies. Do we need a lot of money to be happy? No. People who have a lot of money are not happier than people who do not. Even people who win the lottery are not happier than other people. Money does not solve our problems.

Most people find happiness in work and relationships, not things. Focus on finding a career you enjoy. Focus on building relationships with family and friends. Focus on feeling good about yourself no matter how much or how little money you have.

Take the Next Step Talk to two adults you know about the value of money. Do they think that money can make a person happy? Why or why not? Write down their responses.

For help doing this activity, go to **ewow.glencoe.com/tips** and find the *Smart Tip* for the Chapter 14 *Real-World Connection*.

A Budget Helps You Manage Your Money

A **budget** is a plan to manage your money to reach your goals. Companies have budgets. Governments have budgets. Families have budgets. You need a budget too.

A budget always covers a specific time. For example, companies make their budgets for a year. Most people make their budgets for a month.

Make a budget with three columns. In column 1, list your income and expenses. List your estimates in column 2. Write the actual figure in column 3. **Figure 14.1** on page 337 shows the budget of Adena Williams. Adena goes to community college and works at a library 25 hours a week.

Make and Keep a Budget in Four Steps

Making a monthly budget is not difficult. You can make and keep a budget in four steps. Making a budget will help you plan how you spend and save money.

While You Read

Question What does *estimate* mean?

Step One Is to Estimate Your Income

Step one is to estimate your income for a month. Your income is the amount of money you will make. To *estimate* means to figure out as exactly as you can. Your income may be the same each month or it may be different each month. You need to know how much you have before you decide how much you can spend. Write your estimated income in the "estimated" column of your budget.

Income can come from many sources. You may earn wages or a salary. You may earn tips or commissions. You may receive an allowance. You may receive money from the government.

Adena Williams earns $875 per month at the library. She receives $35 from her parents to help with the bills. She also gets $250 from a student loan. Her income adds up to $1,160 a month. She writes this information at the top of her budget under "Income."

Figure 14.1

Budget With Estimated Amounts

	Estimated	Actual
Income		
Earnings	875	
Allowance	35	
Student Loan	250	
TOTAL MONTHLY INCOME	1,160	
Expenses		
Short-Term Savings	40	
Long-Term Savings	20	
Fixed Expenses		
Rent	350	
Car Payment	90	
School Tuition	65	
Utilities (electricity, gas, water)	25	
Groceries	130	
Phone	39	
Car insurance	125	
Health insurance	86	
Total Fixed Expenses	910	
Flexible Expenses		
Health care (doctor's visits, medication)	25	
Dental care (dentist's visits)	8	
Clothing	30	
Laundry	10	
Personal hygiene (haircut, makeup, etc.)	15	
School supplies (textbooks, etc.)	35	
Eating out	39	
Books and magazines	5	
Entertainment (movies, sports, etc.)	23	
Total Flexible Expenses	190	
TOTAL MONTHLY EXPENSES	1,160	

Income Equals Expenses In a balanced budget, expenses are the same amount as income. What happens if your expenses are more than your income?

Step Two Is to Estimate Your Expenses

expenses ■ Things you spend money on.

Your next step is to plan how you will spend your income. Things you spend money on are **expenses**.

There are four types of expenses: short-term savings, long-term savings, fixed expenses, and flexible expenses. Write all your estimated flexible expenses in the "estimated" column of your budget.

Short-Term Savings Is Money for Your Short-Term Goals

savings ■ Money you keep for the future.

Savings is an important expense. **Savings** is money you keep for the future.

Short-term savings is savings for your short-term goals. Imagine that you want to buy a certain item or service. It could be a DVD player, a vacation, or a pair of shoes. It could be an expensive haircut or a tune-up for your car. You need to save money for it. You need to save until you have enough to buy the item or service.

Adena Williams wants to buy a computer. She puts $40 each month into short-term savings.

While You Read

Question How much of your income should you try to save?

Long-Term Savings Is Money for Your Long-Term Goals

Long-term savings is savings for your long-term goals. What are your long-term goals? Do you want to buy a house or a car? Do you want to go to college? You need to start saving now. Save a small amount from each paycheck. You will have a good amount in just a few years.

Long-term savings also help when you have expenses you did not expect. For example, your car may break down and need to be fixed. You may lose your job.

A budget is not complete without savings. Try to save at least 10 percent of your income.

Adena does not have much money right now. However, she puts a little in long-term savings. She saves $20 each month for retirement.

Long-Term Savings Are Important for Retirement

Long-term savings are important for another reason. This reason is retirement. *Retirement* is the time in life when you are finished with your career. Most people retire at age 65 or 70. Some people save more and retire earlier. Start saving now. You will not have to worry about money when you retire.

Fixed Expenses Are the Same Every Month

Fixed expenses are basic expenses that are about the same each month. For example, you need to pay rent every month. You need to pay for *utilities* such as electricity, heat, and phone service. You need to pay for groceries. You may need to pay for health care. You need to pay for transportation. Transportation could include car payments, car insurance, parking, or bus fare.

fixed expenses ■ Basic expenses that are about the same each month.

Some Fixed Expenses Come Every Few Months

Some fixed expenses come a few times a year instead of every month. For example, Adena Williams pays $195 every three months for tuition. She divides $195 by three to get a monthly amount, $65. She writes this amount on her budget.

While You Read

Question Do all fixed expenses come once a month?

Fixed Expenses
Rent, utilities, and transportation are common fixed expenses. For example, a bus pass costs the same amount each month. What fixed expenses do you pay every month?

Flexible Expenses Change From Month to Month

flexible expenses ■
Expenses that change from
month to month.

Flexible expenses are the second type of expenses. **Flexible expenses** are expenses that change from month to month. Clothing, movies, gifts, travel, and eating out are common flexible expenses. You might go out to eat several times in January but only once in February. You might take two trips over the summer but no trips the rest of the year.

While You Read

Connect Do you ever write down what you spend?

Keep An Expense Record Estimate your flexible expenses by keeping an expense record. This is a chart that shows when and where you spend money.

Set up your expense record like Adena's expense record in **Figure 14.2**. Start with a piece of lined paper or graph paper. Draw lines up and down to make columns. Write the days of the week. Write the names of your expenses at the top of the other columns.

Carry your expense record in your wallet. Make a note every time you spend money. Add your totals at the end of the week.

Figure 14.2

Weekly Expense Record

Expense Record January 1–7, 2007

Flexible Expense / Day	Health/ Dental Care	Clothing/ Laundry	Personal Hygiene	School Supplies	Eating Out	Books/ Magazines	Entertainment	Daily Totals
Monday		$4.50	$12.37					$16.87
Tuesday				$2.99	$4.37			$7.36
Wednesday	$12.00				$6.49			$18.49
Thursday					$0.60			$0.60
Friday		$26.78				$5.37		$32.15
Saturday					$12.50		$10.00	$22.50
Sunday							$6.50	$6.50
Expense Totals	$12.00	$31.28	$12.37	$2.99	$23.96	$5.37	$16.50	$104.47

Keep Track of Your Spending An expense record will help you figure out your spending habits. How can you use weekly expense record to help you plan your budget?

Look at Your Expenses Your expense record tells you a lot about how you spend money. Most people learn that they spend more money than they thought they would. For example, you may realize that you spend a lot of money on clothes. You may realize that you spend a lot of money on magazines or snacks.

Prioritize Your Expenses You need to prioritize your spending. To **prioritize** means to decide which things are most important. You need to decide how you really want to spend your money. Can you buy fewer magazines? Can you bring your lunch instead of buying snacks?

Adena kept an expense record for one week. Her flexible expenses were $104.47. Adena noticed that she spent a lot of money on clothing, eating out, and entertainment.

Adena prioritized. She decided that clothing, eating out, and entertainment were not very important. She decided to spend less on these things. She decided that it was more important to save money for a computer. Adena budgeted $30 for clothing. She budgeted $39 for eating out. She budgeted $23 for entertainment. She wrote these numbers in the "estimated" column.

While You Read

Question How much do you think your flexible expenses would be for one week?

prioritize ■ Decide which things are most important.

Prioritize A budget shows you how much money you have to spend on fun things. Would it be hard for you to spend less money on fun things? Explain.

Step Three Is to Follow Your Budget

Now it is time to follow your budget. Keep an expense record each week. Add up your totals as you go. Make sure your spending is following your budget. Look at your budget and your expense records often. Look at your records before you spend money.

For example, imagine that Adena wants to go to the movies. Her budget gives her $23.00 for entertainment. Her expense records show that she has spent $20.00 on entertainment. That means she has only $3.00 left.

Adena decides to stick to her budget. She decides to do something that costs less money than going to a movie. She and a friend rent a DVD. Renting a DVD is cheaper than buying a movie ticket but still fun.

Keep track of all your expenses for the month. At the end of the month, write each amount on your budget sheet. Write the amounts you spent in the "Actual" column. Look how Adena did this in **Figure 14.3** on the next page.

Step Four Is to Adjust Your Budget

Follow your budget for a month. Then adjust your budget if it needs changing. To *adjust* means to make small changes.

Why would you need to adjust your budget? You may have less income than you thought. You may work fewer hours than you planned. You may have more expenses than you thought. For example, you may need to spend more on school supplies. You will need to adjust the amount of money you set aside for them.

Adena earned less this month than she thought she would. She also saved less than she wanted. She decides to adjust her budget to make it more realistic.

Stick to Your New Budget Try your new budget for a month. Then look at your budget again. Is your new budget working? Are you happy with your spending habits? Do your estimates seem accurate? Can you improve your budget even more? Adjust your budget when you need to.

Figure 14.3

Budget With Estimated and Actual Amounts

	Estimated	Actual
Income		
Earnings	875	855
Allowance	35	35
Student Loan	250	250
TOTAL MONTHLY INCOME	1,160	**1,140**
Expenses		
Short-Term Savings	40	**20**
Long-Term Savings	20	**20**
Fixed Expenses		
Rent	350	**350**
Car Payment	90	**90**
School Tuition	65	**65**
Utilities (electricity, gas, water)	25	**23**
Groceries	130	**147**
Phone	39	**39**
Car insurance	125	**125**
Health insurance	86	**86**
Total Fixed Expenses	910	**925**
Flexible Expenses		
Health care (doctor's visits, medication)	25	**25**
Dental care (dentist's visits)	8	**8**
Clothing	30	**14**
Laundry	10	**8**
Personal hygiene (haircut, makeup, etc.)	15	**12**
School supplies (textbooks, etc.)	35	**37**
Eating out	39	**43**
Books and magazines	5	**7**
Entertainment (movies, sports, etc.)	23	**21**
Total Flexible Expenses	190	**175**
TOTAL MONTHLY EXPENSES	1,160	**1,140**

Follow Your Budget Work hard to follow your budget. Check your budget and your expense records before you spend money. In what areas is Adena over budget?

Check your answers online by visiting **ewow.glencoe.com/review** and selecting the Section 14.1 Review.

After You Read

Retell

1. Explain how money helps you reach your goals.
2. What is the difference between short-term savings and long-term savings? Give specific examples.

Think Critically

3. Why might your actual expenses be different from your estimated expenses? Write down as many reasons as you can.

Math Practice

Answer the multiple-choice math questions at **ewow.glencoe.com/math**.

Fixed and Flexible Expenses

Your monthly net pay is $1,200. You spend 37% on rent, 15% on your car payment and 25% on utilities and groceries. How much money do you have remaining each month?

Step 1 Multiply your net pay by each of the fixed budget categories.
$1,200 $\times$ 0.37 = $444; $1,200 $\times$ 0.15 = $180; and $1,200 $\times$ 0.25 = $300

Step 2 Add the dollar amount for each fixed expense.
$444 + $180 + $300 = $924

Step 3 Subtract the fixed expense total from your net pay.
$1200 − $924 = $276

Result You have $276 remaining each month.

Figure It Out

Your monthly net earnings are $2,350. Your fixed expenses total 50% of your budget. Your flexible expenses total 17%. How much cash do you have left over each month?

Understanding Banking and Credit

Ready, Set, Read

Key Terms

balance

savings
  account

deposit

withdrawal

checking
  account

check

check register

account
  statement

credit

credit card

debt

debit card

Main Idea

    Bank accounts help you keep your money safe and pay for things you need. Credit has advantages and disadvantages.

Thought Organizer

    Copy the chart below. As you read, decide whether you want each of the four money tools in the chart. Write a sentence explaining why.

Money Tool	Right for You? Explain Why.
checking account	I need to pay bills each month
savings account	
credit card	
debit card	

A Bank Account Keeps Your Money Safe

    A bank account is a place where people put their money so it is safe until they need it. A bank account keeps your money from being lost or stolen.

Choose the Bank That Is Best for You

    You can open an account at a bank or credit union. A *credit union* is a bank for people who are part of the same organization. For example, some credit unions are for workers at a certain company.

    Choose a bank that offers what you want. Visit the Web sites of several banks. Research what kinds of services the bank offers. For example, many banks offer advice on money matters.

Learn About Fees, Locations, and Hours   Some banks charge fees (money) for their services. Fees are sometimes called service charges. Service charges may depend on your balance. Your **balance** is the amount of money in your bank account.

balance ■ The amount of money in your bank account.

Find out about locations and hours. Where does your bank have locations, also called branches? It is helpful to have a bank branch near home or work. Find out about the bank's hours. The bank should have hours that fit well with your schedule.

While You Read

Connect Have you ever saved money for a goal?

savings account ■ A bank account where you keep money for the future.

A Savings Account Helps You Manage Your Money

The simplest bank account is the savings account. A **savings account** is a bank account where you keep money for the future. Savings accounts earn *interest*. Your bank pays you interest in exchange for using your money. Interest makes your savings grow.

There are several types of savings accounts. Choose a savings account that fits your goals. Find out how much interest you will receive.

Find out what fees you will have to pay. Some accounts charge a fee if your balance falls below a certain amount. Some accounts charge a fee for each deposit and withdrawal. A **deposit** is money you put into your account. A **withdrawal** is money that you take from your account.

deposit ■ Money you put into your account.

withdrawal ■ Money that you take from your account.

Comparison Shop Shop around for a bank. Make sure your bank has the services you want. Why do you think some banks charge higher fees than others?

The Habit of Saving Money

Camel Hunt works as a salon assistant at a day spa. Every week Camel divides up her take-home pay and puts it into three different bank accounts.

Camel has a checking account to pay bills and buy things. Camel also has two savings accounts. "I have a long-term savings account to save for my future. I don't take money out of that account." Camel also has a short-term savings account. "I'm saving for a car," she says. "I'll take money out of that account when I have enough saved."

Every week when she gets paid, Camel puts money into each of her accounts. This way she will meet both her short-term and her long-term goals.

It's Your Turn   Take a field trip to a local bank. Ask the banker to talk to the class about how to open and use checking and savings accounts. After your field trip, write a thank-you note to the banker.

For help completing this activity, visit **ewow.glencoe.com/tips** and go to the *Smart Tip* for the Chapter 14 *Point of View*.

A Checking Account Lets You Write Checks

The other type of bank account is the checking account. A **checking account** is a bank account that lets you write checks. A **check** is a piece of paper you use to tell your bank to pay money to someone else. Your name, address, and account number are printed on your checks.

Checks come in booklets. At the back of the booklets are deposit slips. A *deposit slip* is a form you fill out when you deposit money in your account. You can also get deposit slips at the bank.

checking account ■ A bank account that lets you write checks.

check ■ A piece of paper you use to tell your bank to pay money to someone else.

Figure 14.4

Personal Check

Irma Lopez
325-A Correa Road
Plano, TX 75025

51-160
111

101

PAY TO THE
ORDER OF _____City Market_____ $ | 85.36 |

_____Eighty-five and 36/100_____ DOLLARS

MEMO _groceries_

⑆073000073⑈30 000031⑈ 00003   _Irma Lopez_

Be Safe Always fill out every part of a check before you sign it. A signed check is worth money. Why is it unsafe to send cash through the mail?

Use Checks for Bills and Purchases You can pay your bills with checks. Paying bills by check is safer than sending cash through the mail.

You can also buy things at many stores with checks. For example, most supermarkets accept checks. Turn the page to see a check that Irma Lopez used to pay for groceries.

While You Read

Visualize When was the last time you saw someone write a check to pay for something at a store?

Write a Personal Check Step by Step

Write your checks neatly and in pen. Start with the date. Write the date in the top right corner.

Now find the line that reads, "pay to the order of." Write the name of the person you need to pay.

Write the amount in numbers in the box with the dollar sign. Write out the full decimal amount. For example, write ten dollars as "10.00" rather than "10."

Write the amount in words on the second long line. Write the cent amount as a fraction. For example, Irma Lopez wrote $85.36 as "eighty-five and 36/100."

Now sign the check at the bottom right. You can also add a note at the bottom left. That helps you remember what the check is for. Irma Lopez wrote "groceries."

Record Your Checks in Your Check Register

A **check register** is a record of your checking account. Fill out your check register when you deposit money or write a check.

Look at Irma Lopez's register in **Figure 14.5**. She opened her account on April 25 with $300. On April 27 she bought groceries. She entered the check number in the "number" column. She wrote 4/27 in the "date" column. She wrote "City Market" in the "description" column.

Next, Irma wrote $85.36 in the "payment" column. She subtracted $85.36 from $300. She wrote her new balance, $214.64. On April 29 Irma deposited $50. She added this to her balance. She then had $264.64.

check register ■ A record of your checking account.

Do Not Overdraw Your Account You should always know how much money you have in your account. That keeps you from overdrawing your account. To *overdraw* your account means to write more checks than you have money for. You have to pay large fees when you overdraw your account.

When you write a check that you cannot pay, the check is returned to the bank. This is called *bouncing a check*. Your must pay large fees when you bounce a check.

While You Read

Question What is a bounced check?

Figure 14.5 Check Register

NUMBER	DATE	DESCRIPTION OF TRANSACTION	PAYMENT/DEBIT	√ T (−)	FEE (IF ANY)	DEPOSIT/DEBIT	BALANCE
	4/25						$300.00
101	4/27	City Market	$85.36				85.36
		Groceries					214.64
	4/29	Deposit				$50.00	50.00
		Gift from Aunt Frida					264.64

Stay Organized Use your check register to keep track of your checks and deposits. Why is it important to know how much money you have in your account?

account statement ■ A record of your account.

While You Read

Question How do you balance a checkbook?

An Account Statement Shows the Activity in Your Account

An **account statement** is a record of your account. The statement shows each amount you have put into your account. The statement also shows each amount you have taken out. **Figure 14.6** shows an example of an account statement for a checking account.

You will get an account statement for your account every month. Most banks also let you look at your account statement on the Internet. This makes it easy to check your account at any time.

Use Your Account Statement to Balance Your Checkbook It is important to know exactly how much money you have. That is why you need to balance your checkbook every month.

Balancing your checkbook means checking all your records. Compare the account statement with your check register. Fix any mistakes in your records. Look for any mistakes in the bank records. Tell the bank about any mistakes you find.

Figure 14.6

Account Statement

Southwestern People's Bank

Irma Lopez
325-A Correa Road
Plano, TX 75025

Statement Date: May 15, 2008

Opening Balance: $300.00
Ending Balance: $423.95
Account #: 006117-7

Date	Description	Debit (−)	Credit (+)
4/25	Deposit		$300.00
4/27	Check # 000101	$85.36	
4/29	Deposit		$50.00
5/2	ATM withdrawal	$40.00	
5/2	Electric Co. bill payment	$47.65	

Keep Good Records Keep your account statements together in a place that is easy for you to remember. Why do you think is it a good idea to save your account statements?

Endorse Your Checks You need to endorse a check before you can deposit it or cash it. Sign your name the way it is written on the front of the check. What should you do if you lose a check that someone has given you?

Visit Your Bank to Open an Account

Are you ready to open an account? Visit your local bank branch. A clerk will help you open an account. You can ask the clerk for advice about which account is best for you. Say how much money you plan to keep in your account. Say how many checks you think you will write each month.

You will fill out paperwork for the account. You will need to give your name, address, phone number, and Social Security number. The clerk will also ask you to sign a signature card. A signature card is an official record of your signature.

Deposit Money to Open Your Account You need to deposit money to open your bank account. This money will be your opening balance.

You can deposit cash or a check, such as a paycheck. You need to endorse each check before you deposit it. To *endorse* a check means to sign it on the back. Sign your name the same way it appears on the front.

While You Read

Connect Have you ever endorsed a check?

Credit Lets You Buy Now and Pay Later

credit ■ Money you can use now and pay back later.

Credit is money you can use now and pay back later. Credit lets you buy things now and pay for them later.

Loans are one form of credit. There are loans for many purposes. You might need a student loan. You might need a car loan. You might need a home loan.

credit card ■ A small plastic card that you can use to buy things on credit.

Credit cards are another form of credit. A credit card is a small plastic card that you can use to buy things on credit. Every month you get a bill for the things you bought. If you do not pay the whole bill, you owe more the next month.

Credit Cards Have Advantages

Credit cards are useful. You do not need to carry a lot of cash if you have a credit card. You can make several purchases and pay for them all at once. You can also use credit cards for emergencies.

Having a credit card is one way to build a good credit history. Pay your credit card bill on time each month. You will be able to get a loan when you need it.

While You Read

Connect Have you ever spent too much money and then regretted it?

Credit Cards Have Disadvantages

Credit cards can cause problems. Credit cards can cost money. Some credit card companies charge a yearly fee, or annual fee, to use a credit card.

Credit cards make it easy to spend too much. If you spend too much, you will not be able to pay your credit card bill. Then you will be in debt. Debt means owing someone money. You will owe money to the company that makes your credit card. You will owe the amount you borrowed plus interest.

debt ■ Owing someone money.

Interest Makes Your Debt Grow   Here is an example to show how interest works. Imagine that you buy new furniture for $1,000. You pay for it on your credit card. This is like taking a loan for $1,000. Imagine that you pay 18 percent yearly interest. If you pay $20 a month, it will take you more than seven years to pay for the furniture. Along the way you will also pay over $800 in interest.

Debit Cards Are Similar to Credit Cards

You may get a debit card with your checking account. A **debit card** is a card that takes money directly from your checking account. It is good for making everyday purchases. You can also use debit cards at ATM machines. An ATM machine is a cash machine. Do not spend more with a debit card than you have in your account. You will overdraw your account.

debit card ■ A card that takes money directly from your checking account.

Shop Around for a Credit Card

Make sure you understand all the terms of a credit card before you use it. What is the credit limit? What is the APR? The APR is the interest rate. *APR* stands for Annual Percentage Rate. You will pay a lot of interest if your card has a high APR.

Use your credit card wisely. Pay your bill on time. This will help you build a good credit history.

Making Good Choices

Being Careful With Credit Offers

Lien Lu wanted to buy a computer. He saw an ad that promised "no payments for a year." Lien talked to his dad about buying the computer. Mr. Lu asked Lien what the interest rate would be once the payments started. Mr. Lu also asked if the computer was sold for the same price in other stores. Lien did not know the answers to these questions. Mr. Lu suggested that Lien research prices and save up the money to buy the computer instead of buying it on credit.

You Make the Call Do you think Lien should buy the computer on credit? Or should he wait until he has saved enough money?

For help in answering this question, visit **ewow.glencoe.com/tips** and find the *Smart Tip* for Chapter 14 *Making Good Choices*.

Check your answers online by visiting **ewow.glencoe.com/review** and selecting the Section 14.2 Review.

After You Read

Retell

1. Explain how to open a bank account. Use your own words.

2. Explain the difference between a credit card and a debit card.

Think Critically

3. Why is it a good idea to know how much money you have in your checking account? Think of as many reasons as you can.

Math Practice

Answer the multiple-choice math questions at **ewow.glencoe.com/math**.

Balancing Your Savings

At the beginning of the month you have $345 in your savings account. You make three deposits in the amounts of $45, $40, and $32. You make two withdrawals in the amounts of $200 and $135. What is your balance at the end of the month?

Step 1 Add all the deposits you made during the month to the beginning balance.
$45 + $40 + $32 + $345 = $462

Step 2 Add all the withdrawals you made during the month.
$200 + $135 = $335

Step 3 Subtract the total withdrawals from the balance.
$462 − $335 = $127

Result Your balance is $127.

Figure It Out

Your checking account shows a balance of $560.00 at the beginning of the month. You make 2 deposits in the amounts of $115 and $225. You write seven checks for a total of $656.23. What is your balance?

Senior Vice President and General Manager of Lee Hecht Harrison

John Bateman-Ferry
New York

Career Cluster: Marketing, Sales, and Service

What does your company do?

"We help people with career management and career transitions. My job is the marketing and sales of our services to the community. I also am the manager of a staff of 15."

Why did you choose a career in marketing and sales?

"Most of my life I prepared to be a New York City firefighter like my dad. A car accident left me paralyzed from the waist down. One day I was walking and knew what I wanted. The next day I was disabled. I never want anybody to have that feeling of not knowing what's next. People feel like that after losing their job. I can help them."

What obstacles have you overcome?

"I have to work harder to get people to accept that I can do the work. Sitting in a wheelchair has nothing to do with how well I perform on the job."

What advice do you have for students?

"Have a plan. Know where resources and advocates are in case you need them. Believe in yourself."

Senior Vice President and General Manager of Lee Hecht Harrison

Training
College graduates with related experience, a high level of creativity, and strong communication skills should have good job opportunities in this area.

Skills and Talents
Listening and communication skills are needed in sales and marketing. English and math skills are also needed.

Career Outlook
Employment of marketing and sales managers is expected to grow faster than average through 2012.

Learn More About It
Sales and marketing careers can take you anywhere in the world. Think about a place in the world where you would like to work. Think about what product or service you would like to market. Write a one-page essay about the job and the country you have chosen.

For help with this activity, visit **ewow.glencoe.com/tips**.

Glencoe
Online

Go to **ewow.glencoe.com**
to find online games and
activities for Chapter 14.

Key Term Review

budget (p. 336)
expenses (p. 338)
savings (p. 338)
fixed expenses (p. 339)
flexible expenses (p. 340)
prioritize (p. 341)
balance (p. 346)
savings account (p. 346)
deposit (p. 346)
withdrawal (p. 346)

checking account (p. 347)
check (p. 347)
check register (p. 349)
account statement
  (p. 350)
credit (p. 352)
credit card (p. 352)
debt (p. 352)
debit card (p. 353)

Check Your Understanding

1. Explain why it is important to manage your money.
2. List the four steps to make and follow a budget.
3. Describe a tool you can use to keep track of your spending.
4. Describe the benefits of savings and checking accounts.
5. Explain what credit is and how to use it wisely.

Write About It

6. **Describe Your Goals**   On page 335 you read this sentence: "Many goals cost money." Write a paragraph describing your goals. Talk about your short-term goals and your long-term goals. List all your goals that will require money. Then list all your goals that will not require money.

Role Play

7. **Play a Financial Planner**   Work with a partner. One student plays a financial planner. A financial planner is a worker who helps people use their money wisely. As the financial planner, ask your "client" about his or her long-term goals. Pick the goal that will cost the most money. Help the client plan how he or she will achieve this goal.

Teamwork Challenge

8. **Research Banks**   Find a local bank or credit union. Research the types of accounts they offer. Make a chart describing the plusses and minuses of each type of account. Include information on opening balance, minimum balance, and fees.

Computer Lab

Make an Expense Record   Use a spreadsheet or budgeting program to make an expense record for one week. Use the headings shown in **Figure 14.2** on page 340. Enter all your numbers for the week. Use formulas to add up your totals. Then graph your spending. Show how much you spent on each type of expense.

Personal Career Portfolio

Make a Budget   Use **Figure 14.3** on page 343 to design a budget. Use a spreadsheet program or word-processing program if you can. Estimate all your income and expenses. Put your budget in your Personal Career Portfolio. Make a copy of your budget and keep it with you. Follow your budget for one month.

Go to **ewow.glencoe.com/portfolio** for help.

Chapter 15

Using Technology

You Already Know...

- technology is important in the world of work
- all workers need computer skills
- computers help in many kinds of jobs
- special technology can help people with disabilities

You Will Learn...

- the five parts of a personal computer
- the uses of peripherals and office machines
- the use of several types of computer programs
- what assistive technology is
- why computer ethics are important

Personal Career Portfolio Preview

For your portfolio, you will make a chart of the types of technology you know how to use. As you read, think about what types of hardware and software you have used in the past.

Before You Read

Preview Skim the chapter. Read every blue heading. Make a list of subjects that you will read about in this chapter. Work with a classmate to compare lists.

Technology Basics

Ready, Set, Read

Key Terms

technological
  literacy
personal
  computer (PC)
hardware
disk drive
peripheral
scanner
voice mail
fax machine

Main Idea

Computers are the most important form of technology. Computer systems and peripherals let you input and output information.

Thought Organizer

Copy the chart below. As you read, fill in the five parts of a computer system and their definitions.

Parts of a Computer System

CPU

Technology Plays a Role in Every Job

You know you need literacy to get a good job. Literacy is the ability to read, speak, and write. Did you know you also need technological literacy? **Technological literacy** is the ability to work with technology. Technology is knowledge and tools that make it possible to do new things. People who are technologically literate understand how technology works. People who are technologically literate are also good at learning how to use new technology.

Think about the kinds of technology you use or observe. Our world uses more and more technology each day. You will probably use and observe even more technology when you enter the world of work.

technological literacy ■
The ability to work with technology.

Computers Are a Type of Technology

A *computer* is a machine that stores and processes data such as words, numbers, and pictures. Workers use computers to create, calculate, and organize information.

You do not have to know a lot about computers to start using them. However, the more you know, the more you will be able to do.

PCs Are Computers for Work, School, and Home

There are many types of computers. Some computers are so large that they take up an entire room. Many people can use these computers at the same time.

Most people use PCs, however. A **personal computer (PC)** is a small computer made for a single person to use. PC stands for personal computer.

PCs Come in Three Sizes   PCs fit on a desk or in a small case. PCs that fit on your desk are called desktop computers. Desktops are the size of a large cereal box.

PCs that fit on your lap are called laptop computers. Laptops are the size of a thick spiral notebook.

PCs that fit in your hand are called palmtops or handhelds. They are the smallest PCs.

While You Read

Question What are the three sizes of PCs?

personal computer (PC) ■
A small computer made for a single person to use.

Personal Digital Assistant A PDA can help you stay organized. A PDA can store names, phone numbers, and tasks. How do you remember names, phone numbers, and tasks?

Hardware Is the Physical Parts of a Computer

Hardware is the physical parts of a computer system. Most PCs have five basic parts. The five parts are CPU, monitor, keyboard, mouse, and disk drive. **Figure 15.1** shows the five parts of a desktop PC.

The *CPU* is the brain of the computer. CPU stands for Central Processing Unit.

The *monitor* is a screen that shows text and graphics.

The *keyboard* is a set of keys that you use to type letters, numbers, and symbols.

The *mouse* is a handheld device that you use to point to areas of the screen. Some people use a touchpad, joystick, or mouth stick instead of a mouse.

Figure 15.1 — The Parts of a Computer

These parts are found on most desktop computers. The location of some parts will vary.

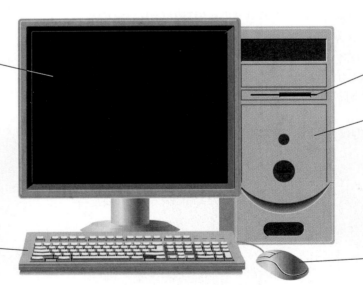

Monitor: Output device that displays text and graphics on a screen.

Keyboard: Input device with an arrangement of letter, figure, symbol, control, function, and editing keys and a numeric keypad.

Disk drive: Input/output device that reads data from and writes data to disk.

CPU (Central Processing Unit): Internal operating unit or "brain" of computer.

Mouse: Input device used for commands and navigation.

Five Basic Parts The CPU, monitor, keyboard, mouse, and disk drives are the five basic parts of a computer system. How could a mouth stick be helpful to people with mobility impairments?

Making a Dream Come True

When he was 14, Fischel Goldstein was paralyzed in a car accident. "I always dreamed of being a lawyer," Fischel says. "For a long time I didn't think that dream would come true."

Fischel learned to use a mouth stick. A mouth stick is a wooden dowel with an eraser on one end and a tube on the other. "I use the mouth stick to type on the computer," Fischel says. "I also use the mouth stick to move papers and turn pages in books."

Fischel now believes in his dream. "I've been accepted to law school. I start a month after I graduate from college."

It's Your Turn Research one type of technology that might help a person with paralysis perform everyday or work tasks. Create a poster that shows when and how this device is used.

For help completing this activity, visit **ewow.glencoe.com/tips** and go to the *Smart Tip* for the Chapter 15 *Point of View*.

A Disk Drive Stores Your Work The fifth part of a computer system is the disk drive. A **disk drive** is a machine that reads from disks and writes to disks. A disk is like a file cabinet. A disk can be full, empty, or in between. You should save your work to a disk to keep from losing it.

Computers have a *hard drive* in the CPU. The hard drive is usually not portable. That means it cannot be taken out of the computer.

Most computers also have disk drives for portable disks. Portable disks include compact disks (CDs), digital video disks (DVDs), and floppy disks. A floppy disk looks like a small plastic square.

disk drive ■ A machine that reads from and writes to disks.

 ewow.glencoe.com/tips

Input and Output
Printing or embossing your work is one way of sharing it with others. You can also send it to another person over the Internet or save it onto a disk. What is the difference between a printer and a Braille embosser?

Peripherals Let You Use a Computer in Many Different Ways

There are many types of hardware beyond the basics. A piece of hardware you can connect to a computer is called a **peripheral**.

Peripherals help with input and output. *Input* is information that you put into the computer. *Output* is information you take from the computer.

peripheral ■ A piece of hardware you can connect to a computer.

Peripherals Let You Put Information Into the Computer

Some peripherals are called input devices. *Input devices* let you put information into the computer. For example, a microphone lets you put words and sounds into a computer. A joystick or mouse changes your hand movements into actions on the computer screen. A **scanner** is a machine that copies words and pictures from paper into a computer.

scanner ■ A machine that copies words and pictures from paper into a computer.

While You Read

Question What do output devices do?

Peripherals Let You Take Information From the Computer

Other peripherals are called output devices. *Output devices* let you see, hear, or feel your work. For example, speakers let you hear words and sounds. A printer or Braille embosser lets you put your work on paper.

Peripherals Let You Share Information Some peripherals give input and output. For example, a rewritable CD lets you put information into the computer. It also lets you copy and store information from the computer.

A modem lets you send and receive information. A *modem* is a peripheral that links computers by wires or cables. Some modems work over phone lines. Other modems work over special digital lines. Physical lines are called *land lines.* You can also get onto the Internet with a wireless modem.

Real-World Connection

What Is Wireless Computing?

Wireless computing lets you use a wireless modem to connect to a computer network without having to be physically plugged into a land line. Once you are connected, you can access files you have on a distant network or connect to the Internet.

Wireless computing lets you use your computer almost anywhere. With wireless technology, travelers can send e-mails in an airport from their laptop computer. Taxi drivers can receive instructions with a PDA. Do you use a cell phone? When you use your cell phone to send a message or a photo, you are using wireless computing.

Take the Next Step Make a list of questions you want to ask about wireless computing. Visit a wireless technology store. Ask an employee to demonstrate wireless computing products. Take notes. Share what you learned with a classmate.

For help doing this activity, go to **ewow.glencoe.com/tips** and find the *Smart Tip* for the Chapter 15 *Real-World Connection.*

Keyboarding is inputting information into a computer using the keyboard. Keyboarding skills are important at school and at work. Improve your keyboarding skills by practicing. Take every opportunity to use a computer at school and at home.

voice mail ■ A system that lets people leave spoken messages when you cannot take a phone call.

While You Read

Connect Have you ever used a touch screen?

fax machine ■ A machine that sends and receives printed information over the telephone.

Today's Office Machines Work Like Computers

Office machines include telephones, photocopiers, and fax machines. All workers need to know how to use these machines.

Today's office machines are a lot like computers. They have small computers inside them. You control the machine by telling the small computer inside what to do.

Voice Mail Lets You Send and Receive Voice Messages   Most of today's telephone systems have voice mail. Voice mail is a system that lets people leave spoken messages when you cannot take a phone call. Voice mail messages are stored in computer memory. You can save a message for a long time. You can share a message with someone else. You can erase a message when you are finished with it.

Photocopiers Scan and Print   Today's photocopiers are like scanners with printers attached. You open the lid and put the paper face-down on the glass. Then you select the options you want from a touch screen. A *touch screen* is a monitor that responds to touch. For example, you can choose how many copies you want. You can choose the paper size. You can make copies lighter or darker. You can make a document bigger or smaller. You can print it on different-sized paper. A small computer in the photocopier stores and remembers your choices.

Fax Machines Send Documents Over the Phone
A fax machine is a machine that sends and receives printed information over the telephone. *Fax* is short for facsimile, which means a copy. A fax machine is like a phone plus a scanner and a printer. When you send a fax, the machine scans your page and sends the information over the phone. The fax machine on the other end prints the page.

Check your answers online by visiting **ewow.glencoe.com/review** and selecting the Section 15.1 Review.

After You Read

Retell

1. Define PC and describe the three sizes of personal computers.
2. Some office machines are printers, scanners, fax machines, and photocopiers all in one. Explain what tasks these machines can do.

Think Critically

3. Do you prefer to keep records on paper or on the computer? Why?

Math Practice

Answer the multiple-choice math questions at **ewow.glencoe.com/math**.

Interest

You take out a loan to buy a computer system. The loan amount is $8,000. The rate of interest is 8%. The term is for six years. How much interest will you pay?

Step 1 Multiply the loan amount by the rate of interest to determine the interest each year.
$8,000 × 0.08 = $640

Step 2 Multiply the interest each year by the term.
$640 × 6 = $3,840

Result You will pay $3,840 in interest. The total cost of the computer system will be $11,840.

Figure It Out

You purchase accessories for your computer. You borrow $1,200 at a rate of 0.20 that is calculated monthly. You pay for the equipment over a 12-month period. What is the interest? What is the total cost of the accessories?

Computer Applications

Key Terms

software
file
folder
word
  processing
graphics
spreadsheet
database
e-mail
assistive
  technology
computer
  ethics

Main Idea

Software applications are tools that let you do specific tasks on the computer. Understanding assistive technology and computer ethics is part of technological literacy.

Thought Organizer

Copy the chart below. As you read, fill in the blanks with the names of the applications described in the chapter.

Applications

1. word processing
2. _____
3. _____
4. _____
5. _____
6. _____

Software Makes Computers Work

software ■ A set of instructions for a computer.

Hardware is one part of computers. Software is the other part of computers. Software is a set of instructions for a computer.

All computers use software called an operating system. An *operating system* is a program that directs the computer's activities. It also controls how the hardware and software work together. Most PCs use either Microsoft® Windows or Mac OS. Windows is used on IBM-compatible PCs. Mac OS comes with Apple computers. Both of these programs use windows. The picture on page 371 shows a window.

Computers also use software called applications. *Applications* are programs for specific tasks. There are applications for all kinds of tasks. Web designers use software to design Web sites. Accountants use software to write checks and file tax returns.

Explore Icons and Menus

One way to learn software is to experiment with a program. Most software is easy to use. You use icons and menus to make your choices. An icon is a small picture that you click on to take an action. For example, you can click on an icon of a printer to print a document.

A menu is a list of options. For example, the "File" menu gives you the choice to open, close, or save a document. Most programs have a "Help" menu with information about using the program.

Use Files and Folders to Organize Your Work

A document you name and save using software is called a **file**. You save a file by giving it a name and a location. The location can be any drive, such as the hard drive or the CD drive. Save your files often so that you do not lose any work. It is a good idea to save two copies of a file. Save one copy on a CD or a floppy disk.

Create folders on each disk to organize your files. A **folder** is a group of related files. Folders make it easy to find the files you need. Putting computer files in folders is like putting paper files in folders. All these folders go onto a disk, which is like a filing cabinet.

Give your files and folders names that are easy to remember. Use the "Search" or "Find" feature if you lose track of your work.

Save Your Work
This computer user is saving files. Why is it a good idea to save your files on a CD or floppy disk?

Word-Processing Programs Let You Create Text and Graphics

word processing ◼ Writing and editing text on the computer.

Word-processing programs are the most common type of software. Word processing is writing and editing text on the computer. A word-processing program lets you type, move sentences around, check your spelling, and more.

At work you can use word-processing programs to write letters and reports. You can add tables and columns to make your document more interesting. You can also add graphics. Graphics are pictures and symbols. Drawings, charts, and photos are types of graphics. You can even add multimedia. *Multimedia* means two or more media such as text, graphics, sound, and video.

graphics ◼ Pictures and symbols.

Word-processing programs let you choose from many interesting fonts. A font is a special style of letters and numbers. The font of the text you are reading right now is called Palatino. You can change the font size and color. You can also add **bold**, *italics*, or underlining.

While You Read

Question How could a spreadsheet program help you keep a budget?

spreadsheet ◼ A program that works with numbers and math functions.

Spreadsheet Programs Let You Organize Numbers

A spreadsheet is a program that works with numbers and math functions. Spreadsheets are useful for keeping records. A teacher might use a spreadsheet to keep records of students' scores. Businesspeople could use a spreadsheet to keep a record of money earned and spent.

Spreadsheets are flexible. You can add or delete rows and columns. You can make columns wider or narrower. You can also add formulas. A *formula* is a math function. A formula can add, subtract, multiply, or divide.

Spreadsheets use rows and columns to organize information. Each column has a letter such as A, B, or C. Each row has a number such as 1, 2, or 3. When a column and a row form a rectangle, it is called a *cell*. The photo on the next page shows a group of cells.

	A	B	C	D	E	F
1	River	Continent	Miles	Kilometers		
2						
3	Nile	Africa	4145	6669		
4	Amazon	South America	4000	6436		
5	Yangtze	Asia	3964	6378		
6	Mississippi	North America	3740	6017		
7	Yenisei-Angara	Asia	3442	5538		

Columns and Rows This small spreadsheet shows information about the five longest rivers in the world. Each row lists a different river. Each column lists a piece of information about the river. What information is in cell A6?

Databases Let You Store, Sort, and Find Information

A **database** is a collection of information on a certain topic. A database could be a contact list. A database could be information about items for sale in a store.

Each column in a database is called a *field*. Each field has one type of information. For example, a field might contain names, phone numbers, or addresses. Each row in a database is called a *record*. A record is a group of fields. A record might contain a person's name, phone number, address, and e-mail address.

Databases let you search your information to find what you need. Databases also let you sort your information in different ways. For example, you could sort your contacts by last name or by addresses.

A database is a good way to keep information organized. For example, you might use a database to keep track of your job leads. You could input information for each lead. You could sort jobs by company type or company name.

You will probably use a database at work. Stores and other companies use databases to keep track of customers and process orders. They use databases to figure out what kinds of products or services they have.

database ■ A collection of information on a certain topic.

Presentation Software Helps You Give Oral Reports

Presentation software lets you give multimedia computer reports. Each display in a presentation is called a *slide*. You can make a short presentation with a few slides or a long presentation with many slides. Your slides can have text, art, photos, sound effects, and video clips. You can also add links to Web sites.

You can present your slide show on your computer. You can also project your slide show on the wall or on a screen.

While You Read

Connect Where do you go to use the Internet?

Web Browsers Let You Explore the World Wide Web

You need a Web browser and an *ISP* to connect to the Internet. A *Web browser* is software that lets you view Web pages. An ISP is a service that lets you connect to the Internet. ISP stands for Internet Service Provider. America Online is one well-known ISP. You pay a fee each month to an ISP for the Internet service.

Communications Software Lets You Share Information

Communications software lets you communicate with other computer users. For example, some programs let you receive faxes on your computer.

The most popular way to communicate by computer is e-mail. **E-mail** is sending and receiving messages by computer. E-mail is short for electronic mail. You can use e-mail to send and receive text and graphics. You can also attach files to e-mails to share them with others. You can create folders in your e-mail program to store messages you want to save.

e-mail ■ Sending and receiving messages by computer.

You need an e-mail account to send and receive e-mail. Several Web sites offer free e-mail accounts. You can use these accounts to send, receive, and store e-mails. You will need to create a *username* and password for your account. A username identifies you. It is usually the first part of your e-mail address.

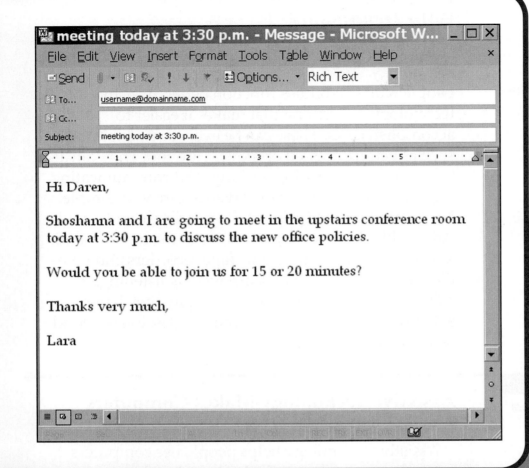

Send an E-Mail   Start an e-mail message by opening a new message window. Most e-mail programs have a "New" icon you can click to start a new message.

Now enter the e-mail address of a recipient. Your message will be returned to you if the address is not correct. You can enter one or more addresses on the *To*: line. You can also enter one or more addresses on the *Cc*: line. *CC* stands for "carbon copy." Use this line for people who you want to see the message.

Write the subject of the e-mail on the subject line. The subject line lets people know what the message is about. Write your text in the message window. You can also copy text from a word-processing program.

Reread your message before you click "Send." Make sure your message is clear and polite.

Assistive Technology Helps People With Disabilities

assistive technology ■
Tools that help people with disabilities function better.

Another important kind of technology is assistive technology. **Assistive technology** is tools that help people with disabilities function better. Assistive technology is anything that makes it easier to accomplish tasks. These can be everyday physical tasks such as getting dressed or moving around. They can also be tasks such as reading, writing, and communicating.

Some assistive technology devices are very simple. For example, pencil grips make pencils easier to hold. Adjustable desks let each person put the monitor and keyboard at the right height. Tape recorders and tape players help people who learn well by listening. Talking calculators help people be sure they have entered the right numbers. Even eyeglasses are a kind of assistive technology.

While You Read

Visualize What would it feel like to type with one hand?

Assistive Technology Makes Computers Accessible to Everyone

Assistive technology helps people use computers better. For example, special keyboards help people who need to type with one hand. Mini keyboards help people who have limited motion.

Many Web sites are designed to help people with disabilities. For example, graphics on Web pages can help people who learn better through pictures than words. Text-only versions of Web sites describe pictures and graphics using words. This helps people with vision impairments.

Spell-check and grammar-check in word-processing programs help people who need help with writing. Screen enlargers let people with vision impairments see text more easily.

A lot of software has assistive technology features. For example, most Web browsers let you choose a font that is the best size for your eyesight. Most operating systems let you input commands and information with a microphone or touch screen.

Computers Are for Everyone New technology makes using computers easier to learn. Here a group of students is learning how to use the Internet by listening to a recording. Do you learn better by reading or by listening? Explain.

Computers Can Read Text Out Loud *Screen readers* let computers speak text out loud. This helps people who have vision impairments. They can also hear descriptions of pictures and moving graphics. Hearing text is also helpful for people who are better listeners than readers. It can also help people who like to read and listen at the same time.

Computers Can Understand Spoken Words
Voice-recognition software lets people use a microphone instead of a keyboard. You talk into a microphone. The computer changes the sounds into typed text. You can then read the text and fix any mistakes you might find. Voice-recognition software helps people who have trouble writing or typing on a keyboard.

While You Read

Question Who could benefit from voice-recognition software?

Computer Ethics Are Standards of Right and Wrong Computer Use

Computers are powerful tools. The way you use computers can affect other people. That is why it is important to think about computer ethics. **Computer ethics** are standards of right and wrong computer use.

Computer hackers are people who do not follow computer ethics. They break into a computer systems without permission. They may break into a system just for fun. They may break into a system to steal money or information.

Computer hacking is against the law. Some hackers try to spread computer viruses to other people's computers. A *computer virus* is a program that goes onto your computer without your knowledge and destroys or changes information. Most computer viruses are transmitted, or passed on, by e-mail. Be careful about opening e-mails or documents that come from people you do not know.

computer ethics ■
Standards of right and wrong computer use.

While You Read

Connect Have you ever used a computer that was part of a network?

Respect Other People's Work

You may work on a computer network at your job. A *network* is two or more computers linked together. There may be files from many different people stored on the network. Do not look at other people's files without permission. Do not delete files or programs that belong to others.

Respect Copyrights Most software programs have a copyright. The © symbol tells you that a product has a copyright. This means that a person or company owns the software. You need permission to copy this software. Copying or using software without permission is called *software piracy*. It is stealing from the developer of the software.

People's ideas belong to them too. You are stealing if you copy other people's words or graphics without permission. Always list the source when you use text or graphics from the Internet.

Abdel Yassin works in an insurance company. He needed an immediate answer about an account when he was away from his desk. He asked Sylvia if he could use her computer. Sylvia agreed to let Abdel use her computer while she was at the copy machine. Abdel accidentally saw an e-mail on Sylvia's computer. The e-mail stated that Sylvia was stealing company funds. Abdel thought he should report the theft, but he worried he would get into trouble because it is against company policy to look at coworkers' e-mail.

You Make the Call What options does Abdel have in this situation? What do you think Abdel should do?

For help in answering this question, visit **ewow.glencoe.com/tips** and find the *Smart Tip* for Chapter 15 *Making Good Choices*.

Follow Your Company's Computer Rules

Most companies have rules for how their workers can use their work computers. For example, you should not use work e-mail for personal messages. You should not reveal secret information about your company. You should not surf the Internet on work time. Never use e-mail or the Internet for inappropriate content. You could be fired. Your company could be sued.

Use E-Mail Etiquette   Be careful when you write e-mail. Write when you are calm, not when you are in a hurry or upset. Use standard English. Be brief and clear. Use correct grammar, spelling, and punctuation. Do not write in all capital letters. People will think you are shouting.

Remember that your writing reflects on your company. Be polite. Sign your e-mail with your name.

 ewow.glencoe.com/tips

Check your answers online by visiting **ewow.glencoe.com/review** and selecting the Section 15.2 Review.

After You Read

Retell

1. Describe the two main types of softwa▢
2. Explain why companies have rules sayin▢ workers can and cannot do with company▢ and Internet programs.

Think Critically

3. Making a copy of copyrighted software is called piracy. It is illegal. Do you think it is wrong to use software you did not buy? Why or why not?

Math Practice

Answer the multiple-choice math questions at **ewow.glencoe.com/math**.

Computers at Work

You use your computer to track your business's gross income and net income. If your gross sales for one year totals $56,000 and the company's income tax is 29%, what is the net profit?

Step 1 Multiply gross sales by the income tax.
$56,000 × 0.29 = $16,240

Step 2 Subtract the income tax from the gross profits.
$56,000 − $16,240 = $39,760

Result Net profits equal $39,760.

Figure It Out

Your business will donate 12% of its net profit to the community for every dollar it makes over $250,000. If the company makes $467,982, what is the total amount that will be donated?

Career Facts

Chemist

Judy Summers-Gates

Pennsylvania

Career Cluster: Science, Technology, Engineering, and Mathematics

What does a chemist do?

"I work in a lab. I analyze color additives in food, cosmetics, anything with color added. I work for the Food and Drug Administration. We make sure the color added to products is safe for consumers."

Why did you choose a career as a chemist?

"I was always fascinated with what things are made of. When I was a little kid I had a million questions. I wanted to know things like why bananas grow on trees and peanuts grow underground."

What obstacles have you overcome?

"Because of damage from multiple sclerosis, I have attention deficit disorder. Also I'm visually impaired, have non-clotting blood so I bleed for hours when I'm bruised, and I use either crutches or a wheelchair. People think I can't do something, or wouldn't want to do something because of my disability."

What advice do you have for students?

"Don't buy into the negative expectations people have of you. Even if something is hard, you can get through it."

Chemist

Training
A bachelor's degree in chemistry or a related field is required. Many research jobs require a master's degree or a Ph.D.

Skills and Talents
Chemists need good science and math skills. Curiosity, creativity, and attention to detail are also helpful.

Career Outlook
Employment of chemists will grow at an average rate through 2012. There will be jobs in medicine and in scientific research.

Learn More About It
Work with a partner. Use the Internet to research careers in science, technology, engineering, or mathematics. With your partner, design a graphic organizer that shows different jobs under one of these main four careers. Include the title of the job, a short description, the job outlook, and education needed. Display your graphic organizers around the room.

For help with this activity, visit **ewow.glencoe.com/tips**.

Glencoe Online

Go to ewow.glencoe.com to find online games and activities for Chapter 15.

Key Term Review

technological literacy (p. 360)
personal computer (PC) (p. 361)
hardware (p. 362)
disk drive (p. 363)
peripheral (p. 364)
scanner (p. 364)
voice mail (p. 366)
fax machine (p. 366)
software (p. 368)

file (p. 369)
folder (p. 369)
word processing (p. 370)
graphics (p. 370)
spreadsheet (p. 370)
database (p. p. 371)
e-mail (p. 372)
assistive technology (p. 374)
computer ethics (p. 376)

Check Your Understanding

1. Sketch and label the five parts of a personal computer.

2. List and define three peripherals or office machines.

3. Describe the main uses of word-processing software, database software, spreadsheet software, and presentation software.

4. Define assistive technology and give two examples.

5. Explain why it is important to use computers ethically.

Write About It

6. **Write an Acceptable Use Policy** An acceptable use policy says what workers may and may not do on their work computers. For example, it says what types of Web sites workers may visit. It says what types of things they should not say in e-mail. Pretend that you are starting a company. Write an acceptable use policy for your employees.

Role Play

7. **Show Your Technology Skills** Work with a partner. One student plays an interviewer. The other student plays a job applicant. As the interviewer, ask the applicant specific questions about his or her computer skills. As the applicant, describe the hardware, software, and office machines you know how to use.

Teamwork Challenge

8. **Set Up an Office** Imagine that you and your team want to start a business. You need office machines and a computer. Plan what your business will do and what hardware and software you will need. For example, will you need word-processing software? Will you need a scanner? Write a summary of the technology you will need. Research prices on the Internet and add them to your plan.

Computer Lab

Make a Web Page Most word-processing programs let you create simple Web pages. Use a word-processing program to format your résumé as a Web page. Format your résumé with graphics.

Personal Career Portfolio

Create a Technology Skills Chart Use a spreadsheet to make a chart of the technology you know how to use. Make a chart with three columns. In the first column, list the name of the technology. In the second column, give the definition of the technology. In the third column, explain how much experience you have with the technology.

Go to **ewow.glencoe.com/portfolio** for help.

Chapter 16

Planning Your Future

You Already Know...

- living on your own makes you more independent
- renting an apartment costs money
- doing community activities is fun
- many agencies offer help in your community
- voting is a citizen's right

You Will Learn...

- the meaning of self-determination and independence
- four things to consider when you rent a place to live
- how to get involved in your community
- several sources of help in your community
- how to register and cast a ballot

Personal Career Portfolio ⟩ Preview

For your portfolio, you will make a transition plan for your life after high school. As you read, think about how you would like your life to be in the future.

Living on Your Own

Ready, Set, Read

Key Terms

transition plan
self-
   determination
independence
commute
lease
utilities
security deposit

Main Idea

You may choose to live at home, with a roommate, or on your own. There are many tasks and costs involved in renting your own place.

Thought Organizer

Copy the chart below. Write what you would like and dislike about living on your own.

I would like	I would dislike
• more independence	• more expenses
• _____	• _____
• _____	• _____
• _____	• _____
• _____	• _____
• _____	

Prepare for Life After High School

transition plan ■ A plan that lists your goals for after high school and says how you will reach those goals.

The end of high school is a time of transition, or change. Do you have a transition plan? A transition plan is a plan that lists your goals for after high school and says how you will reach those goals. All students with an Individual Education Plan (IEP) have a transition plan. Everyone should have a plan for after high school.

You need to answer some important questions as you make your plan. Will you continue your education? Will you work full-time or part-time? Will you live at home, on your own, or with help? It is important to have a plan.

Self-Determination Is Power Over Your Life

Self-determination is the power to make decisions about your own life. Making your own decisions will feel good. You will set goals and work toward them. You will control your life. You will be an adult.

Making your own decisions can be scary, too. You might make a wrong decision. That is okay. You will learn more each day.

self-determination ■ The power to make decisions about your own life.

Independence Is Relying on Yourself

Self-determination goes along with independence. **Independence** means relying on yourself. It means taking care of your own needs.

Having your own money helps you to be independent. Having your own place to live helps you to be independent also.

While You Read

Question What is the difference between self-determination and independence?

independence ■ Relying on yourself.

Real-World Connection

Working for Yourself

An *entrepreneur* is someone who starts a business. As an entrepreneur, you would work for yourself. You would also have the responsibility to make your business work. You would lose your job if your business does not make money.

Starting a business takes a lot of time, energy, and knowledge. You would need to learn about finance and management. You would need to work hard to make your business a success.

Take the Next Step Find someone who is self-employed. Ask that person about the plusses and minuses of self-employment. What traits would help a person be a good entrepreneur? Why?

For help doing this activity, go to **ewow.glencoe.com/tips** and find the *Smart Tip* for the Chapter 16 *Real-World Connection*.

Plan Where You Will Live

You may want your own apartment when you get a new job. Many young people like to live on their own. They like the feeling of independence.

Living independently can be difficult, however. Can you pay all your bills on time? Can you manage shopping, cooking, and cleaning?

Think about the plusses of living away from home. Think about the minuses. Then decide if it is for you.

Living at Home Saves Money

Many young people live at home after they finish school. At home you can share expenses. You do not have to buy furniture of your own. You might share a television and a car. At home you can also share chores. You could take turns shopping, cooking, and cleaning.

While You Read

Connect Would you rather live alone or with a roommate?

Having a Roommate Saves Money

Many people share an apartment with a roommate. You might rent an apartment with a friend. You might move in with someone who already has a place.

Sharing a home with a roommate has plusses. You and your roommate share expenses. That saves money. You are more independent than you would be if you lived at home. You have someone to help with shopping, cooking, and cleaning.

Sharing a home with a roommate has minuses. You are less independent than you would be if you lived alone. You may have disagreements with your roommate. For example, you may disagree about noise.

Choose a Trustworthy Roommate Your roommate should be someone you can trust. Your roommate should respect your privacy.

Talk ahead of time about your living habits. How often will friends visit? Is it okay to play loud music?

Decide ahead of time how you will divide the expenses and the chores. Make sure you do not have to pay or do more than your share.

Choose an Apartment Carefully

Do you want to live on your own? Finding the right place takes some time and effort. You need to think about location, safety, lease terms, and cost.

Think About Location

First think about *location*, or where you want to live. Your apartment should be near a grocery and other stores. You may want to be near family and friends, too.

Think about how you will commute to work. To **commute** means to travel back and forth to your job. Can you walk to work? Is there a bus route nearby?

While You Read

Connect Would you mind commuting a long time to work each day?

commute ■ Travel back and forth to your job.

Point of View

Planning for Independence

Mia Gomez knew she wanted to live on her own someday. "I grew up in a large family. I wanted to have my own space," says Mia. "But I knew it would take a lot of money to live on my own."

Mia went to a career college in Plano, Texas, to train as a dental assistant. She lived with her older sister, Lupe, while she went to school. "I helped take care of my nephews." Mia then got a full-time job. "I helped my sister with the bills, but I also saved 20 percent of my net income. At the end of the year, I had $4,500. This was enough for me to move into my own place."

It's Your Turn Find out the average rent of a one-bedroom apartment with utilities in your area. What would this cost you each month?

For help completing this activity, visit **ewow.glencoe.com/tips** and go to the *Smart Tip* for the Chapter 16 *Point of View*.

Think About Safety and Comfort

Think about your personal safety and comfort. The house or building should be in good repair. It should be safe. Look for fire escapes. Are there locks on windows and doors? Are there lights inside and outside? Visit the area after dark. Ask the police if the area is safe.

Choose a Home That Fits Your Needs   The building should be right for your individual needs. You will need wheelchair access if you use a wheelchair. You will need to make sure you can get outside quickly in an emergency. You may need an apartment without carpeting if you have asthma or allergies. You may need a quiet building if you are sensitive to noise.

Many buildings have apartments designed for people with disabilities. The National Accessible Apartment Clearinghouse (NAAC) can help you find an accessible apartment.

Think About the Terms of the Lease

lease ■ A written contract for a place you rent.

You must usually sign a lease to move into an apartment. A lease is a written contract for a place you rent. The contract is between a tenant and a landlord. The *tenant* is the renter. The *landlord* is the owner or manager.

A lease tells you what rules you must follow. For example, the lease tells you when you must pay rent. The lease tells you whether you may have pets.

Most leases last for a year. You must pay a fee if you want to move out before then.

A lease can be hard to read. Ask an adult to help you study it. Make sure you understand it before you sign it.

While You Read

Question About how much should you budget for housing?

Think About Cost

The main cost of housing is rent. How much rent can you afford? Budget about one-third of your income for housing. Remember that you will also need money to buy things for the apartment. For example, you will probably need furniture, bedding, and kitchen supplies.

Utilities Are Essential Services Utilities are another cost of renting. **Utilities** are services for a dwelling such as electricity, heat, and water. You may also need to pay for garbage pick-up.

Your landlord may pay for some or all of the utilities. Find out about how much you will have to pay for utilities each month.

utilities ■ Services for a dwelling such as electricity, heat, and water.

Use Creativity to Find a Place to Live

There are many ways to find a place to live. One way is to ask your family and friends for help. Someone may know of a room or apartment for rent.

Is there an area of town that is convenient? Look around that area. Look for "For Rent" signs. Call the telephone number on the signs. Ask if you can see the apartment or room that is for rent. Some Web sites help people find places to live and roommates, too.

Always look closely at an apartment before you rent. Make sure the unit is safe and comfortable. Make sure it is worth the money.

While You Read

Question Why should you always look closely at an apartment before renting?

Making Good Choices

Choosing a Roommate

Jake's friend Micah invited him to share his apartment. Micah's apartment is close to Jake's new workplace. The rent is low, too. Micah already has furniture, so Jake would not have to buy any.

The price and location are very appealing to Jake. Unfortunately, Micah has a lot of parties. He rarely cleans. Jake worries that he would not like living with Micah.

You Make the Call Should Jake move in with Micah? Why or why not?

For help in answering this question, visit **ewow.glencoe.com/tips** and find the *Smart Tip* for the Chapter 16 *Making Good Choices*.

Read the Housing Ads

Another way to find a new home is to read the newspaper classified ads. Look in the "Rental" or "For Rent" section.

Some listings are for apartments to share. Other listings are for unfurnished apartments. Still other listings are for furnished apartments. Most unfurnished apartments have a stove and a refrigerator. Furnished apartments also have furniture and some appliances, such as a microwave. Most apartment buildings have a coin-operated washer and dryer.

Like job ads, rental ads use abbreviations. **Figure 16.1** shows several abbreviations.

Figure 16.1

Housing Ads

AC = air conditioning	incl. = including	ref. = references
appt. = appointment	ldry. = laundry	refrig. = refrigerator
apt. = apartment	incl. = included	req. = required
bdrm., br = bedroom	mo. = month	rom. = room
bldg. = building	neg. = negotiable (to be	sq. ft. = square feet
dep. = deposit	agreed upon)	unfurn. = unfurnished
furn. = furnished	occ. = occupancy	util. = utilities

ROOMS FOR RENT

Share 2 bdrm, 1 bath near Church and Main. Upper unit, lots of light, parking. 1/2 rent and utils. Non-smoker. $500/mo. plus deposit. Avail 9/3. 337-0135 ask for Wendy.

APARTMENTS, FURNISHED

Nicely furnished, carpeted 1 BR apt. near Beckman Institute and Mercy Hospital, $980/mo includes utils. Off-street parking. 12-mo lease. Deposit. Avail. Aug. 15. Call 384-0178.

APARTMENTS, UNFURNISHED

GREAT CAMPUS LOCATION
Furnished 1, 2, 3 bdrm apts. All units with dishwasher, stove, refrig., AC. Patio. No pets. Short-term leases available with immediate occupancy. $850-$1375. Call 688-0136 for appt.

Quiet, cozy 1 bdrm. apt in Lynwood with garage, small patio. Heat, water, and garbage paid. Near bus lines. Ideal for student. $765 plus deposit. Call 251-9100 or 359-0122.

Finding a Home Classified ads tell you the location, rent, and other details of an apartment. Why should you always visit a place before you decide to rent?

Fill Out a Rental Application

To rent a new home, you will need to fill out a rental application form. You will give your name, address, Social Security number, and employment history. You will also give information about your income. You may need to pay a small application fee.

Sometimes rental applications are turned down. However, discrimination in housing is illegal. It is illegal to discriminate based on race, color, national origin, religion, gender, family status, or disability. Contact the Department of Housing and Urban Development if you think you are being discriminated against.

Find Out About Deposits Ask about the security deposit before you rent. A **security deposit** is money to pay for possible damage to the apartment. This deposit is usually the same amount as one month's rent.

There may be other deposits, too. For example, there may be a cleaning deposit. There may be a pet deposit.

security deposit ■ Money to pay for possible damage to the apartment.

Make Your New Place a Home

You will get the keys to your place after you sign your lease and pay the deposits and rent. Now it is time to set up your household.

It takes time to get settled in a new place. You may feel a little lonely at first. This is normal. Soon your new place will feel like home.

While You Read

Visualize Imagine how you would you feel during your first night in a new apartment.

Set Up Your Household

You have several things to do after you move in. Call the utility companies to set up service. Call the telephone company to get a phone line. Plan where to put your things. Buy basics such as furniture, groceries, and cleaning supplies.

Use your money wisely. Buy healthy foods for your kitchen. Look for used or inexpensive furniture.

Borrow items if you can. Comparison shop for large items. To *comparison shop* means to compare items to find the best price and quality.

Being Part of Your Community

Ready, Set, Read

Key Terms

community service

lifelong learning

self-advocacy

support network

unemployment insurance

vocational rehabilitation

register

ballot

Main Idea

You can enjoy life more by getting involved with your community. You can help others and get help in return.

Thought Organizer

Copy the chart below. As you read, list four types of help you can find in your community.

job help at a One-Stop Career Center

Community Help

Join Your Community

Everyone needs to be part of a community. A *community* is a group of people who have something in common. You may be part of a community in your neighborhood, at school, or at work. You may be part of a community with people who have similar needs.

Participating in community activities is important. People who are involved in their communities are usually happier than people who are not involved in their communities. You can be involved in your community in many ways. You can join a club or faith group. You can be active in politics. You can take a class. You can go to a show or sports event.

Clubs and Faith Groups Help You Get Involved

Every community has clubs and faith groups where you can meet people. For example, your community might have a bicycling club or an arts group. Your community might have a religious youth group or a group for senior citizens. National groups have local chapters all over the country. For example, the Sierra Club has activities all over the country. You could go on hikes or camping trips with your local club members.

Many communities have neighborhood associations. A *neighborhood association* is a group of people who live in a certain area. The association works to make the neighborhood a better place to live. For example, a neighborhood association might organize a neighborhood clean-up day.

Community Service Helps You Get Involved

Community service is an important way to get involved. **Community service** is volunteer work that makes your community a better place to live. You might clean up a park. You might read to children at the library. You might help with a local garden. You might answer phones or walk dogs at an animal shelter.

You can even do community service online. You could translate a document into another language, design a brochure, or give online tutoring. It feels good to give to others in the community.

Lifelong Learning Helps You Get Involved

Lifelong learning means continuing to learn after you finish school. There are many ways to learn. You could learn by talking to people in your community. You could take a night class at the adult school in your community. You could take a course at your local university or community college.

Lifelong learning helps you get ahead in your career. It also helps you become part of your community. It helps you make friends and contacts.

While You Read

Connect Do you think everyone should do community service?

community service ■
Volunteer work that makes your community a better place to live.

lifelong learning ■
Continuing to learn after you finish school.

Find Transportation in Your Community

You need transportation to get involved in your community. Will you need a car? Having a car can be expensive. You will have car payments. You will also need to pay for insurance, fuel, and repairs. This could be several hundred dollars each month.

Join a Car Pool or Vanpool   Another way to get to work is to join a car pool. You would ride to work with someone else. You would pay part of the cost of driving. You could also join a vanpool. A *vanpool* is a group of people who commute together in a van. One person drives the van. The other people pay a fare.

Save Money With Public Transportation   Public transportation is the least expensive choice. Buy a monthly pass if you ride public transportation often. This will save you money.

Public transportation is usually accessible to people with disabilities. For example, buses often have lifts for wheelchair users.

What if public transportation is not accessible? Find out about paratransit. *Paratransit* is transportation for people who cannot use regular transit because of a disability. Paratransit comes to your door and takes you where you need to go.

Sharing the Ride
Good transportation helps you to live independently. Do you think having a car is worth the expense? Why or why not?

Get Help From Your Community

Your community is also a place to get help. You can make friends and find support. You can get training and job help. You can get help finding a place to live.

Getting help for yourself is part of self-advocacy. **Self-advocacy** means speaking up for what you want and need. It means that you can make decisions about yourself. It means that you can take responsibility for your own life.

self-advocacy ■ Speaking up for what you want and need.

Build a Support Network

Work to build a support network in your community. A **support network** is a group of people who can help you when you need it. You can help them when they need it, too. Your support network could include family, friends, teachers, and neighbors.

support network ■ A group of people who can help you when you need it.

Get Job Help at a One-Stop Career Center

You can find job help at the One-Stop Career Center in your community. A *One-Stop Career Center* is a job and training help center. There are One-Stop Career Centers in every state. There is probably one near you. One-Stop Career Centers have resources for everyone, including people with disabilities and people who speak limited English. Sometimes a One-Stop Career Center may set up an interview for you. Career Centers help both the employer and the job seeker. You can find your local One-Stop Career Center on the Internet or by calling your state's public employment agency.

While You Read

Question How can you find your local One-Stop Career Center?

Unemployment Insurance Helps You When You Lose Your Job   One-stop career centers can also give you information about unemployment insurance. **Unemployment insurance** is a government program that helps you if you lose your job. You can get help if your job ended or if you had to leave your job. You will get payments and help finding a new job.

Each state has its own program. Contact your State Unemployment Insurance office to learn more.

unemployment insurance ■ A government program that helps you if you lose your job.

Independent Living Centers Help People With Disabilities

Independent living centers are nonprofit organizations that help people with disabilities live independently.

Independent living centers can help you find housing and transportation. They can give you job training. Independent living centers can also help you get other services. For example, an independent living center could help you get housing assistance. An independent living center could help you apply for Supplemental Security Income (SSI). SSI is a program that helps people who cannot work to earn money.

Vocational Rehabilitation Helps You Prepare for a New Career

vocational rehabilitation ■
A government program that helps people with disabilities get and keep a job.

Vocational rehabilitation is a government program that helps people with disabilities get and keep a job. You can receive services such as counseling, medical and mental health services, and job training.

Look for your state's Vocational Rehabilitation office on the Internet or in the blue pages of your phone book. A vocational rehabilitation counselor may even have an office at your high school.

While You Read

Connect Do you think it is okay not to vote?

register ■ To sign up to be a voter.

Register to Vote

Voting helps you be part of the community, too. Voting is every citizen's right.

You must be a U.S. citizen age 18 or over in order to vote. You must also register to vote. To **register** means to sign up to be a voter. You fill out a voter registration form. You can get a voter registration form on the Internet. You can also get a voter registration form at most post offices and public libraries. Fill out the form, sign it, and send it to the address marked on the form. You will receive a voter registration card in the mail.

After you register, you are given the address of a polling place. A *polling place* is the place where you will vote. Make sure you know how to find the polling place. Make sure you know what hours you can vote.

Cast Your Vote
Voting gives you a voice. It helps you feel like a part of your community. How should a voter decide how to vote in an election?

Cast Your Ballot

What happens when you go to the polling place? First you check in with an election worker. You give your name and address. The election worker finds your name in the voter list. You sign your name on the list.

Next the election worker gives you a ballot. A **ballot** is a piece of paper used to cast your vote. You mark your choices on the ballot.

ballot ■ A piece of paper used to cast your vote.

Today some ballots are electronic. You vote by touching a screen or clicking with a mouse.

Find an Accessible Polling Place   Do you have a disability? Make sure your polling place will be accessible to you. You can request another polling place that is accessible.

Early voting is often available to people who have difficulty walking or standing. You can also ask for curbside voting. *Curbside voting* is when an election worker brings your ballot to your car outside the polling place.

While You Read

Question What does *accessible* mean?

Check your answers online by visiting ewow.glencoe.com/review and selecting the Section 16.2 Review.

Retell

1. List the costs of having a car.
2. Describe two advantages of lifelong learning. Use your own words.

Think Critically

3. How is voting related to self-advocacy?

Math Practice

Answer the multiple-choice math questions at ewow.glencoe.com/math.

Paying for Lifelong Learning

Courses at your community college cost $13.00 per unit. The registration fee is $27.00 per quarter. How much will a four-unit course cost?

Step 1 Calculate the course fee.
$13.00 × 4 = $52.00

Step 2 Add the registration fee to the course fee.
$52.00 + $27.00 = $79.00

Result A four-unit course will cost $79.00.

Figure It Out

You add a second course this quarter. This course is three units. How much will the second course cost?

Vehicle Product Specialist

Ian Minicuci
Michigan

Career Cluster: Transportation, Distribution, and Logistics

What does a vehicle product specialist do?

"I tour with auto shows and answer questions about vehicles."

Why did you choose a career in the automobile industry?

"I'm a wheelchair user. I was working in a mobility program helping manufacturers make vehicles more accessible to people who have difficulty with mobility. I was offered a job to work with original equipment manufacturers (OEM) at the auto shows. Now I work in the OEM mobility program for Pontiac and GMC."

What obstacles have you overcome?

"Transportation can be a challenge. I travel a lot and hotels can sometimes be a problem. I travel with other people, so they help me."

What advice do you have for students?

"Know who you are and be okay with who you are. Ask for assistance when you need it. No one can do everything alone. Never stop dreaming because I know you can reach the stars. I'll see you there."

Vehicle Product Specialist

Training
A high school education is needed to be a vehicle product specialist. Vehicle manufacturers provide training.

Skills and Talents
Product knowledge, communication skills, and people skills are needed to be a vehicle product specialist.

Career Outlook
Employment in the auto trade is expected to grow at an average rate through 2012.

Learn More About It
What features would you change about a vehicle to make it the perfect vehicle for you? For example, if you have trouble getting in and out of a car, what would you do to make it easier? Write a three- to five-minute presentation about your design changes. Explain what they are and why you want them. Give your presentation in class.

For help with this activity, visit **ewow.glencoe.com/tips**.

Glencoe Online

Go to **ewow.glencoe.com** to find online games and activities for Chapter 16.

Key Term Review

transition plan (p. 384)
self-determination (p. 385)
independence (p. 385)
commute (p. 387)
lease (p. 388)
utilities (p. 389)
security deposit (p. 391)
community service (p. 395)

lifelong learning (p. 395)
self-advocacy (p. 397)
support network (p. 397)
unemployment insurance (p. 397)
vocational rehabilitation (p. 398)
register (p. 398)
ballot (p. 399)

Check Your Understanding

1. Define self-determination and independence.
2. Describe the four things to consider when you rent a place to live.
3. List four ways to get involved in your community.
4. Describe four sources of help in your community.
5. Explain how to register and how to cast a ballot.

Write About It

6. **Write About Your Support Network** A support network is a group of people who can help you when you need it. Describe your support network. Explain whether you have people who help you when you need help. Tell whether you would like to have a larger support network. List ideas for making your support network larger and stronger.

Role Play

7. **Explain Your Transition Plan**   Work with a partner. One person plays a counselor. Explain to the counselor what your plans are for after high school. Explain where you will live, what training or education you will get, and what kind of job you will do. Explain how you will be involved in your community. Switch roles with your partner.

Teamwork Challenge

8. **Create a Service Guide**   Make a guide to the services available in your community. Choose one of these areas: housing assistance, employment assistance, or assistance for people with disabilities. Include services by the government and services by nonprofit organizations. Include a name, address, phone number, and Internet address for each service.

Computer Lab

Organize Household Tasks   Make a list of all the household chores you must do each month. Research the subject on the Internet to make sure your list is complete. Then use a word-processing program to create a checklist of daily, weekly, and monthly chores. Compare your list with your classmates' lists.

Personal Career Portfolio

Write a Transition Essay   Write a one-page essay describing your future goals. Describe the education or training you will receive. Describe the lifestyle you would like to have. Describe the career you plan to have. Describe where you will live and how you will be involved in your community.

Go to **ewow.glencoe.com/portfolio** for help.

Unit 4 Review

Chapter Summaries

Chapter 13 Your Paycheck and Your Taxes

Most workers must pay taxes on the money they earn. Your employer will take out tax money from your earnings and send it to the government. Your paycheck tells you how much money was taken out for taxes. At the end of the year, you must fill out a tax return and send it to the government.

Chapter 14 Managing Your Money

A budget is a plan for spending and saving. A budget helps you balance your income and expenses. A bank account keeps your money safe. A savings account helps you save. A checking account lets you write checks to pay bills and buy things. Credit cards are convenient but make it easy to overspend.

Chapter 15 Using Technology

Computers are the most common form of technology. Many workers work with personal computers and peripherals. Software lets you do word processing, create spreadsheets and databases, make presentations, browse the Web, and send and receive e-mail. Assistive technology makes computers accessible to people with all kinds of disabilities.

Chapter 16 Planning Your Future

You may live on your own after you get a job. You will need to find a safe, comfortable, and affordable place to live. You will need to balance work and personal tasks. You will also join the community. You can help out in your community and find help for problems such as discrimination and job loss.

These are the topics you read about in this unit. What did you learn?

Chapter 13
Your Paycheck and Your Taxes
- Understanding Your Paycheck
- Filing Your Taxes

Chapter 14
Managing Your Money
- Making a Budget
- Understanding Banking and Credit

Chapter 15
Using Technology
- Technology Basics
- Computer Applications

Chapter 16
Planning Your Future
- Living on Your Own
- Being Part of the Community

Glossary

A

account statement A record of your account.

accurate Truthful and without errors.

active listening Paying attention and responding to what someone says.

adult education Training courses for people age 18 and over.

apprenticeship An on-the-job training program in which you learn from an expert worker.

appropriate Correct for the situation.

assertive Direct, honest, and polite.

assistive technology Tools that help people with disabilities function better.

associate degree A title you receive when you complete a two-year program at a community college.

B

bachelor's degree A title you receive when you complete a four-year program at a college or university.

balance The amount of money in your bank account.

ballot A piece of paper used to cast your vote.

benefits Extras that workers receive on a job.

body language The messages that your movements send.

budget A plan to manage your money to reach your goals.

business Selling goods or services.

C

career All the related jobs you do during your life.

career cluster A group of related occupations.

career college A private postsecondary school that offers training programs for service occupations.

career evaluation A chart showing of the plusses and minuses of a career.

career goal A goal for the work you want to do.

career plan A chart showing all the steps you will take to reach your career goal.

character A person's ethics and behavior.

check A piece of paper you use to tell your bank to pay money to someone else.

check register A record of your checking account.

checking account A bank account that lets you write checks.

chronological résumé A résumé that lists your achievements in time order.

classified ad A short notice that appears in a section of the newspaper.

cold-calling Calling without a lead or referral.

college A postsecondary school that offers classes in several interest areas.

commission Pay based on how much you sell.

communication Sharing thoughts and feelings.

community college A public postsecondary school that offers two-year programs in many subjects.

community service Volunteer work that makes your community a better place to live.

commute Travel back and forth to your job.

compromise An agreement where both sides give in a little.

computer ethics Standards of right and wrong computer use.

conflict A strong disagreement.

constructive criticism A comment about things you can do better.

contact A person you know who can give you information about jobs.

contact information How to reach a contact: a phone number, an address, or an e-mail address.

contact list A list of all your contacts.

cooperate To work well with others to reach a goal.

cooperative education A program that combines school with a part-time job.

courtesy Politeness and respect.

cover letter A letter of application that says why you are a good match for the job.

credit Money you can use now and pay back later.

credit card A small plastic card that you can use to buy things on credit.

D

database A collection of information on a certain topic.

debit card A card that takes money directly from your checking account.

debt Owing someone money.

decision A choice among several options.

decision-making process A series of steps that you take to make a good decision.

deduction An amount taken from your gross pay.

defensive Closed to other people's opinions.

dependent A person who is supported by someone else.

deposit Money you put into your account.

Glossary

disability A long-lasting impairment that limits a major life activity.

disk drive A machine that reads from and writes to disks.

distance education Education in which the teacher and the student are not together in a classroom.

diverse Varied and different.

dress code A description of the clothes that are appropriate for work.

E

e-mail Sending and receiving messages by computer.

emergency A serious and sudden event that calls for quick action.

emotions Strong feelings.

empathy The ability to imagine yourself in another person's shoes.

employability skills Basic skills that you need to get a job, keep a job, and do well at a job.

employment agency An organization that matches workers with jobs.

engineering Using science and mathematics to make things that help people.

enthusiasm Interest and eagerness.

enunciate To speak each syllable clearly.

equal opportunity Fair treatment for everyone.

equipment All the objects, such as machines and tools, that you need to do a job.

ethics Knowing right from wrong.

expenses Things you spend money on.

experiences Activities you have tried.

F

fax machine A machine that sends and receives printed information over the telephone.

feedback Information about how well you are doing your job.

FICA Social Security tax.

file A document you name and save.

finance Managing money.

fire extinguisher A container of chemicals that will put out a small fire.

first aid Medical help that a person needs right away after an injury.

fixed expenses Basic expenses that are about the same each month.

flammable Easy to set on fire.

flexibility The ability to change when the world around you changes.

flexible expenses Expenses that change from month to month.

folder A group of related files.

follow up To finish something or do the next step.

Form 1040EZ The simplest federal income tax form.

Form I-9 A form showing that you are allowed to work in the United States.

Form W-2 A form that shows how much you earned and how much your employer withheld for taxes.

Form W-4 A form that tells your employer how much money to withhold for taxes.

G

goal Something you want to achieve.

gossip Saying bad things about people behind their backs.

graphics Pictures and symbols.

gross pay The amount of pay you earn.

H

hardware The physical parts of a computer system.

harassment Unwelcome behavior that creates a hostile environment.

hazard Anything that might harm someone.

health science Helping people stay healthy and recover from sickness.

high voltage A large and dangerous amount of electricity.

hospitality and tourism Services for people who are traveling.

hygiene The care you give your health and cleanliness.

I

identity The way other people know you.

income tax Tax on the money you earn.

income tax return A form that you fill out to show how much income tax you owe.

independence Relying on yourself.

information technology Designing and using computer systems.

informational interview A discussion with a person who has a job that interests you.

initiative Doing work without being told.

interests Things you like to do.

Internal Revenue Service (IRS) The part of the federal government that collects taxes.

Internet A worldwide network of computers.

internship A short-term job or work project.

interviewer The person who interviews you.

J

job Work you do for pay.

job accommodations Things that help workers with disabilities to do their jobs.

Glossary

job applicant A person applying for a job.

job application form A printed sheet with blanks that you fill in to apply for a job.

job board A collection of job listings on the Internet.

job interview A meeting between an employer and a job applicant about a job.

job lead Information about a job opening.

job listing A written notice of a job opening.

job objective The type of job you want.

job opening A job that is vacant.

job shadowing Spending time with a worker on the job.

K

knowledge Understanding facts.

L

labor contract A written agreement about wages, hours, and working conditions.

leadership Motivating others to work toward a goal.

learning styles The different ways people naturally think and learn.

lease A written contract for a place you rent.

leisure Free time.

lifelong learning Continuing to learn after you finish school.

lifestyle The way you spend your time, energy, and money.

long-term goal A goal that will take a year or more to reach.

loyalty Being on the side of something or someone.

M

management Making decisions and planning.

manufacturing Making products by hand or machine.

marketing Deciding which goods and services people will want to buy.

material safety data sheet (MSDS) A document that describes a chemical and how to handle it.

medium-term goal A goal that will take between three months and a year to reach.

N

negotiate To try to get better terms.

net pay The amount of pay you receive on your check.

networking Asking your contacts for help and information about jobs.

O

occupation The type of work you do to earn a living.

online job application form A job application form on the Internet.

on-the-job training Training (education in a specific skill) at work.

orientation A program that introduces new employees to a company.

OSHA The part of the government that sets safety rules and inspects workplaces.

overtime Extra pay that you get when you work more than 40 hours in a week.

P

part-time job A job where you work up to 30 hours per week.

performance review A meeting where your boss tells you how well you have been doing your job.

peripheral A piece of hardware you can connect to a computer.

personal career profile A list of your career information.

personal computer (PC) A small computer made for a single person to use.

personal fact sheet A list of all the information about yourself that you will need for a job application form.

personal protective equipment Safety wear that protects you from hazards.

personality The way you think, feel, and act.

positive attitude A cheerful view of life.

postsecondary education Study after high school.

prejudice A negative attitude toward a group of people.

prioritize To decide which things are most important.

promotion A move to a job with more responsibility and higher pay.

punctuality Being on time.

R

raise An increase in pay.

receptive Open to other people's opinions.

reference A person who will tell an employer that you will do a good job.

referral A new contact that you get from an old contact.

refund A return of money.

register To sign up to be a voter.

research Collecting information.

respect High esteem.

responsibility Working hard and setting high standards for yourself.

résumé A one-page summary of your skills, work experience, and education.

right Something the law says you should have.

RTK label A chemical safety label.

S

salary An amount of pay for each month or year you work.

savings Money you keep for the future.

savings account A bank account where you keep money for the future.

scanner A machine that copies words and pictures from paper into a computer.

security deposit Money to pay for possible damage to a rented home.

self-advocacy Speaking up for what you want and need.

self-awareness Knowing your thoughts, feelings, and actions.

self-determination The power to make decisions about your own life.

self-esteem A positive feeling about yourself.

self-image How you see yourself.

service industry All the businesses that provide activities for a fee.

service learning A program that combines school with volunteer work.

short-term goal A goal that will take three months or less to reach.

skills Abilities to do specific tasks.

skills résumé A résumé that lists your achievements by type of skill.

Social Security A government program that helps disabled and retired people.

Social Security number A nine-digit number that helps the government keep a record of your earnings.

software A set of instructions for a computer.

spell check A computer tool that finds misspelled words and suggests correct spellings.

spreadsheet A program that works with numbers and math functions.

standard English The form of English taught in school.

supervisor A boss or manager.

support network A group of people who can help you when you need it.

T

talents Natural gifts.

tax liability The amount of tax you owe.

tax preparer A person you can pay to fill out your tax forms.

taxes Money that you must pay to the government.

team A group of people who have a common goal.

technical school A private postsecondary school that offers training programs for specific occupations.

technological literacy The ability to work with technology.

technology Knowledge and tools that make it possible to do new things.

temp job A job that is not permanent.

temp-to-hire job A job that changes from a temp job to a permanent job.

tentative Flexible and not final.

terms The details of an offer.

time management Using time to reach your goals.

tip Money that a worker receives from a customer for doing a good job.

tolerance Treating everyone fairly and equally.

training Education in a specific skill.

transition plan A plan that lists your goals for after high school and says how you will reach those goals.

tuition The fee you pay to a school for each unit or course.

U

unemployment insurance A government program that helps you if you lose your job.

uniform An outfit that shows you work for a certain company.

utilities Services for a dwelling such as electricity, heat, and water.

V

values Things that are important to you.

ventilation Fresh air flowing into a closed space.

vocational rehabilitation A government program that helps people with disabilities get and keep a job.

voice mail A system that lets people leave spoken messages when you cannot take a phone call.

volunteer work Work you do without receiving pay.

W

wages An amount of money you receive for every hour you work.

withdrawal Money that you take from your account.

word processing Writing and editing text on the computer.

work Any useful activity.

work ethic The belief that work has value.

work permit A card showing that you are allowed to work in the United States.

workers' compensation An insurance program that helps you if you are hurt at work.

working conditions The conditions in which you spend your workday.

Glosario

A

account statement/estado de cuenta Registro de tu cuenta.

accurate/preciso Verídico y sin errores.

active listening/escucha activa Prestar atención y responder a lo que alguien dice.

adult education/educación de adultos Cursos de entrenamiento para personas de 18 años de edad o mayores.

apprenticeship/aprendizaje Programa de entrenamiento en el que aprendes de un trabajador experimentado.

appropriate/apropiado Adecuado para la situación.

assertive/afirmativo Directo, honesto, y cortés.

assistive technology/tecnología asistencial Aparatos que ayudan a personas con incapacidades a desenvolverse mejor.

associate degree/diploma asociado Título que recibes cuando terminas un programa de dos años en un colegio comunitario.

B

bachelor's degree/diploma de bachiller Título que recibes cuando terminas un programa de cuatro años en un colegio universitario o universidad.

balance/saldo Suma de dinero en tu cuenta bancaria.

ballot/papeleta (de votación) Papel utilizado para dar tu voto.

benefits/beneficios Extras que reciben los trabajadores en un empleo.

body language/lenguaje corporal Mensajes que revelan tus movimientos.

budget/presupuesto Plan para administrar tu dinero y alcanzar tus metas.

business/negocio Venta de bienes o servicios.

C

career/carrera Todos los trabajos relacionados que ejerces durante tu vida.

career cluster/rama ocupacional Un grupo de ocupaciones relacionadas.

career college/colegio ocupacional Escuela postsecundaria privada que ofrece programas de entrenamiento para ocupaciones de servicios.

career evaluation/evaluación ocupacional Gráfica que muestra los pros y contras de una carrera.

career goal/meta ocupacional Meta para el trabajo que quieres realizar.

career plan/plan ocupacional Plan que muestra todos los pasos que darás para alcanzar tu meta ocupacional.

character/carácter La ética y la conducta de una persona.

check/cheque Pieza de papel que usas para decirle a tu banco que le pague cierto dinero a alguien.

check register/registro de cheques Informe de tu cuenta de cheques.

checking account/cuenta de cheques Cuenta bancaria que te permite escribir cheques.

chronological résumé/résumé cronológico Curriculum vitae que enumera todos tus logros ordenados por fechas.

classified ad/anuncio clasificado Aviso corto que aparece en una sección de un periódico.

cold-calling/llamar "en frío" Llamar sin tener una pista o referencia.

college/colegio universitario Escuela postsecundaria que ofrece cursos en varias áreas de interés.

commission/comisión Pago basado en cuánto vendes.

communication/comunicación Intercambiar ideas e impresiones.

community college/colegio comunitario Escuela postsecundaria que ofrece programas de dos años en muchas asignaturas.

community service/servicio comunitario Trabajo voluntario que hace que tu comunidad sea un mejor lugar para vivir.

commute/viajar (al trabajo) Ida y vuelta al trabajo.

compromise/compromiso Un acuerdo mediante el cual ambas partes ceden un poco.

computer ethics/ética de computación Reglas para el uso correcto e incorrecto de las computadoras.

conflict/conflicto Un desacuerdo mayor.

constructive criticism/crítica constructiva Comentario sobre cosas que puedes hacer mejor.

contact/contacto Persona a la que conoces que te puede dar información de empleos.

contact information/información de contactos Cómo comunicarse con un contacto: un número de teléfono, una dirección, o una dirección electrónica.

contact list/lista de contactos Una lista de todos tus contactos.

cooperate/cooperar Trabajar bien junto a otros para lograr una meta.

cooperative education/educación cooperativa Programa que combina la escuela con un trabajo a tiempo parcial.

courtesy/cortesía Buenas maneras y respeto.

cover letter/carta de presentación Carta de solicitud laboral que explica por qué eres buen candidato para un trabajo.

credit/crédito Dinero que puedes usar ahora y pagar más tarde.

credit card/tarjeta de crédito Pequeña tarjeta plástica que puedes usar para comprar cosas a crédito.

D

database/base de datos Colección de información sobre un cierto tema.

debit card/tarjeta de débito Tarjeta para sacar dinero directamente de tu cuenta de cheques.

debt/deuda Deberle dinero a alguien.

decision/decisión Selección entre varias opciones.

decision-making process/proceso de toma de decisión Serie de pasos que llevas a cabo para tomar una buena decisión.

deduction/deducción Cantidad extraída de tu salario bruto.

defensive/defensivo Cerrado a las opiniones de otros.

dependent/dependiente Persona que es mantenida por otra.

deposit/depósito Dinero que pones en tu cuenta.

disability/incapacidad Impedimento físico o mental a largo plazo que limita una o más actividades importantes de la vida.

disk drive/lector de discos Unidad que lee y escribe en discos.

Glosario

distance education/educación a distancia Educación en la cual el maestro y el estudiante no están juntos en un salón de clases.

diverse/diverso Variado y diferente.

dress code/código de vestir Descripción de la ropa que es apropiada para trabajar.

E

e-mail/correo electrónico Envío y recepción de mensajes por medio de una computadora.

emergency/emergencia Suceso serio e imprevisto que requiere atención inmediata.

emotions/emociones Sentimientos fuertes.

empathy/empatía/simpatía por alguien La habilidad de ponerse uno en la situación de otra persona.

employability skills/destrezas laborales Destrezas que necesitas para conseguir un trabajo, mantenerlo, y tener éxito en ese trabajo.

employment agency/agencia de empleos Organización que contrata a empleados apropiados para trabajos específicos.

engineering/ingeniería Usar la ciencia y las matemáticas para crear cosas que ayudan a la gente.

enthusiasm/entusiasmo Interés y buena disposición.

enunciate/enunciar Pronunciar cada sílaba claramente.

equal opportunity/oportunidades iguales Tratar por igual a todos.

equipment/equipo Todos los objetos, como máquinas y herramientas, que necesitas para realizar un trabajo.

ethics/ética Distinguir lo correcto de lo incorrecto.

expenses/gastos Cosas que compras con tu dinero.

experiences/experiencias Actividades que has realizado.

F

fax machine/máquina de faxes Máquina que envía y recibe información impresa por teléfono.

feedback/opiniones de otros Información acerca de cómo te está yendo en un trabajo.

FICA/FICA Impuesto del Seguro Social.

file/archivo Documento que nombras y guardas ("save").

finance/finanza Administrar el dinero.

fire extinguisher/extinguidor de incendios Contenedor con químicos para apagar un pequeño incendio.

first aid/primeros auxilios Asistencia médica que necesita una persona inmediatamente después de una lesión.

fixed expenses/gastos fijos Gastos básicos similares de cada mes.

flammable/inflamable Fácil de prenderle fuego.

flexibility/flexibilidad La habilidad de cambiar cuando cambian las condiciones alrededor.

flexible expenses/gastos flexibles Gastos que cambian cada mes.

folder/carpeta Grupo de archivos relacionados.

follow up/continuación Terminar algo o dar el próximo paso.

Form 1040EZ/Formulario 1040EZ El formulario más simple de los impuestos federales de ingresos.

Form I-9/Formulario I-9 Formulario que muestra que tienes permiso para trabajar en los Estados Unidos.

Form W-2/Formulario W-2 Formulario que muestra cuánto has ganado y cuánto tu empleador te dedujo de impuestos.

Form W-4/Formulario W-4 Formulario que le dice a tu empleador cuánto tiene que deducir de impuestos.

G

goal/meta Algo que quieres lograr.

gossip/chismorreo Decir cosas malas de la gente detrás de sus espaldas.

graphics/gráficas Dibujos o fotos y símbolos.

gross pay/salario bruto Cantidad de pago global que ganas.

H

hardware/hardware (equipo) Las partes físicas de un sistema de computadora.

harassment/hostigamiento Conducta inoportuna que crea un ambiente hostil.

hazard/peligro Cualquier cosa que pueda hacerle daño a alguien.

health science/ciencia de la salud Ayudar a la gente a permanecer saludables y a recuperarse de una enfermedad.

high voltage/alto voltaje Cantidad considerable y peligrosa de electricidad.

hospitality and tourism/hospitalidad y turismo Servicios para personas que están de viaje.

hygiene/higiene Cuidados que les prestas a tu salud y limpieza.

I

identity/identidad La forma en que otra gente te conoce.

income tax/impuestos de ingresos Impuestos sobre el dinero que ganas.

income tax return/declaración de impuestos Formulario que llenas para mostrar cuánto debes en impuestos sobre tus ingresos.

independence/independencia Confiar en ti mismo/a.

information technology/tecnología de la información Diseñar y usar sistemas de computadoras.

informational interview/entrevista informativa Discusión con una persona que tiene un trabajo que te interesa.

initiative/iniciativa Hacer un trabajo sin que te lo pidan.

interests/intereses Las cosas que te gustan.

Internal Revenue Service (IRS)/Servicio Interno de Ingresos (IRS) La parte del gobierno federal que colecta impuestos.

Internet/Internet Red mundial de computadoras.

internship/puesto de interno Empleo o proyecto de trabajo a corto plazo.

interviewer/entrevistador La persona que te entrevista.

J

job/empleo Trabajo que haces por un pago.

job accommodations/acomodaciones de trabajo Cosas que ayudan a empleados con incapacidades a hacer sus trabajos.

job applicant/solicitante de empleo Persona que está solicitando un empleo.

job application form/formulario de empleo Hoja impresa con espacios en blanco que debes llenar al solicitar un empleo.

job board/tablero de anuncios de empleos Colección de listados de trabajos en Internet.

job interview/entrevista de trabajo
Encuentro entre un empleador y un/a solicitante de empleo acerca de un trabajo.

job lead/pista de un empleo Información sobre una oportunidad de trabajo.

job listing/listado de empleo Aviso escrito de una oportunidad de trabajo.

job objective/objetivo de trabajo El tipo de empleo que deseas.

job opening/oportunidad de empleo Empleo que está vacante, disponible.

job shadowing/hacer sombra en un trabajo Pasar cierto tiempo con otro trabajador en un empleo.

K

knowledge/conocimiento Entender los hechos, la realidad.

L

labor contract/contrato laboral Acuerdo escrito sobre salarios, horas, y condiciones de trabajo.

leadership/liderazgo Motivar a otros a trabajar para lograr una meta.

learning styles/estilos de aprendizaje Las diferentes formas en que la gente piensa y aprende naturalmente.

lease/arrendamiento Contrato escrito para alquilar un local.

leisure/ocio Tiempo libre.

lifelong learning/aprendizaje de por vida Continuar aprendiendo después que termines la escuela.

lifestyle/estilo de vida La forma como usas tu tiempo, energía, y dinero.

long-term goal/meta a largo plazo Meta que tomará un año o más para alcanzar.

loyalty/lealtad Estar del lado de algo o alguien.

M

management/gerencia Tomar decisiones y planificar.

manufacturing/fabricar Crear productos a mano o a máquina.

marketing/comercialización Decidir qué productos y servicios quiere comprar la gente.

material safety data sheet (MSDS)/hoja de datos sobre la seguridad de los materiales (MSDS) Documento que describe una sustancia química y cómo manipularla.

medium-term goal/meta a medio plazo Meta que tomará entre tres meses y un año para alcanzar.

N

negotiate/negociar Tratar de obtener condiciones más ventajosas.

net pay/salario neto Cantidad de pago que recibes en tu cheque.

networking/establecer conexiones Pedir ayuda e información sobre empleos a tus contactos.

O

occupation/ocupación El tipo de trabajo que haces para ganarte la vida.

online job application form/formulario de solicitud de empleo en línea Formulario de solicitud de empleo en Internet.

on-the-job training/entrenamiento laboral Entrenamiento (educación en una destreza específica) en el trabajo.

orientation/orientación Programa para presentar nuevos empleados a una compañía.

OSHA/OSHA Sector del gobierno que establece las reglas de seguridad e inspecciona los lugares de trabajo.

overtime/tiempo suplementario Pago extra que recibes cuando trabajas más de 40 horas por semana.

P

part-time job/empleo a tiempo parcial Empleo donde trabajas 30 ó menos horas por semana.

performance review/evaluación laboral Reunión en la que tu jefe te dice cómo estás haciendo en tu trabajo.

peripheral/periférico Un componente que puedes conectar a una computadora.

personal career profile/perfil ocupacional Lista de tu información ocupacional personal.

personal computer (PC)/computadora personal (PC) Computadora más pequeña construída para ser usada por una persona individualmente.

personal fact sheet/hoja de datos personales Lista con toda tu información personal que necesitarás para llenar una solicitud de empleo.

personal protective equipment/equipo de protección personal Equipo de seguridad que te pones para protegerte de riesgos y peligros.

personality/personalidad La forma en que piensas, sientes, y actúas.

positive attitude/actitud positiva Perspectiva alegre de la vida.

postsecondary education/educación postsecundaria Estudios realizados después de la escuela preparatoria (high school).

prejudice/perjuicio Actitud negativa hacia un grupo determinado de personas.

prioritize/priorizar Decidir qué cosas son las más importantes.

promotion/promoción Cambio en un empleo con más responsabilidad y mejor pago.

punctuality/puntualidad Llegar a tiempo.

R

raise/aumento (de salario) Mejora en el pago.

receptive/receptivo Receptivo a las opiniones de otra gente.

reference/referencia Persona que le dirá a un empleador que realizarás un buen trabajo.

referral/recomendación Nuevo contacto que obtienes por medio de un viejo contacto.

refund/reembolso Devolución de dinero.

register/registrarse Firmar para ser votante.

research/investigación Recoger información.

respect/respeto Alta estimación.

responsibility/responsabilidad Trabajar duro y establecer altos principios personales.

résumé/curriculum vitae Sumario en una hoja de tus destrezas, experiencia laboral, y educación.

right/derecho Algo que la ley dicta que debes tener o recibir.

RTK label/etiqueta RTK Etiqueta de seguridad en ciertos productos químicos.

S

salary/salario Cantidad de pago por cada mes o año que trabajas.

savings/ahorros Dinero que guardas para el futuro.

savings account/cuenta de ahorros Cuenta bancaria donde guardas dinero para el futuro.

scanner/escáner Maquina que copia palabras y gráficas de un papel a una computadora.

security deposit/depósito de seguridad Dinero que se paga por posibles daños a un hogar rentado.

self-advocacy/auto-abogacía Defender lo que uno quiere y necesita.

self-awareness/auto-conocimiento Estar bien al tanto de tus propios pensamientos, sentimientos, y acciones.

self-determination/auto-determinación El poder de decisión sobre tu propia vida.

self-esteem/auto-estimación Sentimientos positivos acerca de ti mismo/a.

self-image/imagen de sí mismo/a Cómo te ves a ti mismo/a.

service industry/sector de servicios Todos los negocios que proveen actividades por un precio.

service learning/aprendizaje práctico Programa que combina la escuela con trabajo voluntario.

short-term goal/meta a corto plazo Meta que tomará tres meses o menos para alcanzar.

skills/destrezas Habilidades para realizar ciertas tareas.

skills résumé/curriculum vitae de destrezas Currículo que enumera tus logros según el tipo de detreza.

Social Security/Seguro Social Programa del gobierno que ayuda a la gente incapacitada y a los que se retiran.

Social Security number/número del Seguro Social Número de nueve cifras que ayuda al gobierno a mantener un registro de tus ingresos.

software/software (programas de computadora) Serie de instrucciones para una computadora.

spell check/revisión ortográfica Una herramienta en las computadoras que encuentra palabras con faltas de ortografía y sugiere correcciones.

spreadsheet/hoja de cálculos Programa que trabaja con números y funciones matemáticas.

standard English/inglés corriente El tipo de inglés que se enseña en la escuela.

supervisor/supervisor Un jefe o gerente.

support network/red de conexiones Grupo de gente que puede ayudarte cuando lo necesites.

T

talents/talentos Dones naturales personales.

tax liability/obligación de impuestos La cantidad de impuestos que debes.

tax preparer/preparador de impuestos Persona a la que le pagas para llenar tus declaraciones de impuestos.

taxes/impuestos Dinero que tienes que pagarle al gobierno.

team/equipo Grupo de gente con una meta común.

technical school/escuela técnica Escuela postsecundaria privada que ofrece programas de entrenamiento para ocupaciones específicas.

technological literacy/capacidad tecnológica La habilidad de trabajar con tecnología.

technology/tecnología Conocimientos e instrumentos o herramientas que hacen posible crear nuevas cosas.

temp job/empleo temporal Empleo que no es permanente.

temp-to-hire job/empleo temporal-a-contratado Empleo que cambia de empleo temporal a empleo permanente.

tentative/tentativo Flexible y no definitivo.

terms/términos Detalles y condiciones de una oferta.

time management/utilización del tiempo Usar el tiempo adecuadamente para alcanzar tus metas.

tip/propina Dinero que recibe un trabajador de un cliente al realizar un buen trabajo.

tolerance/tolerancia Tratar a todos justa y equitativamente.

training/entrenamiento Educación en una destreza específica.

transition plan/plan de transición Plan que enumera las metas para después de la escuela preparatoria y cómo alcanzar esas metas.

tuition/matrícula Dinero que pagas a una escuela por cada unidad o curso.

U

unemployment insurance/seguro de desempleo Programa del gobierno que te ayuda si pierdes tu empleo.

uniform/uniforme Ropa que muestra que trabajas para una cierta compañía.

utilities/utilidades Servicios para una vivienda tales como electricidad, calefacción, y agua.

V

values/valores Las cosas que son importantes para ti.

ventilation/ventilación Aire fresco que circula hacia un espacio cerrado.

vocational rehabilitation/rehabilitación vocacional Programa del gobierno que ayuda a gente con incapacidades a conseguir y mantener un empleo.

voice mail/correo de voz Sistema que le permite a la gente dejar mensajes hablados cuando no pueden responder una llamada telefónica.

volunteer work/trabajo voluntario Trabajo que realizas sin recibir pago por él.

W

wages/sueldo Cantidad que recibes por cada hora que trabajas.

withdrawal/retirada de fondos Dinero que sacas de tu cuenta.

word processing/tratamiento de texto Escribir y editar texto en la computadora.

work/trabajo Cualquier actividad útil.

work ethic/ética laboral La creencia de que el trabajo tiene un valor.

work permit/permiso de trabajo Tarjeta que muestra que te está permitido trabajar en los Estados Unidos.

workers' compensation/compensación laboral Programa de seguros que te ayuda si te lesionas en el trabajo.

working conditions/condiciones de trabajo Las condiciones en que pasas tu jornada de trabajo.

CAREER CLUSTERS

Education and Training

There are three pathways in the education and training career cluster.

Teaching and training is showing people how to learn a subject or a skill.

Professional support services provide counseling and assistance to people seeking education and training.

Administration and administrative support manage the day-to-day activities and goals of schools and other educational and training facilities.

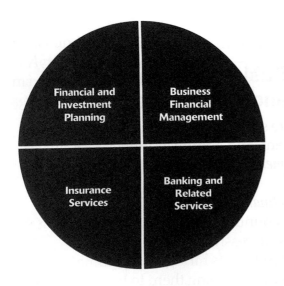

Finance

There are four pathways in the finance career cluster.

Financial and investment planning is providing advice about money and what to do with it.

Business financial management is creating accounting systems used to make financial decisions for businesses.

Banking and related services provide banks, loans, and credit services.

Insurance services provide financial protection from loss.

Government and Public Administration

There are seven pathways in the government and public administration career cluster.

Governance is creating and enforcing laws and public policies.

National security is being a member of the armed forces and protecting our country.

Foreign service workers represent the interests of our country to other nations.

Planning is making goals and plans for how to use land and resources.

Revenue and taxation is collecting and monitoring taxes from citizens and businesses.

Regulation makes sure that industries, utilities, buildings, the environment, and technology are properly used, maintained, and protected.

Public management and administration is running agencies or companies that deal with public resources, such as a city or utility.

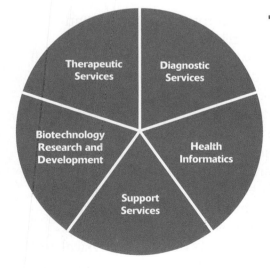

Health Science

There are five pathways in the health science career cluster.

Therapeutic services maintain and improve health over time by providing care, treatment, counseling, and health information.

Diagnostic services detect, diagnose, and treat medical conditions.

Health informatics includes health care administration as well as the collecting and managing patient and health care information and technology.

Support services provide an environment for health care delivery.

Biotechnology research and development involves studying, discovering and creating health conditions, treatments, information and services.

Career Clusters Appendix

Hospitality and Tourism

There are four pathways in the hospitality and tourism career cluster.

Restaurant and food/beverage services provide places and services where customers can eat and drink.

Lodging is all the services involved in providing a place to live for one or several days.

Travel and tourism employees develop and manage places, guides, and services for travelers.

Recreation, amusements, and attractions are services on location for leisure activities such as sports, festivals, or amusement rides.

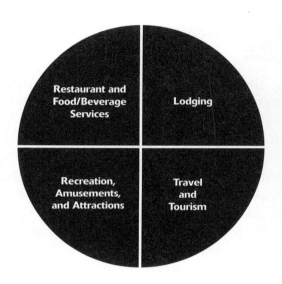

Human Services

There are five pathways in the human services career cluster.

Early childhood development and services is all the services that provide for the care and nurturing of young children.

Counseling and mental health services assist people with issues, decisions, and problems.

Family and community services provide assistance and care for human beings and their social needs, such as financial or family counseling, employment training, and disabled-access services.

Personal care services deal with physical and emotional well-being. These services can include hairstylists, dentists, dance teachers, and funeral attendants.

Consumer services help people make decisions about their finances and their purchases.

Career Clusters Appendix

CAREER CLUSTERS

Information Technology

There are four pathways in the information technology career cluster.

Interactive media deals with digital media such as the World Wide Web, DVDs, and CD-ROMs.

Programming/software engineering is designing and maintaining computer operating systems and software.

Network systems deal with the maintenance of computer networks.

Information support and services deal with creating, maintaining, and providing technical assistance for computer systems.

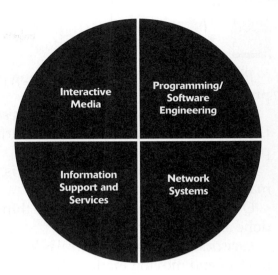

Law, Public Safety, and Security

There are five pathways in the law, public safety, and security career cluster.

Correction services workers manage and help individuals who are in or have been in corrections facilities such as jail.

Emergency and fire management services protect the public in case of fires and other emergencies.

Security and protective services work to protect public and private property such as museums or businesses.

Law enforcement services maintain public order and protect lives and property.

Legal services assist individuals or businesses in seeking legal help in civil or criminal matters.

CAREER CLUSTERS

Manufacturing

Production is making or assembling parts or products.

Manufacturing production process development is designing products and manufacturing processes.

Maintenance, installation, and repair is maintaining equipment.

Quality assurance is making sure things are done and made correctly.

Logistics and inventory control is keeping track of and moving manufacturing products and materials.

Health, safety, and environmental assurance is making sure that the workplace is safe.

Marketing, Sales, and Service

There are seven pathways in the marketing, sales, and service career cluster.

Management and entrepreneurship is forming and running businesses.

Professional sales and marketing is developing and promoting products for sale.

Buying and merchandising is the service of getting products to the customer.

Marketing communications and promotion is getting information out to the public about a good or service.

Marketing information management and research is understanding people's needs and wants and developing products for them.

Distribution and logistics is moving and keeping track of products and materials.

E-marketing is using electronic tools such as e-mail for marketing.

Science, Technology, Engineering, and Mathematics

There are two pathways in the science, technology, engineering, and mathematics career cluster.

Science and mathematics is using science and math skills to perform research, create products, and solve problems.

Engineering and technology is using and applying scientific principles and processes in the real world.

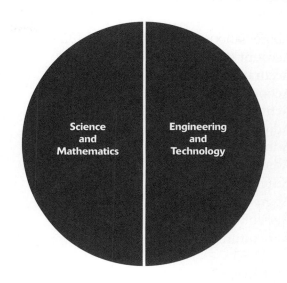

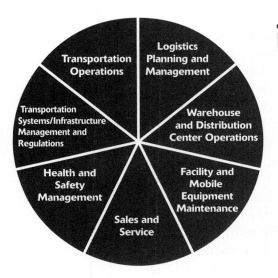

Transportation, Distribution, and Logistics Career Cluster

There are seven pathways in the transportation, distribution, and logistics career cluster.

Transportation operations is getting things and people safely from one place to another.

Logistics planning and management is distributing and transporting materials.

Warehousing and distribution center operations keep track of and manage cargo.

Facility and mobile equipment maintenance is making sure transportation vehicles are working and functional.

Transportation systems/infrastructure planning, management, and regulations is managing and designing public transportation.

Health, safety, and environmental management is handling and planning for risks.

Sales and service is marketing and selling transportation services.

Index

Index

F

Family, 10, 30
Farming consultant, 23
Fax, 366
Fax machine, 366
Federal Insurance Contribution Act (FICA), 313
Feedback, 296–298
FICA. *See* Federal Insurance Contribution Act
Fiction, 274
Field, database, 371
Files, 369
File tax return, 320–328
Finance, 57, 147
Fire extinguisher, 247
Fire prevention, 247
First aid, 253
Fixed expenses, 339
Flammable, 250
Flexibility, 18
Flexible expenses, 340
Floppy disk, 363
Folders, 369
Follow through, 143–144
Follow up, 199
Food processing, 55
Form 1040EZ, 323–325
Form I-9, 219–220
Formula, 370
Form W-2, 321
Form W-4, 316–318
Four-year college. *See* Bachelor's degree
Friends, 9, 30

G

Gender, 261
Getting along with others, 258–279
  avoid gossip, 263
  be positive, 263
  be same person each day, 265
  build teamwork skills, 266

  cooperate, 266–267
  laugh, 265
  show empathy, 262
  show interest in others, 261
  show respect, 264
  tolerate differences, 261
Goal(s), 112–118
  defined, 112
  general or specific, 113
  long-term, 115
  medium-term, 115
  short-term, 115
Goods, 15
Gossip, 263
Government and public administration, 58, 177
Government Web sites, 136
Graphics, 370
Greeting, to cover letter, 172
Gregg Reference Manual, The, 175
Gross pay, 312

H

Harassment, 289
Hard drive, 363
Hardware, 362–363
Hazard, 240
Heading
  in chronological resume, 164
  to cover letter, 172
Health, 10, 30
Health habits, 290–291
Health science, 59, 203
Hearing loss, 239
Helping others, 29
Hidden job market, 139
High voltage, 246, 249
Hobby, 35
Home, 386–388. *See also* Housing
Honesty, 290
Hospitality and tourism, 59, 231
Hotel employee, 231
Housing

Index

Index

Index

Index

Credits

Cover

Background photo: Royalty-free/CORBIS

Clockwise from top: Billy Hustace/Getty Images; Virgo/Masterfile; David Roth/Getty Images; Kwame Zikomo/SuperStock; Ariel Skelley/ CORBIS.

Bill Aron/PhotoEdit **xiii**(t), **308–309, 323, 346, 351, 405**(t); Paul Barton/ CORBIS **xv, 45**; Peter Byron/PhotoEdit **286**; Ken Chernus/Getty Images **266**; Jim Cummins/CORBIS **42**; Keith Dannemiller/CORBIS SABA **81**; Darama/CORBIS **197**; Lon C. Diehl/PhotoEdit **291**; Randy Faris/CORBIS **xii**(b), **306–307**; Getty Images **399**; Glamour International/Age Fotostock America, Inc. **361**; Glencoe/McGraw-Hill **10**; Jeff Greenberg/PhotoEdit **xiv**(b), **382–383, 405**(b); Charles Gupton/CORBIS **xvi, 94**; Craig Hammell/ CORBIS **16**; Brownie Harris/CORBIS **85**; Will Hart/PhotoEdit **vii**(t), **78–79, 123**(m); John Henley/ CORBIS **396**; Christian Hoehn/Getty Images **297**; Henryk T. Kaiser/Age Fotostock America, Inc. **66**; Christina Kennedy/ PhotoEdit **167**; Bob Krist/CORBIS **56**; David Lees/Getty Images **141**; Lester Lefkowitz/CORBIS **237**; James Leynse/CORBIS **153**; Ian Logan/Getty Images **vii**(b), **100–101**; Jan Logan/Getty Images **123**(bc); Kaz Mori/Getty Images **103**; Robin Nelson/PhotoEdit **284**; Michael Newman/PhotoEdit **ix**(t), **130, 150–151, 207**(m), **364, 392**; Steve Niedorf/Getty Images **189**; Gabe Palmer/CORBIS **vi**(t), **26–27, 123**(b); Jose Luis Pelaez, Inc./CORBIS **31**; Mark Richards/PhotoEdit **227**; Jon Riley/Getty Images **210–211, 305**(t); Andersen-Ross/Getty Images **270**; Bob Rowan; Progressive Image/CORBIS **21, 38**; Royalty-free/CORBIS **375**; Royalty-free/Digital Vision/Getty Images **vi**(b), **52–53, 123**(tc), **183**; Glencoe/McGraw-Hill **34**; Royalty-free/ Photodisc/Getty Images **6, 156, 262**; Andy Sacks/Getty Images **xxii–001**; Chuck Savage/CORBIS **v, 2–3, 123**(t), **174**; Ariel Skelley/CORBIS **x, 195, 208–209**; Ariel Skelley/Masterfile **314**; David Stoecklein/CORBIS **113**; SuperStock **xi**(b), **xii**(t), **124–125, 246, 258–259, 280–281, 305**(b), **305**(bm), **341**; LWA-Dann Tardif/CORBIS **xiv**(t), **358–359, 405**(bm); Jaime Vilklaseca/Getty Images **xi**(t), **305**(tm), **324–325**; Terry Vine/Getty Images **215**; Tom Wagner/CORBIS SABA **92**; Ben/Marcos Welsh/Age Fotostock America, Inc. **369**; LWA-Stephen Welstead/CORBIS **viii, 126–127, 207**(t), **273**; David Young-Wolff/PhotoEdit **ix**(b), **xiii**(b), **136, 180–181, 207**(b), **218, 225, 332–333, 339, 405**(tm); Eric K. K. Yu/ CORBIS **59**.